THREE AGAINST
THE THIRD REPUBLIC

Three Against
The Third Republic

Sorel, Barrès, and Maurras

———————

BY MICHAEL CURTIS

PRINCETON · NEW JERSEY

PRINCETON UNIVERSITY PRESS

1959

Printed in the United States of America
by Princeton University Press, Princeton, N.J.

Library of Congress card 59-11075

Publication of this book has been aided by
the Ford Foundation program
to support publication, through university presses,
of works in the humanities and
social sciences.

CONTENTS

THREE AGAINST
THE THIRD REPUBLIC

CHAPTER I

INTRODUCTION

POLITICAL theory is essentially the outcome of dissatisfaction with existing conditions, at once the autobiography of its time and the commentary on it. A state of contentment or the belief that an appropriate number of opportunities are present in a society is not likely to foster the growth or even allow the existence of a systematic ideology. An unusually large intellectual expression of dissatisfaction was shown in the French Third Republic between 1885 and 1914, for, if the republican positivist school of Renouvier and Littré is excluded, there were no major thinkers who were not reacting in some fashion against the revolutionary or democratic current stemming from the French Revolution.

Anti-Republican intellectuals had little but contempt for the political regime or for the bourgeois spirit it embodied— "né homme, mort épicier," was their epithet for M. Homais— and felt little but disillusionment with the results of the French Revolution. Even if not all intellectuals would have seen fit to shelter in an ivory tower as Flaubert advised, or to agree with the Goncourts that the Republican regime brought about a lowering of intelligence, the number of converts to Catholicism, from Léon Bloy to Max Jacob, was itself a remarkable commentary on a regime which had anticlericalism as at least a semiofficial creed. It was not surprising that the *idéologues* were as suspect to the Republican politicians at the end of the nineteenth century as they were to Napoleon at the beginning.

But if the attack on the Third Republic came from men of letters rather than from political figures,[1] neither the workers, who in 1899 had celebrated the Triumph of the Republic, nor the peasants had much enthusiasm for it by 1914. The indictment that those who were hostile brought against the Republic was a formidable one: inefficient and corrupt politi-

---

[1] H. J. Laski, *Authority in the Modern State*, New Haven, 1919, p. 169.

3

cal institutions, stagnant economy, aimless drifting, lack of glory, absence of general interest or the dominance of private interests, increase of social evils, the amorality of life, the power of the Church or the power of the masons, the influence of coteries, the lack of preoccupation with social questions, the financial scandals, the venom of the subsidized press, the growth of revolutionary movements challenging the whole basis of the system.

The Third Republic fought a war on two fronts: against those for whom the Revolution had been a calamity and who desired above all a return to the past, and against those for whom the task of the Revolution had not been completed. And these two struggles were being waged with little ideological support behind the regime. France slipped into, rather than chose, the Republic. If some, like Jules Siegfried, wealthy Protestant businessman, accepted it with confidence, for many the very word "Republic" held terror. The country became Republican because of the fear of militant clericalism,[2] and because, as Thiers had shrewdly observed, "It is the regime that divides us least." It occasioned little loyalty and less enthusiasm, and the remarkable thing about it was that, like Sièyes, it survived. In every election except 1885, those parties supporting the Republic increased in number, until in 1914 there were few elected opponents of the Republic. But a hundred years after 1789, the inheritors of the spirit of Chouannerie and the old part of the Vendée were still opposed to Revolution and the Republic.[3]

Yet if the Republic occasioned little loyalty in the period 1885 to 1914, the nature of the two major crises, Boulangism and the Dreyfus Affair (described in Chapter II), forced a division of opinion so that the blocs for and against the system stood revealed. The threat, in the first crisis, of an individual dictatorship, and in the second, of a challenge by military leaders to civilian authority, led to the formation of

[2] Albert Thibaudet, *Les Idées politiques de la France*, Paris, 1932, p. 34.

[3] André Siegfried, *Tableau politique de la France de l'ouest sous la Troisième République*, Paris, 1913, p. 510.

blocs, the Left supporting, the Right challenging, the existence of the Republic.

Definition of political terminology, especially the concepts of Left and Right, can never be wholly exact because of the number of variables entering into any given situation. In France the problem is made more acute than elsewhere because national and religious issues cut across economic and political ones. Moreover, the same words—nationalism, pacifism, militarism—have been adopted at different times by conflicting groups for varying purposes. Terminology undergoes a constant change of meaning. To trace the word *progressiste* from 1885 to 1906 is to witness a political somersault from a left-wing group to a conservative group supporting clericalism. In 1890 the Radical-Socialists were the political extreme Left— the mantle of neo-Jacobinism draped, or was clung to, by them; in 1914 it was the Socialist party which picked up the mantle. When in 1906 a majority was formed for the first time exclusively by those Left groups created after 1877, all the other parties were pushed further to the Right.

Yet a difference of emphasis between Left and Right is at all times discernible. They differ on the conception of human nature and the perfectibility of man, on the possibility of systematic solutions, on the relative merits of tradition and progress and of duties and rights, on the meaning of liberty, on the stress on hierarchy and command, on the value and extent of the educational process, on the usefulness of initiative and collective wisdom.

A relative position in the French political spectrum is educed from a combination of attitudes toward the extent of economic and social reform, centralization of the power of the state, the nature of the parliamentary system, the desirability of political parties, the relation of Church and State, the responsibility of authority, the use of force or coercion, national power versus international collaboration.

The Republic, based on the concept of the sovereignty of the people,[4] was opposed to a monarchical system, to political

[4] A sovereignty that was acknowledged even by the sceptical, cf. the remark of Jules Ferry, "la canaille . . . je veux dire la sainte canaille."

power resting in the hands of an obsolete landed aristocracy, to irrational or authoritarian ideas. Against *le presbytère et le château*, it was secular in its opposition to the social and political power of the Church; the peasants, uninterested in theological dogma, were still afraid of the restoration of Church lands. Little concerned with the social problem, the Republicans had in 1879 captured all political positions for the first time, but instead of proposing social reforms, they attacked clericalism. Mme de Villeparisis, so much more liberal than the majority of the middle class, "did not understand how anyone could be scandalized by the expulsion of the Jesuits."[5] The attempts of Léon Bourgeois in 1896 and of Caillaux in the years before 1914 to introduce an income tax and financial reforms were doomed to failure. The underlying philosophical support for the Republic was positivism, bitterly opposed to and by the Church. A semiofficial creed, the operating premise of the Ecole Polytechnique (of which both a politician like Freycinet and a philosopher like Littré were products), Sorel and Maurras were in different ways influenced by it.

Although there may not have been a program, the Republic had a certain political and social orientation. Its slogans, "marcher de l'avant," "aller à gauche," "combattre la réaction," "lutter pour la démocratie," "écraser le clericalisme," indicated that Republicans of principle would always oppose reaction and threats to the regime, resisting Boulanger in 1889, and refusing to follow the Progressists in alliance with the Right in 1902. The middle class occupied the center of the political stage, and was the focal point of this republicanism. It is noticeable that between 1893 and 1906, only Casimir-Périer and Waldeck-Rousseau came from the upper-bourgeoisie. This dominance of the middle class was such that after the sixteenth of May, it became clear to the Right (limited to the army, the Church, diplomacy, the magistrature, and the world of finance), that it could not gain power legally, and that a *coup d'état* would be the only possibility.

[5] Marcel Proust, *Within the Budding Grove*, London, 1924, vol. 2, p. 8.

INTRODUCTION

This book is a study of three writers, Charles Maurras, Maurice Barrès, and Georges Sorel, in the years between 1885 and 1914, and of their reactions to the deficiencies they saw in the Third Republic and in the system of democracy. It begins in 1885 with the appearance of certain new political factors. This was the year when Jaurès entered politics, when state support of primary education began, when Leo XIII dissuaded Albert de Mun from forming a Catholic political party, when Republican discipline was first manifested at the ballot box, when the credits for Tonkin were passed by a narrow majority of 6, when Clemenceau abandoned Paris as a constituency, and a chair at the Sorbonne for the history of the Revolution was founded by the City of Paris. The study ends in 1914 because the three writers had by this time made their original contributions to the thought of the country, if not their total political impact. Their remaining contributions, even in the case of Maurras, who lived the longest period after 1914, were to a large extent concerned with exposition or amplification. Moreover, the outbreak of World War I brought an added dimension into their work and a temporary reconciliation with the regime for the sake of the defense of France.

Barrès, Maurras, and Sorel are important not only because they provided the chief ideological weapons for the attack on the regime but also, in a wider context, because they contribute significantly to an understanding of a later period of European political history. In their contemporary significance, they illustrated the various attitudes of the conservative, the reactionary, and the moralist. Barrès was the conservative, Nationalist, and traditionalist; but he was also the aesthetic dilettante stressing the value of individual sensibility. Maurras was the counter-revolutionary, Nationalist, and monarchist, concerned with the preservation of a state of equilibrium and convinced that order was heaven's first law. Sorel, vacillating in his political convictions but making his deepest impression while a syndicalist, was the dedicated moralist who denounced decadence and stressed the importance of individual action.

7

The hostility of the three to the regime was the measure of the division of the country and of the existence of real economic and political difficulties. The writers made many valid criticisms, possessed in some ways profound psychological insight, and attempted to penetrate behind the myths of the Third Republic, but they failed to deal with many of the real economic and social problems. In spite of the realism they thought they brought to bear on political problems, which in the case of Maurras amounted to a science of politics, they nowhere appreciated the value of Gambetta's method of "serialization," the attack on each problem successively when the time was ripe.[6]

However, the criticism of these three writers was not limited to attacks on the Third Republic and its deficiency in political personnel and institutions. It also included attacks on the French Revolution and on the principles of democracy as a social system and a method of governmental operation. All three were basically irreligious writers, and each, attempting to solve the political, social, or psychological problems of the day, was in his individual way preoccupied with the quest for the Holy Grail of certainty.

Though this study does not investigate the influence or even examine the writings of the three after 1914, except where such investigation helps to elucidate meanings or illuminate personal behavior, it is abundantly clear that the attitude of Maurras, Barrès, and Sorel to the society of their own day, and the solutions they proposed, were remarkably prophetic of those to be adopted by later totalitarian regimes.

The need for dictatorship or the strong man, the stress on action, even purposeless action, the cult of energy, the concept of the elite, the denial of the realism, or the possibility, of political equality, the bitter anti-Semitism, even the idea of national socialism—all are to be found in the works of the three writers. It is unfair and unrealistic to juxtapose these ideas and theses with those of totalitarian regimes and thus to regard Barrès, Maurras, and Sorel as embryonic Fascists,

[6] John Eros, "The Positivist Generation of French Republicanism," *Sociological Review* (December 1955), 3:255-273.

Nazis, or Communists. Many of the ideas and activities of the later political movements would have been anathema to the writers, but their significant anticipations and relationships cannot be wholly discounted.

THE LOVE OF FRENCH CULTURE

All three writers were proud heirs to French greatness and culture. They illustrated—Sorel less so than the other two—by their life and writings both the habitual interconnection in France of politics and culture and therefore the political importance of literature and the habitual limitations of the culture.

Since 1635, when Richelieu created the French Academy, as much for political as for literary reasons, and Queen Mother Marie de Médicis intrigued against Richelieu in the auction room as well as in the palace, there has been an historic association between politics and culture in France. Literary tastes and cultural differences may well be the key to political differences, as they were in the eighteenth century when the dispute over the respective merits of Gluck and Piccini was both cause and effect of the break between Rousseau and the Encyclopédistes. Napoleon himself had the wit to say of Beaumarchais' *Le Mariage de Figaro* that it was the Revolution already in action. "There is no question of knowing if it is the duty or the advantage of writers to seek to exercise an influence on the politics of the country. One states it, as a fact, that they exercise that influence," said Barrès.[7] For Sorel, the literary quarrel of "the ancients and the moderns" became an important event in the history of philosophy.[8] The traditional association between politics and culture was continued in the Third Republic, as was demonstrated when the performance of Sardou's *Thermidor* in 1891, regarded by the Left as a counter-revolutionary manifesto, led to an important debate in the Chamber on political principles.

[7] Maurice Barrès, "L'Elite intellectuelle et la démocratie," *Revue politique et littéraire* (November 19, 1904), 41:246.
[8] *Georges Sorel, Les Illusions du progrès*, Paris, 1927, pp. 35-36.

The relationship between intellectual and political figures in the 1885 to 1914 period was an extraordinarily close one. Clemenceau, novelist, art patron for the Louvre, friend of Debussy, companion of Daudet and Goncourt; Viviani and Jaurès, reciting by heart the whole of *Phèdre*; the rigid Marxist, Guesde, writing Baudelairian verse; Hanotaux, both Foreign Minister and historian; Quesnay de Beaurepaire, both magistrate and novelist—these are not exceptional figures. It was typical that Clemenceau, forming his Cabinet in October 1906, should find his Minister of War, Picquart, staying in Vienna with Gustav Mahler.

No account of French socialism can neglect the influence of the Ecole Normale Supérieure and of its librarian, Lucien Herr, who attempted to make it a Port-Royal of science and philosophy, as Massis said. Indeed, in some sense, political differences can be seen as an outcome of the struggle between the Rue d'Ulm and the Rue Saint-Guillaume.

"The heir to the Bourbons," said Maurras, "is the man of letters," and in fact, at the end of the nineteenth century, many of the influential men in France, Clemenceau, Drumont, Rochefort, Father Bailly, Cassagnac were newspaper editors. In the absence of strong, disciplined parties, the career of a political figure depended upon his popularity, and the press was the best way in which this could be developed. Barrès himself conducted his literary and political campaigns at the same time. The considerable number of frustrated aesthetes left unemployed by the publishing crisis at the end of the nineteenth century, who turned to political anti-Semitism or joined the Action Française,[9] was a portent of the *déclassé* intellectual of the 1930's.

"Beneath every literature there is a philosophy," said Taine. The tastes of Maurras and Barrès in literature and of Sorel in historical periods may have been more influential in their thinking than they were willing or able to confess. It was, after all, Barrès' article in *Le Figaro* in 1892, "La Querelle des Nationalistes et des Cosmopolites," dealing not with a

[9] R. F. Byrnes, *Anti-Semitism in Modern France*, New Brunswick, 1950, i: 287.

political question at all but with the differences between those
poets supporting the classical French tradition and the admirers of Tolstoy and Ibsen, that led to the transition from
literary to political nationalism.

Barrès, Maurras, and to a lesser degree, Sorel, were all concerned with the French literary tradition and its correct expression, and the first two could both say of their former
mentor and political enemy, Anatole France, "Above all, he
preserved the French language." They agreed with France
that "our French culture . . . the noblest and most delicate
thing in the world . . . is becoming impoverished."[10] All these
writers had a deep love for the soil and heritage of France,
and exemplified the aphorism of Mauriac, "Cybele has more
worshippers in France than Christ."

It was this appreciation of the greatness of France and of
its historic place in the world, coupled with a concern about
the relative decline of the country and with what appeared
to be signs of decadence, that allowed the three writers to
be characteristically representative of French thought. In a
country where even the revolutionary theories move in nar-
rowly prescribed directions, where political events may be
commemorated by annual excursions to the Père-Lachaise
cemetery, where the question of the resting place of the Unknown Soldier has profound political meaning, and the tombs
of the illustrious dead provide one of the major tourist at-
tractions, these three writers could all claim to be inheritors
of one of the varieties of French tradition. Sorel was in the
tradition of Proudhon, of resistance to the State and the dislike of politics; Barrès in the tradition of Stendhal and Chateaubriand, of individual sensibility; and Maurras in the tradition of de Maistre, Comte, Fustel de Coulanges, of order
and stability. Almost in spite of themselves, they illustrated
the truth of Péguy's argument in *Notre Jeunesse* that the
Revolution was not the dividing line between good and bad,
that tradition did not end or liberty begin in 1789.

But these writers possessed the disadvantages as well as the
advantages of French culture and tradition. Provincial, steeped

[10] Anatole France, *On Life and Letters*, New York, 1911, I: 247-248.

in and proud of their inheritance, they argued within the context of a limited sphere of knowledge, which resulted in surprisingly poor judgment and a remarkable blindness to actual conditions. The opinions of Barrès on German philosophy or of Maurras on the British constitutional monarchy betrayed the fact that their knowledge was often both secondhand and inadequate. "Barrès' criticism of Descartes, Kant, and Comte in *Le Jardin de Bérénice* is completely wrong," wrote Parodi,[11] and in fact one can have little faith in the criticism of a writer who judges Fourier on the basis of a preface by Charles Gide, Lassalle by a photograph, and Marx by the kitchens of German restaurants. Barrès, in the first issue of his journal, *Les Taches d'encre*, November 5, 1884, wrote, "We have intellectual fathers in all countries. Kant, Goethe, Hegel rank alongside the first of us," and at different times claimed among those who had influenced him Seneca, Loyola, Pascal, Montesquieu, Constant, Disraeli. But one finds in his thought little trace of this broad intellectual parentage, little appreciation of foreign culture for their own sake. As late as 1923, he was using a scholar, Gustave Cohen, to translate a book into English for him. Similarly, Maurras, denying the Nietzschean influence that critics had detected in his first book, *Le Chemin de paradis*, confessed he had never heard of the German, let alone read him, when he wrote his book.

The stress of these writers on literary classicism often led to surprisingly bad judgment, adulation of second-rate writers over important figures, and neglect of the novel. What a comment on Barrès' literary judgment that he should dismiss Proust as "de nouveau," although the latter had dedicated a book to him! In an era when interest in foreign cultures—in Wagner, Ibsen, and Dostoevsky, in Japanese art and the Russian ballet—was developing, the parochialism of the Nationalists becomes even more striking.

With the partial exception of Sorel, all three writers had an almost total disregard for real economic and social condi-

11 D. Parodi, "La Doctrine politique et sociale de M. Maurice Barrès," *La Revue du mois* (January 1907), 3:34.

tions, little realization of the industrial changes occurring in the world, little conception of the underlying shift in power relations, especially between France and Germany, borne out in figures of production and trade. All misread both history and contemporary conditions to support their attacks, all had a highly limited view of political reality, and were almost devoid of practical suggestions.

Yet besides the limitations of interest of the three themselves, it was also the novelty of the problems, two of which were of outstanding importance, that precluded any significant thinking. Externally, there was the problem of the relative decline of France in the hierarchy of nations, especially in relation to Germany. Internally, there was the problem of the rise of working-class movements and the appearance of the mass on the political scene. Underlying both problems were the deficiencies in the economic system, and the social problems to which they gave rise.

ECONOMIC AND SOCIAL DIFFICULTIES

Economic Difficulties

Though Rist called the period 1897 to 1912 one of great progress and industrial advance,[12] this cannot be substantiated in any comparative sense. It is true that foreign trade doubled in value from 7½ million to 15 million francs, and that from 1885 to 1912 coal mining doubled, iron and steel production tripled, and 10,000 kilometers of railroad tracks were added, but the corresponding increase in Germany and England was far greater. France remained almost self-supporting, but at a price, paid in stagnant exports and failure to develop home industries connected with the handling of imported foods. The enterprising economic ideas of Jules Siegfried, Alsatian Protestant, were, as his son remarked, "to a certain degree ideas foreign to France."[13] Even colonial expansion was due more to individual initiative than to the

[12] Charles Rist, "Nos Ressources financières," *La Revue de Paris* (December 1, 1915), 23:660.

[13] André Siegfried, *Mes Souvenirs de la Troisième République*, Paris, 1946, p. 25.

13

deliberate will of parliamentary assemblies, and allowed France, at least in appearance, to conserve its place among the great states.[14] To some extent until 1914, says Goguel, the inconveniences of a feeble and divided political regime were hardly noticeable. The power of the Parisian financial market and customs protection masked the backwardness of the productive capacity of France and its inability to face its rivals in the international markets.

The lack of progress was due to several factors. France was short of raw materials, except iron ore, vital for expansion, and imported over one-third of the total coal used. Its coal reserves were one-tenth those of Great Britain, and one twenty-fifth those of Germany. Its rivers could not sustain large shipping traffic. The price of fuel was high, it was often not good for coking, and France had insufficient water power. There was inadequate scientific application to industrial problems, and little attention given to the development of French inventive genius. Serious scientific teaching was limited. Méline, "whose heart beat only for cereals," and whose solution to the economic problem was protection, held in his book, *Le Retour à la terre et la surproduction industrielle*, that since the manufacturing industry no longer had any future and provided contemptible dividends of only two to three per cent, there should be more investment in land.

The conservative economic behavior, the lack of speculation, and the desire for a moderate regular income meant a high rate of book amortization, a shortage of risk capital, a holding by the banks of too much ready money, and an export of capital. From one-third to one-half of French savings were invested abroad; in the period from 1889 to 1908, over 24 billion francs worth of foreign stocks were bought, and only 15 billion of French. There were about 17 billion francs spent on Russian bonds, one quarter of which were in government bonds, giving a second motive to the Russian alliance. (Ferry's youthful indiscretion in shouting "Vive la Pologne!" in the Czar's face was discreetly forgotten for both

[14] François Goguel, *Le Régime politique français*, Paris, 1955, p. 16.

commercial and diplomatic reasons.) But there was considerable criticism of the loans to Germany, which were being used both for German industrial development and to cement German relations with Turkey. There was a working relationship between French and German banks, but "the male sex was always on the other side of the Rhine."[15]

The relative lack of change in the economy—64 per cent of the population was living in rural areas in 1886 and 56 per cent in 1911—suggested rigidity rather than equilibrium. France was the only great Western country that remained largely rural, and the normal scale of economic organization, both agricultural and industrial, was small. Of the seven million owners of land, 29,000 owned 30 million acres among them, while five million farmers owned six million acres. In 1895, 85 per cent of farms were less than 25 acres in size, and 39 per cent only 2½ acres.[16] The average French entrepreneur was a small businessman, operating by himself or with partners. In 1896, 534,000 of the 575,000 industrial establishments employed fewer than 10 persons,[17] while fewer than one per cent of plants had over 500 workers. By 1906, only 41 per cent of all industrial employees worked in establishments of over 100 workers. The 1880's had seen the opening of large shops like the Bonheur des Dames portrayed by Zola, which constituted a severe competitive challenge to small business, but France was still a nation of small enterprises with few great industrial concentrations, until 1906, when the Union des Industries was created by the Comité des Forges, a steel trust grouping 44 companies in several industries. For the Radicals, the word *petit* had a certain *mystique*; it is not surprising that six major newspapers had *petit* in their titles. The political significance of this small-scale economy lay in the fact that the small businessman would continually vacillate between the appeals of reaction and radicalism.

[15] Lysis, *Les Capitalistes français contre la France*, Paris, 1916, p. 34.
[16] W. F. Ogburn and W. Jaffé, *The Economic Development of Post-War France*, New York, 1929, p. 472.
[17] S. B. Clough, *France: A History of National Economics 1789-1939*, New York, 1939, p. 232.

Social Evils

The lack of a strong economic base gave rise to serious social problems: depopulation and overcentralization, antagonism between workers and owners of businesses, and alcoholism.

There was a constant concern over the failure of the French population to increase, especially when it was compared with the rapid expansion in Germany. In 1885 there was little difference in numbers between the two countries; by 1912, Germany had a population of 68 millión while France had only 39 million, an increase of little more than one million from 1886. Moreover, the population was aging. In 1900 35.6 per cent of the people were over 40.

The concern was not limited to the stagnation of the total population. It also included an awareness of the fact that after 1875 the rural population had begun both an absolute and a relative decline. By 1890 the population in more than half of the departments was not replacing itself. This meant that a large number of aliens were working on the land; in 1911, for instance, there were 12,000 Italians working in the Grenoble area alone.

The city began to make its impact on French life and thinking.

> Lorsque les soirs
> Sculptent le firmament de leur manteaux d'ébène,
> La ville au loin s'étale et domine la plaine.
>
> C'est la ville que la nuit formidable éclaire,
> La ville en plâtre, en stuc, en bois, en fer, en or,
> Tentaculaire.
> —VERHAEREN

But it was not the growth of cities as such that caused discontent. In 1911 there were still only five towns with over 200,000 population. It was the growth of Paris, and the political problems that followed from this growth, that were alarming. "By 1789," Tocqueville had written, "Paris was

France."[18] Louis XIV had on six occasions attempted to check the growth of Paris and had failed. Its population had doubled in half a century, being one million by 1850. From 1870 to 1900 its growth accounted for half the total increase in France.

The political implications of this concentration soon became evident. "When one is born in a great town like Paris one has no country . . . one has only a street," said Dumas. The uprootedness of individuals of which Barrès became the spokesman, the presence in Paris of highly literate and articulate coteries,[19] the absorption of the intellectual life of the whole country led to the concentration of discontent, an increase of political activity against the regime, and criticism of the political centralization which was one of its major characteristics. Napoleon in Moscow could sign the decree directing the Comédie Française; a Ministry in the early 1900's in Paris could decide the color of latrines in Toulon.[20]

A serious inadequacy was the reluctance to frame social reforms. The erroneous belief that Gambetta had declared there was no social question was widespread, and not until 1881 did Clemenceau produce the cry, "Vive la République démocratique et sociale." But social evils, like the housing problem in Paris, where more than one-third of the houses were unhealthy, and a million Parisians lived without the necessary air space,[21] went unattended. Probably the most serious complaints were raised against the menace of alcoholism.

In 1872, there had been 179,000 shops selling drink. After the removal of all restrictions in 1881 on the number of saloons and public houses, there were 410,000 in 1889 and 483,000 in 1913. Paris itself had one for every four houses. At the beginning of the twentieth century, there were at Menilmontant

[18] Alexis de Tocqueville, *L'Ancien régime*, Oxford, 1949, p. 80.

[19] R. F. Byrnes, *op.cit.*, pp. 40-41. In 1900 there were over 120,000 people working for newspapers.

[20] Robert de Jouvenel, *La République des camarades*, Paris, 1914, p. 121.

[21] P. M. Boujou and H. Dubois, *La Troisième République 1870-1940*, Paris, 1952, p. 49.

INTRODUCTION

14 cafes out of 20 shops. The number of people engaged in distilling had grown from 90,000 in 1869 to over one million in 1913.[22] The average consumption in 1889 was four liters per person. This growth in alcoholism had had, it was held, a detrimental effect on the health of the people, leading to a rise in tuberculosis, early mortality and criminality. Moreover, it was believed to be one of the factors in the fall of population growth. To the Right, the tavern was a bulwark of anticlerical democratic aspirations.[23] A correlation was observed between the development of the alcohol peril and the progress of socialist ideas, and this was a menace that could not be neglected, because "one changes one's religion more easily than one changes one's cafe."

Moreover, wine production brought political problems with it. The hazards of wine production and the phylloxera disease caused a reduction in the area under cultivation of 33 per cent between 1873 and 1900,[24] leading to demands for protection from the formerly free-trade South, and to political demonstrations. During the most important crisis in 1907, Marcellin Albert, "Redeemer of the South," threatened the regime, but had neither practical advice to offer nor organizational ability to guide the movement, the serious nature of which was shown by the burning of a town hall, the partial mutiny of two regiments, and the resignation of Under-Secretary of State Sarraut.

But the major defect was the failure to ameliorate conditions of work and the reluctance of employers to make concessions to their workers. Working conditions were far from pleasant. There were few holidays, and the working day in 1900 was long—11 hours in the North, 10 in the South, and on the railways a continuous work period of 20 hours was not unknown. In 1898 there were 6,000 infringements of the laws regulating factories; so-called "charity" organizations employed children of four and five; and hygiene regulations

[22] The supply was greatly increased by the removal of excise taxes from all alcohol produced for private consumption.
[23] H. Leyret, *La République et les politiciens*, Paris, 1909, pp. 120-122.
[24] J. H. Clapham, *The Economic Development of France and Germany 1815-1914*, Cambridge, 1928, p. 180.

were widely disregarded. The industrial accident rate was vastly increased in the 1890's: in 1898 alone there were 35,000 accidents, of which 643 were fatal. Inspection was made difficult because, of the 309,000 establishments in 1899, 270,300 employed fewer than 11 persons.

The response of the working class to these conditions and to their precarious situation was an increase in acts of violence, the idea of the General Strike, and the growth of trade unions and Socialist groups. It was only toward the end of the first decade of the twentieth century, when the working-class movements were increasing in strength and in influence and constituted a possible threat to the regime, that concessions were made and important social legislation passed. The regime had been late to recognize the Aristotelian truth that any person or body adding new power to the state would tend to produce sedition.

The Rise of Caliban

Until 1877 politics for the workers consisted solely in supporting the Republican parties. Thiers had said, "One no longer talks of socialism . . . we have got rid of it," but events were soon to belie him. The return of the condemned of the Commune to France in 1880, which caused Cassagnac to launch the slogan incessantly repeated by the Right, "The assassins and the incendiaries are returning; the priests are departing!" the leadership by Jules Guesde of the Café Soufflet group, gave an impetus to working-class organizations and activities.

Important strikes at Decazeville and Vierzon had broken out in 1886 and stoppages of work were becoming increasingly frequent. Between 1890 and 1893 they had doubled in number: in the latter year there were 634 strikes involving over 170,000 workers. The May Day demonstration of 1891 produced the "massacre of Fourmies," where several workers were killed. Clemenceau, who had been acute enough in 1885 to abandon Paris as a constituency and transfer to Draguignan in the Var, spoke of the Fourth Estate which was arising, and which either had to be rejected with violence or welcomed with open arms.[25] Acts of terrorism by anarchists began to make the middle class worry, not only about income tax proposals but about bombs.

In 1887 the Duval incident, a case of robbery, arson, and murder, had led to a difference of opinion between Guesde and the Socialists, Séverine and the anarchists. In 1892, Ravachol had robbed a sepulchre and murdered a hermit beggar. On December 9, 1893, Vaillant threw a bomb during a meeting of the Chamber of Deputies, producing a declaration from the President of the Chamber, Charles Dupuy, "Messieurs, la séance continue," which was soon to make him Prime Minister. The Duchesse d'Uzès, the patroness of Boulanger, declared that she was ready to take care of the orphan of Vaillant.

On February 5, 1894, Emile Henry threw a bomb in the Hotel Terminus; on April 4, 1894, another explosion in the Restaurant Foyot wounded and caused the loss of an eye to the poet, Laurent Tailhade, who, after the Vaillant incident, had written, "What does the death of some unimportant people matter if the gesture is beautiful?" On June 24th, the President of the Republic himself was assassinated.

The principle of the General Strike was affirmed in 1888 at the Bordeaux Congress of the National Federation of *Syndicats*, which had been founded in 1886, and it was supported by other working-class organizations and upheld by Congresses of the C.G.T. (Confédération Générale du Travail) in 1896 and 1897, although it was not supported by the political Socialists. Guesde in particular had denounced it, and in 1904 suggested that the idea of the General Strike did more harm to socialism than did "ministerialism." But even the united Socialist party agreed in 1906 to support the Charter of Amiens with its recognition of class struggle and its emphasis on direct action. Sorel thought the Charter one of the most important dates in the working-class movement because of its antipatriotic, antimilitarist, and antistatist program.[26]

25 *Journal Officiel* (May 8, 1891), p. 816.
26 Edouard Berth, *Les Derniers aspects du socialisme*, Paris, 1923, p. 51.

The strike in France has had an almost mystical value to many workers as an affirmation of class consciousness and class action. But if the period between 1902 and 1909 was really what Cole has called "the heroic period of syndicalism,"[27] it was also one which produced in reaction not only the consolidation of employers through the Comité des Forges, but also governmental action arresting strike leaders and using the army to end the strikes. It is ironic that it was Briand, in 1888 and 1892 so vehement a proponent of the General Strike, who in 1910 broke the threat of such a strike by arresting its committee and calling up 15,000 strikers.

Though the number of *syndicat* members had grown rapidly—in 1906 there were 4,857 *syndicats* with a membership of 836,000, while in 1914 there were 4,846 with a membership of 1,026,000—the membership was still small in comparison to the total of six million workers. The ideas of syndicalism were in fact largely the result of the small, decentralized elitist *syndicats'* constant lack of financial support, and their disillusionment with political organizations.[28] Hostility to all parties, including Socialist ones, was evident, and the degree of this hostility was shown in 1908 when, at a meeting of postal workers on strike, the well-known M. Buisson and a few other Socialist deputies were hooted off the platform. The early development of a bitter antiparty, antiparliamentary attitude toward the Third Republic on the part of many French workers contributed in no small measure to the difficulties of French democracy.

Part of the problem of the French working-class movement was its internal division, no less in the Socialist groups than in the trade union bodies. The rise of Socialist parties after 1885 challenged the claim of Clemenceau to be the political spokesman for the working class.[29] But at the 1899 Paris Socialist Congress, there were still five chief Socialist groups,

[27] G. D. H. Cole, *A History of Socialist Thought*, Vol. III, *The Second International 1889-1914*, London, 1956, Part 1, p. 342.
[28] Lewis Lorwin, *Syndicalism in France*, 2nd edn., New York, 1914, pp. 210-212.
[29] J. A. Scott, *Republican Ideas and the Liberal Tradition in France 1870-1914*, New York, 1951, p. 134.

and numerous minor political groups, labor unions, and cooperative societies. It was not until 1905 that the Socialist schism was healed and that it broke with its Republican allies. The united party advanced rapidly. In 1906 it obtained a total of 878,000 votes and 52 seats; in 1910 it obtained 1,100,000 votes and 76 seats; in 1914 it obtained 1,400,000 votes and 103 seats. When the outstanding leader of the party, Jean Jaurès, was assassinated in 1914, a whole nation mourned.

The fact that France was troubled by these new and complex problems, both external and internal, for which no solution was in sight, meant a considerable degree of dissatisfaction with and opposition to the regime. In this opposition, Sorel, Maurras, and Barrès were prominent in giving voice to the discontent and in attempting to give it direction. Much of the antagonism against the regime was produced in the various crises that France experienced from 1885 to 1914, and it was in the ferment of the Boulanger and Dreyfus crises that the political theories of Maurras, Barrès, and Sorel were to a large extent forged and elaborated.

To examine the case made against the Republic by these three men is to test the appropriateness of their criticisms, the degree of their profundity, and their ability to recognize deficiencies and suggest changes. But since the three writers were all products of French culture with its concomitant advantages and disadvantages, they reacted as do many French thinkers to political problems. It may be that France is an illustration of Bagehot's observation that nations, just as individuals, may be too clever to be practical, and not dull enough to be free. The presence of writers postulating abstract theories which allow no compromise, the refusal to recognize the consequences of their proposals, and the doctrinaire nature of a pure system may be responsible for that lack of contact between theory and action symptomatic of France.

TWO CRISES: BOULANGER
AND DREYFUS

OF THE MANY CRISES which confronted the Third Republic up to 1914, the two most serious, and the two most responsible for the division of opinion in the country, were those in which General Boulanger and Captain Dreyfus became the respective symbols of opposition to or support for the Republic. The Boulanger crisis was an indication of the danger, perpetually lurking just below the surface of French political life, of the ability of the demagogue or the strong man by an appeal to national unity to rally around himself all those bearing resentment toward the regime. The Dreyfus Affair showed the Republicans, and eventually the Socialists, that the union of the former constituent elements of the *ancien régime*—the army, the Church, and the aristocracy—imperiled the life of the Republic.

The two crises were important not only in the political life of France, but also in the formation of political attitudes by Barrès, Maurras, and Sorel. It was the Boulanger crisis that first stirred Barrès, a potential Bonapartist, into political activity, and the image of the energetic and dynamic leader was one that he never lost. It was the Dreyfus Affair that caused Barrès and Maurras to come together as leaders of the antirevisionist movement and as dual spokesmen of the Right. It was the outcome of the same Affair that led Sorel, a Dreyfusard during the years of the crisis, if a somewhat lukewarm one, to adopt a more bitter and extreme antipolitical, antiparliamentarian, and anti-intellectual attitude because of his disappointment at its outcome.

BOULANGER: THE REPUBLIC AROUSED

Sixteen years after the establishment of the Republic, it faced its first severe crisis and survived—thanks to a combination of good fortune, the weakness of the leading figure in the crisis, ineptitude on the part of its attackers, and an unusually astute political maneuver. Boulangism was an incoherent movement linking those dissident elements discontented for various reasons with the existing regime: antirepublicans, antidemocrats and anti-Semites, those wanting constitutional revision, those opposed to the anticlerical bias of the regime, and those whose primary emotion was the memory of the defeat by Germany.

Behind the growth of this first important movement of discontent were the desire for *la revanche* and for national glory, the rise of nationalist sentiment, the continual tension with Germany and the belief that Bismarck was being forced to withdraw through his fear of the possible intervention of a superior force, and a distaste for a regime that had produced a number of scandals, the last of which touched the Elysée itself. Professional patriots like Déroulède, favoring an alliance with Russia as the best defense against Germany, were attracted to it.

Between 1878 and 1889, the most profound emotion in the hearts of the masses was *la revanche*.[1] Mme Adam, the friend of Gambetta, had divided Frenchmen into friends and foes of the idea.[2] But while Gambetta had warned, "Think of it always; speak of it never," the raucous emotionalism of Déroulède made it a nationalist war cry:

> Et la revanche doit finir, lente peut-être
> Mais en tout cas fatale, et terrible à coup sûr;
> La haine est déjà née, et la force va naître:
> C'est au faucheur à voir si le champ n'est pas mûr.

Déroulède, opposed to Ferry's policy of colonial expeditions at the expense of the eastern frontier—"I have lost two children and you offer me twenty servants,"[3] became in 1884

---

[1] Alexandre Zévaès, *Une Génération*, Paris, 1922, p. 9.

[2] G. P. Gooch, "Mme Adam and Gambetta," *Courts and Cabinets,* New York, 1946, p. 351.

[3] Jérôme et Jean Tharaud, *La Vie et la mort de Déroulède*, Paris, 1914, pp. 6-7. It is paradoxical that Ferry, attacked over Tonkin, had had 20,000 copies of Déroulède's poems, *Chants du soldat*, distributed in the schools.

President of the League of Patriots, dedicated to "the preparation of revenge." He offered Boulanger two medals, one of Gambetta and the other of Chanzy, the civilian and the military leader of resistance to the Germans in 1870. The thoughts of the League of Patriots, the witty journalist Séverine said, sought refuge like the storks on the rooftops of Alsace. Certainly Boulanger endeared himself to the patriots by the tears he shed over the five flags of Alsace-Lorraine, draped with black streamers, which were displayed at a gymnastic exhibition in Paris.

But to the original aim of the League, Déroulède added that of the revision of the Constitution by appeal to the nation. France, to be strong, had to have an authoritarian government, not a parliamentary one, and one Nationalist party, not a chaos of conflicting factions. Constantly looking for the strong man, he found him in the man on the black horse. Boulangism attracted all those who wanted constitutional revision. Since the failure of Gambetta in 1881 and 1882 to obtain approval for proposals for constitutional reform, all plans for revision and appeals for strong government were to come from the reactionary, antiparliamentary, and sometimes antirepublican Right.[4]

Like all movements having no genuine or basic ideas of its own, Boulangism appealed to everyone, "un talisman promis à tous les malheureux," as Arthur Meyer said in 1889: to workers protesting against the mechanization of work, to artisans reduced to the condition of employees, to small businessmen impoverished by economic crisis, to manufacturers troubled by imports of German goods, to farmers hurt by the lowering of agricultural prices, bad crops and phylloxeria, to those who had lost their savings in the crash of the Union Générale. The diversity of the movement gave it the appearance of a carnival.[5]

The central figure, Boulanger himself, was all things to all men: Cromwell to the Republicans, Monk to the Royalists,

[4] François Goguel, "The Historical Background of Contemporary French Politics," *Yale French Studies*, No. 15 (July 1955), p. 32.
[5] Georges Bernanos, *La Grande peur des bien-pensants*, Paris, 1931, p. 217.

Saint-Arnaud to the Bonapartists, "Général Revanche" to the patriots, Caesar to his country, and to Marguerite de Bonnemain a neuropathic Anthony.[6] To the religious, he was a savior against the atheistic, intolerant Republic which had introduced educational legislation banning religion from the schools, and which had made primary education free, laic, and compulsory.

To a large degree he inherited that charismatic quality which the French, since the days of Napoleon, have associated with certain individuals. In the early years of the Republic, Gambettism was the direct line of descent from Bonapartism. Siegfried tells of an old man who said, "You see this hand? Gambetta shook it. I have not washed it since."[7] Boulangism was in many ways the heir to Gambettism, though many of Gambetta's followers, like Joseph Reinach, were hostile to Boulanger.

Largely a product of the large towns, Boulangism was of comparatively little importance in the rural areas. The movement appealed to the workers addicted to *la revanche*, love of military glory, and dislike of the parliamentary oligarchy. Extreme Socialist and Blanquist insurrectionists like Roche, Granger, and Elie May, believing in the necessity of a transitory minority dictatorship, were attracted, and old Communards like Pierre Denis and Louise Michel flirted with the movement. At Nancy in 1889 Maurice Barrès made his electoral debut as a Nationalist and a Socialist.

Initially the protégé of the Radicals and of the anticlericals, Boulanger drifted to the Right and entered into negotiations with monarchists, with the Church, and with foreign autocrats. As early as November 29, 1887, Boulanger had reached an agreement at the house of the Comte de Martimprey, the Comte de Mackau representing the Comte de Paris, to restore the monarchy after a *coup d'état* and an appeal to the people. But his duplicity was such that he also paid a secret visit to Prangins to see the Napoleonic pretender.

In a speech at Tours on March 17, 1889, he appealed to

6 Adrien Dansette, *Le Boulangisme 1886-1890*, Paris, 1938, p. 374.
7 André Siegfried, *Mes Souvenirs de la Troisième République*, p. 91.

the Church and declared that the Republic must repudiate its Jacobin heritage. For the Left he became "le Boulanger des curés," "la revanche des Jesuites." His appeal was successful in that the expulsion of the Sisters of Mercy from the hospitals helped him to win the election in Paris.

On August 9, 1889, he wrote to Alexander of Russia, presenting himself as the choice of Providence, who would guarantee law and order and ensure a strong France. He promised to end bribery and corruption by uprooting parliamentarianism and the monstrous abuses resulting from it, and to fight against the growing threat of socialism. The Russian autocrat, soon to visit France and pay respect to the Marseillaise, ignored the letter.

The program of Boulanger was as broad and as vague as these varied appeals. His program of "Dissolution, Constituante, et Révision," loose and obscure, was interpreted differently. The parliamentary regime would be abolished and replaced by one Chamber, with powers limited by Presidential veto and popular referendum, and a Council of State to make the law. Ministers who would be chosen from outside the Council would be responsible to the Head of State. The method of election of the President would be changed. Boulanger became the first leader in modern times to insist on the need for unity of a National party, instead of a nation broken into small groups. He was the first "to call all good Frenchmen to group themselves around me to strengthen the Republic." The support of *la revanche* and of a Russian alliance, and his opposition to colonial expeditions allowed for a time a temporary reconciliation with Clemenceau against the common enemy, Ferry, in 1887. For the first time, Republicans were allied with monarchists against other Republicans. But on social and economic questions, no solution was offered. The Boulangist movement was "a faith for the troops, a means for the lieutenants, an end for the leader, but for no one a doctrine."[8]

The importance of the movement and its danger to the existence of the Republic can be attested to by its remarkable

[8] Adrien Dansette, *op.cit.*, p. 153.

popularity. It was the parade on July 14, 1886, when the soldiers turned their heads right to Boulanger and not left to the President of the Republic, that established his political significance. A three-line announcement in the newspapers sufficed to bring 150,000 to the Gare de Lyon on July 8th to prevent his departure for Clermont-Ferrand where he had been "exiled" by a government that wanted to get him out of Paris.[9] His name literally became a household word with the manufacture of Boulanger soap, pipes, lorgnettes, weapons, toys, playing cards (he was one of the kings), food and liqueur (the only one not containing any German product).

> C'est à Boulanger que tous devront leur pain
> On ne peut se passer de boulanger.

Politics had degenerated into a commercial enterprise.

Boulangism was a movement of the large towns in which the leading part was taken by disgruntled journalists hostile to the regime, like Rochefort, Eugène Mayer, Portalis, Lalou, as much as by professional politicians. The treasury of this Nationalist movement was amply filled by the friend of Arthur Meyer, the Duchesse d'Uzès, whose money flowed as freely as the champagne from which it had been derived, and by Baron Hirsch, an Austrian who sought to emulate in reality the acceptance of Swann by the *haut monde*.

Antiparliamentary, antidemocratic, and, depending upon Boulanger's relation with Drumont, intermittently anti-Semitic in spite of the fact that some of his most important administrative assistants and some of his financial supporters were Jewish, Boulangism constituted the most important single threat to the regime in its early period. It is probable that the fate of the Republic on the evening of January 27, 1889, hung on the lips of the enigmatic Marguerite de Bonnemain.[10] That the movement failed was due to the deficiencies

[9] Fifty years later, the glass from which he had drunk while at the station was on display at a fashionable antique shop in Paris.

[10] Mme de Bonnemain was one of the many women, from Mme Adam to Mme de Portès, who played a role of political importance in the life of the Third Republic. It is improbable that she was either a German spy or an agent of the French Government, as many supposed.

of Boulanger himself, to the lack of a doctrine, to the diversity of its adherents, and to the firm hand of one Republican.

The most curious part of the movement was the leader himself, "a Hitler who failed,"[11] as Raymond Mortimer has called him, who had little understanding of the causes of the movement he was leading. His meteoric rise was due to Clemenceau, who scornfully dismissed him after his suicide as "the general who died as he had lived—a second lieutenant," and to the cabaret singer, Paulus, who as readily wrote songs for the opponents of Boulanger as for Boulanger himself, and who chose as the hero of his songs Boulanger, rather than two other generals almost by accident. One has, commented *La Vie Parisienne*, the comedians that one deserves: Louis XIV had Molière, Napoleon had Talma, Gambetta had Coquelin, and Boulanger had Paulus.

Ambitious, sympathetic, popular, and attractive to many women, Boulanger was singularly deficient in qualities of character and intelligence, a liar, and an intriguer. At one point he was negotiating with future Prime Ministers Freycinet, Goblet, and Floquet, promising a *coup d'état* to the Royalists, and paying a visit to Prince Napoleon. He was a man of action who ran before danger, a political adventurer who dreaded adventures. The disillusion that Mme de Caillavet, the Egeria of Anatole France, experienced after giving an eagerly awaited dinner party for him was not unusual,[12] yet ladies of the aristocracy continued to curtsey to him, to place him at the head of their tables.

Almost as soon as he became Minister of War, he organized a press bureau to record and publicize his actions. His ambition, limited at first to remaining Minister of War, grew by what it fed upon. Meetings were arranged for him with the Francophile Prince of Wales, who had once succeeded in bring-

[11] Raymond Mortimer, "Books in General," *New Statesman and Nation* (August 1, 1942), 24:78. By a curious coincidence, both the Boulangist and the Nazi movements reached their climax about 15 years after the defeat of the two countries in war.

[12] J. M. Pouquet, *The Last Salon: Anatole France and His Muse*, New York, 1927, p. 119.

ing Gambetta and Galliffet together.[13] Carried away by the flattery of the aristocracy and by the ease of his entrance into the house of the Duchesse de la Carrachioli, Countess Bari, and Countess Soboleska, he was drawn further and further from his political origins and merited Emperor William of Germany's scornful dismissal of him as "His Majesty Ernest I." His political career was an unscrupulous vacillation from the black horse of Longchamp to the Black Horse of Ixelles.[14]

Boulanger, hesitant, without the energy or will to prepare or make a *coup d'état*, was content to wait for power to fall into his hands. A Pichegru rather than the Augereau that Clemenceau had at first thought him, lacking that inner toughness without which political preoccupation declines into stagnant sentimentalism, he refused on two occasions to take advantage of circumstances in his favor. History, said Marx, repeats itself, once as tragedy and once as farce. With the Government bewildered, the President preparing to leave the Elysée less than six hundred yards away, even Clemenceau wondering what conditions were like in New Caledonia, the police benevolently neutral if not overtly favorable, the Parisian populace in unusually high spirits, and his own supporters eagerly urging him to action, he was content to remain in the Café Durand at the Madeleine, and refused to follow the precedent of Louis Napoleon.

Thiébaud, one of the chief lieutenants of Boulanger, was correct in prophesying on the night of January 27, 1889, "Minuit cinq, messieurs. Depuis cinq minutes, le boulangisme est en baisse." With the victory almost won, Grouchy did not arrive. "L'Empire est mort de ses origines," argued Boulanger as a reason for not attempting a coup, but Déroulède was more realistic in replying, "Il en a vécue dix-huit ans." The Republic was fortunate that he was only "a comic

[13] M. Reclus, *La Troisième République de 1870 à 1918*, Paris, 1945, p. 110.

[14] Boulanger rode his black horse, Tunis, in the 1886 parade at Longchamp. The Black Horse was a tavern near the suburb of Ixelles, where Boulanger committed suicide on the grave of his mistress.

opera Saint-Arnaud." How apt was the comment of Constans, "È finita la comedia."

Yet the choice of whether to be Cromwell or Monk was one which depended as much on the nature of the movement as on himself. It is difficult to see how the incompatible views of the allied forces could have been reconciled. No one can ride two horses galloping in opposite directions, and the boulevard wit was not alone in saying, "I am with Boulanger up to the 17th Brumaire."

Political institutions can last as long as energetic men are willing to defend them. The alteration of the electoral system to single-member constituencies with a single ballot, the agility of Constans at the Place Beauvau, the skill in his inspired warnings to the frightened leader, the recall of the Duc d'Aumale from exile to divide the monarchist and personal followers of the General, and the confiscation of the papers and legal proceedings against the League of Patriots were sufficient to end the movement as a threat to the state. The Eiffel Tower, the most spectacular feature of the 1889 Exposition in Paris, may have been an outstanding engineering feat, but the survival of the Republic was an even greater political one.

Goguel has commented that Boulangism gave birth both to modern nationalism and to modern socialism in France.[15] Its basic antiparliamentary nature separated the Right from the moderate Republicans, while the discontent of the laboring masses against the system of economic liberalism produced a form of national socialism. The experience of the Commune and the enthusiasm of Gambetta had left a legacy of patriotism associated with the Left. The French had maintained their faith in the army, and even elected as their first President "the only Marshal who had been defeated more times than Bazaine."[16]

At first a popular movement seemingly in the tradition of the generals of the Committee of Public Safety, Boulangism

[15] François Goguel, *La Politique des partis sous la Troisième République*, Paris, 1946.
[16] Philip Guedalla, *The Two marshals: Bazaine, Pétain*, New York, 1943, p. 231.

was animated by the sentiments of anticlericalism and patriotism; Boulanger, the general of the Radicals, was the minister of *curés-sac-au-dos*. But reversing itself and becoming clerical and reactionary, Boulangism led to a situation in which the army, military power, and national defense became the prerogative of the Right, and the League of Patriots led by Déroulède the prototype of nationalist, antidemocratic organizations. The Departments of the East, from the electoral point of view formerly Republican, now began to vote for the Right.

The Boulangist crisis also illustrated the historic dilemma of Socialist parties, whether to remain intransigently uninterested in matters not connected with the making of the social revolution, or to support the lesser evil and ally with the Republicans against the threat of the Right. The Socialist parties were divided on the issue.

Support for the Republic came from Brousse and the Possibilists, who proclaimed that the first task was the struggle against Boulanger, and therefore formed an alliance with Constans and Ferry, who on October 14, 1883, had said the peril was on the Left. The Possibilists declared, "We workers are ready to forget the sixteen years during which the bourgeoisie has betrayed the hopes of the people, we are ready to defend and to conserve by all means the weak germ of our republican institutions against military threats. Long live the social Republic."[17]

In May 1888, on the initiative of Joffrin, Clemenceau, and de Ranc, the Société des Droits de l'Homme et du Citoyen was founded. A committee of direction including Socialists like Allemane, Brousse, Joffrin, and Paulard and non-Socialists like Clemenceau, Pelletan, Labordère, Mathé, and Révillon issued a manifesto declaring, "We believe that an entente between all those who remain faithful to the Republic is necessary to put an end to the Boulangist adventure so humiliating for our country. The entente will last as long as the peril. . . . The object of the Société is the defense of the

[17] As cited in Alexandre Zévaès, *Histoire du socialisme et du communisme en France*, Paris, 1947, p. 166.

Republic by the merciless struggle against any kind of reaction or dictatorship."[18]

The Blanquists were divided, some, like Granger and Roche, following Rochefort in an opportunist move to destroy the system, and others, like Vaillant and Landrin, joining the Guesdists in neutrality. A plague on the Rue de Sèze (the Boulangist headquarters), and the Rue Cadet (home of the Société des Droits de l'Homme). In the vital electoral contest in Paris on January 27, 1889, the Guesdists and Blanquists refused to support either Boulanger or Jacques, "the candidate of the Republic," and nominated their own candidate. For Guesde, "both the *epauletier* Boulanger and the boss Jacques belong to the same enemy class which for a century has caused proletarian France to be hungry and downtrodden." There was an air of unreality in Vaillant's election-day attack on both Boulanger and his opponent, the candidate of the Floquets and the Ferrys, of the bourgeois oligarchy. "Every good citizen must vote against personal power and against bourgeois reaction, against imperialism and opportunism, for the social Republic."[19]

The Republic was saved in spite of the extremists and neutralists, who were only too content to sit like patience on a monument. An important feature of the 1893 election was to be the appearance of over 50 Socialists. The political strength of the conservatives was reduced, and at the ensuing election, fewer than 20 candidates dared to run as monarchists. In 1893, the reaction against Boulangism produced the greatest Republican electoral triumph, ended the possibility of an immediate return of monarchy, and turned the interest of politicians in other directions. But Boulangism, with its radical origins, its appeal to class collaboration, its raucous self-advertisement, its direct appeal to the people, was to be a forerunner of all future mass political movements.

THE DREYFUS AFFAIR: A CALL TO ARMS

Léon Blum said, "One cannot understand the Dreyfus Affair unless one remembers that it broke out less than eight

[18] *loc.cit.*   [19] *ibid.*, pp. 170-172.

years after the failure of a revolution . . . the Boulangists were looking for revenge . . . and the discredit of institutions and parties."[20] The origin of the mystery of the Affair still lies buried in obscurity. Art could not follow the incredibly melodramatic complexity of nature, as Anatole France was to find when writing *Penguin Island*. Indeed it is even possible that the Affair was born on the day in 1892 when at the bridge of Charmes (the birthplace of Barrès!) army officers were jealous of the long conversation between General Boisdeffre and the officer Alfred Dreyfus who had so obviously impressed him with his knowledge of the maneuvers that were taking place. But its political importance lies in the defense of the Republic against the many-sided onslaught on it. It may be true that the 1898 general election was in no sense a referendum for or against Dreyfus, but it is difficult to believe that the Affair failed to affect the political life of the country, as Mr. Fox has claimed.[21] The most important political battles were fought outside the Chambers, and the degree of its importance was shown when Jaurès, bringing the Affair into the electoral campaign, lost his Parliamentary seat.

It divided France in a way which no other problem had done. When Proust in 1901 gave a dinner party to which 60 guests of differing political persuasions were invited, Léon Daudet wrote, "I doubt if anyone except Proust could have accomplished that feat."[22] In 1909 the ardent Dreyfusard, Jules Renard, still refused the friendship of the influential critic Jules Lemaître, an antirevisionist. It took some years before Rodin agreed to visit Anatole France again. The nonpolitical André Gide signed a petition in favor of Dreyfus, but confessed he was censured severely by his family. In December 1897, Barrès agreed to dine with Zola, France, and Bourget only on condition that there was no talk of the Dreyfus Affair.

20 Léon Blum, *Souvenirs sur l'affaire*, Paris, 1935, pp. 65-67.

21 E. W. Fox, "The Third Force 1897-1939," *Modern France*, ed. E. M. Earle, p. 132.

22 Léon Daudet, *Memoirs*, trans. A. K. Griggs, London, 1926, p. 267.

The division was as complete in the political as in the literary world. In the Chamber, the Minister of Labor, who had stopped to speak to Scheurer-Kestner for a moment, was obliged to say that it was only to get the address of a pastry shop.[23]

The Affair produced a considerable amount of violence, a number of duels in which politicians and journalists were antagonists (some of which showed that Clemenceau's skill as an adversary had been greatly exaggerated), anti-Semitic attacks in many of the large towns, suicides and attempted assassinations, several demonstrations and legal proceedings, and an unprecedented degree of abuse. One of the most distressing features of the Affair was the imputation of unworthy motives to the prorevisionists. For Brunetière, intellectuals had taken up Dreyfus from "exasperated vanity." Ideas of honor, justice, duty, and interest of the nation were found to have conflicting interpretations, producing the kind of callous cynicism shown by Paul Claudel, speaking of the harm the Affair had done France abroad. To Renard's question, "Mais la tolérance?" he replied, "Il y a des maisons pour ça."[24] For Bernanos, Zola's *J'Accuse* was a terrible blow at French morale; for Daudet, General Mercier had the surest and most scrupulous judgment.

The issue in the Affair was a confused one, the belief in the innocence or guilt of an individual being merely the starting point for more general differences of opinion. There was passion on both sides, the passion, Halévy said, of a race on one side, and that of a caste on the other.[25] There were differing motives behind the Dreyfusards—love of abstract justice or national honor, as with Péguy, love of truth irrespective of the consequences, as with Picquart, antimilitarism, which had been growing since Boulanger, and reaction against the nationalist, clerical, and anti-Semitic threats. In the opposing camp, the combination of the old Boulangists, the army, the

[23] Nicolas Halasz, *Captain Dreyfus*, New York, 1955, p. 110.
[24] Jules Renard, *Journal, Vol. 3 1901-1905*, Paris, 1927, p. 554.
[25] Daniel Halévy, "Apologie pour notre passé," *Cahiers de la Quinzaine* (1910), 11th Series, No. 11.

professional anti-Semites, the Church and some intellectuals—
supported by the mob, or what Anatole France called "Pecus"
—was a more consistent body because largely a negative one.
The antirevisionist belief, partly the crystallization of anti-
intellectual reaction to the excessive faith in science of the
nineteenth century, was in large measure a desire to maintain
the order of traditional authorities.

Yet sometimes it is difficult to account for the presence
of a person in a particular camp. Logically, one of the leaders
of the antirevisionist movement should have been Clemenceau—the man concerned with the national interest rather
than the fate of individuals, the man "little accessible to pity,
who pursued misanthropy to a cruel cynicism," as Blum said
—if he had not been aware of the elements dangerous to the
Republic in the movement. A Bonapartist like Paul de Cassagnac or an anti-Semite like Octave Mirbeau joined the
Dreyfusards, in opposition to most of their kind. An aesthete
like Barrès, the youthful maître, broke with most of his disciples in joining the antirevisionist group.

While the strength of the Dreyfusards was provincial, republican, and plebeian, drawing considerable support from the
literary world and the universities, the antirevisionists were
largely Parisian and upper middle class, including Royalists
and most of the French Academy. Anatole France, whose one
political certainty was the innocence of Dreyfus, would rarely
attend the Academy meetings after the Affair. The former
Boulangists, discontented with parliamentarianism and believing in plebiscitary rule, entered into the new movement,
led by Déroulède, Barrès, Rochefort, and Millevoye. As Péguy
wrote, there was much Caesarism in anti-Dreyfusism. The
Royalists, including Philippe of Orleans, were strongly antirevisionist, although some of their leaders, like the Empress
Eugènie and the Duc d'Aumale, possessing that inside knowledge of Dreyfus' innocence common to the European royal
circles, refused to join them.

The professional anti-Semites like Drumont and Guérin,
and those believing that "the aim of the Jewish-Masonic-
Protestant Syndicate is to discredit the army, in dishonoring

the General Staff, most of whose members are old students of congregational schools,"[26] were active participants against Dreyfus. Both the contemporary and future leaders of the army were antirevisionist. It was an augury of things to come that Pétain was on the General Staff of the military government of Paris in 1895 to 1899, and that Weygand, future member of the Action Française, subscribed to the Henry Memorial. Even Barrès remarked in 1897 that it was striking that the Republican government tolerated the reactionary spirit in the army. Democracy saw in the soldier its most dangerous rival, for the republican mind and the military mind are contradictory and incompatible.

The virus of anti-Semitism itself grew to such a degree that it turned the elegant Viennese journalist, Theodor Herzl, into the founder of political Zionism. The Affair "showed an accumulated hatred of the Jews far beyond the measure we had suspected in France."[27] What he discovered on September 9, 1899 was that "it is possible to deny justice to a Jew for no other reason than that he is a Jew." Violent outbreaks in Algiers (where, in four days, 158 shops were plundered) and in other North African towns were followed by similar attacks in metropolitan France. The Prince of Guermantes, soon to become a Dreyfusard, kept saying that all the Jews ought to have been sent back to Jerusalem. Proust's Albertine, for reasons of snobbery, falsely pretended her family did not allow her to visit Jews.

The Royalist *Gazette de France* had as early as July 19, 1894 held that the proportion of Jewish officers in the army was 10 times as great as it ought to have been. To Thiébaud in the *Eclair*, the Dreyfus agitation was but a pretext for the establishment of the permanent rule of the Anglo-German Jewish and Protestant group in France. Anti-Semitism was regarded as patriotism by the Right, and Jews were even thought of as British spies.

The French bishops allowed the Church to identify itself

[26] E. Renauld, *Le Péril Protestant*, as cited in Alexandre Zévaès, *L'Affaire Dreyfus*, Paris, 1931, p. 10.
[27] Theodor Herzl, *Welt*, December 24, 1897.

with the cause of the General Staff and the forgers, and even put the vitriolic Drumont in a position to pose as the spokesman of French Catholicism. There were over 300 priests who subscribed to the Henry Memorial, and 30,000 who subscribed to Drumont's *La Libre parole*.[28] The Jesuit school in the Rue des Postes educated many officers and was in close touch with Drumont's paper. There were 96 Ultramontane soldier clubs, holding both religious services and social functions. Although only a minority of the General Staff came from Catholic schools—in 1898, out of 40 officers, 10 were pupils of the Jesuits—neither General Boisdeffre nor General Gonse took any important decision without consulting his Jesuit confessor. On the desk of the ambitious Father du Lac, said Anatole France, there was a single book, the *Annuaire*.[29]

The ecclesiastical and political leaders of the Church defended the authority of the army. The Archbishop of Paris was the patron of the "Labarum League" of anti-Semitic officers. The Archbishop of Toulouse in his 1898 Lenten Pastoral criticized the campaign against the military leaders. In August 1898, the Bishop of Nancy attacked "those miserable people who have been gathering mud to throw at the army, to throw in the face of Mother France!" In July, at a prize-giving ceremony at Arceuil, Father Didon had declared that "the army is a holy force whose mission is to make right prevail," and attacked the "unrestrained liberty which is impatient at force and revolts against it." In the Chamber, the Catholic Party was led by de Mun, a *rallié* who became convinced that the Jewish peril was worse than the possibility of endangering the Republic. The interview that the Pope gave to *Le Figaro* in 1899, indicating that good Catholics might support revision, was a rare example of the Church denying that anti-revisionism was the beginning of wisdom.

Before the Affair, the army leaders had tolerated the Republic out of prudence rather than enthusiasm. A caste with a remarkable degree of intermarriage and continuity—a comparison of the army list of 1890 with the army of Condé in

28 Albert Thibaudet, *Les Idées politiques de la France*, p. 46.
29 Anatole France, *Le Parti noir*, Paris, 1904, p. 20.

1791 to 1792 showed over a thousand names common to both
—it emphasized conformity. When Lyautey, in an unsigned
article in the *Revue des deux mondes*, March 15, 1891, wrote
that the officer must also be the educator of the nation,
morally obliged to produce the most salutary consequences
from the social point of view, he was duly found a post in
Indochina, as one in Tunisia was to be found for the dis-
obedient Picquart. The attitude of the army did much to
justify Clemenceau's gibe that the incapable and ignorant
generals knew of nothing but that their sabres were sprinkled
with incense.

The army showed a complete lack of interest and understanding of civil life, expressing an undisguised contempt for
"les pekins," as everyone who did not wear a uniform was
called. "General de Boisdeffre . . . felt it distinctly odd that
he should be living at a time when he must join in showing
deference to the President of the Municipal Council, who
was a mere nobody."[30] A regime in which deputies were placed
before Field Marshals on ceremonial occasions was not likely
to endear itself to the military. The army officers were interested in foreign affairs because of the close relation to
military affairs, but unless they happened to belong to a reactionary or clerical milieu, they were indifferent to internal
affairs. Although the army had given no backing to Boulanger, whom it regarded as an undisciplined officer, and had
not supported an attempt at dictatorship, the restraint and
loyalty exercised was to a considerable degree the result of
the diversion produced by the colonial expeditions. Jules
Ferry, as the minister most responsible for these expeditions,
deserved more than he received from an ungrateful nation.[31]

Mr. Chapman, a writer not unsympathetic to the army,
states, "The army was at best neutral to the regime."[32] Republicans were becoming only too ready to agree with Tocqueville that it was the greatest obstacle to the foundation and

[30] Marcel Proust, *Jean Santeuil*, London, 1955, p. 325.
[31] The curious combination of the anarchist Louise Michel and the
nationalist Déroulède had been formed to march on the Elysée if Ferry
had been elected President.
[32] Guy Chapman, *The Dreyfus Case*, London, 1955, p. 39.

stability of the Republic in France. Among literary works this distaste for militarism was shown in Abel Hermant's *Cavalier Miserey*, Charles Leroy's *Colonel Ramollot*, and Lucien Descaves' *Sousoffs*. Yet if Rémy de Gourmont's anti-patriotic article ("Le Joujou patriotisme," *Mercure de France*, April 1891) on his unwillingness to give up for Alsace-Lorraine the little finger with which he knocked the ash off his cigarette is often quoted, it is normally forgotten that he lost his job at the Bibliothèque Nationale because of it. Moreover, Rémy de Gourmont himself later wrote to Barrès, confessing his error in having written the article.[33]

The eager, active, ambitious army with its heritage of past victories inevitably made a parliamentary republic, with no aristocratic prestige and with a peaceful intent, afraid for its mere existence. The army, resenting control of its policy by politicians, believed war might deliver France from the "parliamentary yoke." Hostile to socialism, pacifism, parliamentarianism, and to Germany, it attacked "humanitarianism and utopian notions of universal peace."

The Affair developed into a crisis partly because of the lack of courage of those in power. Freycinet had already given up control over army appointments to the army itself. Léon Bourgeois suspended the Dean of the Faculty of Letters of the University of Bordeaux for having made a Dreyfusard speech over the tomb of his predecessor. Hanotaux cashiered members of the Diplomatic Corps who had doubts and were willing to express them. Méline was present but silent in the Chamber when Cavaignac proclaimed the Henry forgeries to be genuine. The kind of neutrality displayed by Dupuy in wanting the Affair to be regulated strictly juridically would have been satisfactory only if there had been impartial justice on both sides.

Some of the Opportunists might have been doubtful about the guilt of Dreyfus; they spoke of "liberating their conscience," but the liberation would be very discreet, on the day after victory had been won. The Radicals were hostile

[33] Maurice Barrès, *Mes Cahiers*, Paris, 1929-1957, XIV, 97.

to revision, from Bourgeois, whose underlying philosophy of *Solidarité* provided him with an attitude of agonizing indecision, to Brisson, convinced of the guilt of Dreyfus until the Henry letter, and Cavaignac, still convinced even after it had been shown to be a forgery. The antirevisionist speech of Cavaignac, "the heir to two generations of murder," as he was called, was voted *affichage*.

The danger to the regime lay not simply in the negative obscurantism of the Nationalists but in the failure of the Socialist or working-class movements to support the regime at once. It was Jaurès who, at the time of the original sentence, had complained that it was not severe enough. In a manifesto of January 19, 1898, the Socialists held that the Affair was a convulsive struggle, hypocritical and fraudulent, of two rival bourgeois parties. The clericals were lying when they called patriotism what was only a shameful appetite for positions and salaries. The Opportunists lied when they invoked human rights. Opportunists and clericals were in agreement to dupe and subdue democracy. Proletarians were to stand aside from the bourgeois civil war. Only later, realizing that the true danger came from the Nationalists, did Jaurès urge that the task of revolutionary Socialists was to support the side of the revisionists, since it served not only humanity, but also the working class when they protested against illegality.

Even the doctrinaire Jules Guesde came to recognize that Zola's letter was the greatest revolutionary act of the century. The Socialist parties formed in 1898 a Joint Vigilance Committee to protect the Republic, with the object of giving to the country the impression of a united Socialist party, ready to face any eventuality. Later, the Comité d'Entente began to reunite all the active forces of French socialism.

But if the Republicans and Socialists were hesitant, intellectuals rushed in where politicians feared to tread. As Thibaudet observed, the Affair was "a tumult of intellectuals" in which writers lined up on both sides, although the majority, energetically supported by the Ecole Normale Supérieure and Lucien Herr, were Dreyfusards. Sometimes, as with Albert Sorel, fanatically antirevisionist, there was a break between

41

the worlds of which intellectuals had been a part, in his case that of the political historian and that of the historian of politics.[34] The Affair was a mirror in which writers looked at themselves.[35] Among the antirevisionists, Brunetière, editor of the *Revue des deux mondes*, kept back his book on Calas and, since the strain of Voltairian descent was passing into the revisionist camp, even began to doubt the innocence of Calas. Until the Affair the lawyer was all-powerful in politics; after it, the professor became a political rival.

The Affair was the effective end of *fin de siècle*. The lassitude, lack of idealism, and distaste for action characterized in nineteenth-century literature by Bourget, Maupassant, Verlaine, and the playwright Henri Becque came to an end.

The Affair added moral fervor to the political struggle, "a moral crisis," William James called it, and produced a number of masterpieces of a warm humanity: Zola's *J'Accuse*; Anatole France's *Monsieur Bergeret à Paris*; the *Journal* of Jules Renard; Jaurès' collected articles, *Preuves;* the passages on Swann and the Guermantes in Proust; and, at a later stage, Roger Martin du Gard's *Jean Barois*. The Affair was to give a new lease of life to the Republic, to provide it with an enthusiastic vigor equivalent in many ways to the Wesleyan revivals in the Anglo-Saxon countries,[36] and to bolster its support, even though it also gave birth to the most formidable intellectual opposition in the Action Française movement, and strengthened the attachment of the Right to the *mystique* of nationalism.

The Affair heightened the anticlericalism and the antimilitarism of Republicans. It led to violent antireligious sectarianism against the alliance of the Catholic Right with the would-be destroyers of the Republic of Méline, and to the anticlerical Republic of the ex-theological student Combes. If the political world had formerly been divided on most questions, it had been united on patriotism, and the credits for the army

[34] Albert Thibaudet, *La République des professeurs*, Paris, 1927, p. 18.
[35] Cecile Delhorbe, *L'Affaire Dreyfus et les écrivains français*, Paris, 1932, p. 341.
[36] Albert Thibaudet, *Les Idées de Charles Maurras*, Paris, 1919, p. 121.

had been voted almost unanimously.[37] But many now came to believe that a republic led by generals like Boisdeffre and Pellieux was more dangerous than the dictatorship of a single general, Boulanger.

Urbain Gohier, one of the writers for *L'Aurore*, published a pamphlet entitled "The Army Against the Nation," in which he declared, "The barracks are the schools of all debauchery and vice."[38] The development of antimilitarism (formerly limited to intellectuals) and of pacifism subordinated the army to political control, and subjected it to popular hostility. On March 16, 1913, at Pré-Saint-Gervais, a crowd of 120,000 demonstrated against militarism and the three-year military service bill.

The mob had entered into politics, both on the Left and on the Right. For the Right, the streets became a possible battleground, as Guérin had shown when he and a band of antirevisionists had physically defied the police by arming their building. The barricades would no longer be exclusively the possession of the Left. But the power of the working class had made itself felt, and contact was established between it and the intellectual elite, leading to the fusion of the Socialist parties in 1905. The most important single political result of the Affair was that it brought the workers, at least temporarily, back to the Republic, for they had found a fatherland. When on November 19, 1899 a bronze statue by the revolutionary sculptor Dalou, symbolizing the triumph of the Republic, was unveiled, 300,000 gathered by the statue at the Place de la Nation. After the violent attacks on Loubet by Baron Christiani at Auteuil on June 4, 1899, the defense of the President became the concern of the Paris populace. The Grand Prix at Longchamp the Sunday following the attack became a Republican and Socialist demonstration in his honor.

Among the important political results of the Affair was the shift of the country to the Left, and Socialist support for participation in government. The combination of Millerand

[37] J. Chastenet, *Histoire de la Troisième République*, Paris, 1954, 2:331.
[38] E. Beau de Loménie, *Les Responsibilités des dynasties bourgeoises*, Paris, 2:297.

and Galliffet in the same administration was of historic importance, and it split Socialist movements throughout Europe. The Socialists, becoming a party of reform rather than of revolution by accepting Millerand's Saint Mandé program, agreed to the alliance between the left Progressists and the Union of the Left, in which the latter became the controlling force. At the 1902 election, the Radicals and the Radical Socialists emerged triumphant, and Clemenceau re-entered political life as a dominating figure. The petty bourgeoisie was ready to modify its institutions, but not to overthrow them.[39] The battle had been not for or against Dreyfus, for or against revision, but for or against the Republic, secularism, and militarism.[40]

The Republic was saved at the cost of some fanaticism. For a time the lines of demarcation were more clearly outlined, and royalism and nationalism were discredited. The *Ralliement* was virtually killed, the political influence of Catholics reduced, but a powerful political Catholic Left was made impossible. From the Affair, Halévy deduced the observation that the country would be in danger if it did not have a true conservative party.[41] The anticlerical, antimilitarist radical bloc was the Republican bloc, and the lack of a powerful constitutional Right was a handicap from which France has not even yet ceased to suffer. Nationalism joined hands with conservatism and became the defender of ancient institutions. As Blum said, the old agitators of Boulangism and Panama became men supporting the old order.[42] For the regime this combination was dangerous; but a permanent danger, as Barrès knew, could render a useful service to the Republic in making its survival more likely.

[39] Jean-Paul Sartre, *What Is Literature?*, New York, 1949, p. 201.
[40] Léon Blum, *Souvenirs sur l'affaire*, p. 173.
[41] Daniel Halévy, *op.cit.*, p. 113.
[42] Léon Blum, *Oeuvre, Vol. 1*, Paris, 1954, p. 500.

CHAPTER III

THE MEN: SOREL, BARRÈS, MAURRAS

THE ATTACK on the Republic made by Sorel, Barrès, and Maurras was not a concerted one, and there were many differences in their respective approaches. However, not only was there a great deal of overlapping in their attitudes toward political and social problems, as the ensuing chapters attempt to show, but there was also a certain interplay among the three in their political and literary life.

Between Barrès and Maurras there was a close but not intimate link. They worked on parallel lines, but were not bound in political alliance. Maurras often acknowledged his debt to the slightly older Barrès. "Without Barrès," he said, "what would I have become? Without his warning, where would I not have gone astray?"[1] Maurras wrote one of the first appreciative reviews of *Sous l'oeil des barbares*, Barrès' first novel, and was amazed to find his hero only six years his senior. He dedicated one of the stories in *Le Chemin de paradis* to Barrès, and collaborated with him on the journal *La Cocarde*. Together, they became the chief intellectual spokesmen of anti-Dreyfusism and nationalism, Barrès publishing 13 articles in the *Revue d'action française* between 1899 and 1903. Indeed, it was to Barrès, as the possible leader of the movement, that the original statement of the four fundamental principles of the Action Française were addressed on November 15, 1899. Maurras acknowledged also the role of Barrès in the attempt to save French culture. "If impressionism, naturalism, and all other forms of degenerate romanticism have been defeated in French intellectual life between 1885 and 1895, it is to Barrès and to Barrès alone that the chief honor of the triumph is due," he wrote.[2] On the death of Barrès, Maurras wrote that one of the columns of France had fallen, and a great support of morals and intelligence had departed.[3]

[1] Henri Massis, *Maurras et notre temps*, Paris-Geneva, 1951, I:46.
[2] *Gazette de France*, April 9, 1905.
[3] *L'Action française*, December 6, 1923.

Barrès in return had great respect for Maurras and thought that "in the literary field, it was Maurras who had begun the campaign against romanticism, that dazzling literary blaze which was so foreign to French tradition and so fleeting,"[4] while in the political field, he had high praise for *Enquête sur la monarchie.* He paid him a great compliment by using the visit that Taine had paid to Maurras as a basis for a description in *Les Déracinés* of the visit paid by Taine to Roemerspecher. But on the question of monarchy, the Action Française movement, the degree of rigidity of doctrine, and the nature of individualism, their views were incompatible. "Ah, it is my shame . . . Barrès is not a monarchist," lamented Maurras,[5] but Barrès' complaint of the "durs petits esprits" that Maurras was creating as disciples was amply justified. He contrasted the influence of Maurras and himself. Whereas the former was concerned with training disciples, he was interested, not in making people think like him, but in leading them to their highest point of perfection.[6]

The link between Sorel and Maurras was ephemeral and peripheral. In 1908, explaining to Georges Valois why he was not a monarchist, Sorel argued that one event dominated everything—the event of 1871, when a Royalist assembly caused the massacre in Paris of over 30,000 men, a massacre which determined the whole history of the Third Republic.[7] But Sorel became aware in 1909 of the similarities between himself and Maurras in some of their political attitudes. In a letter to Croce[8] on June 27, 1909, he wrote, "Maurras and his friends are well educated, and people are becoming disgusted with the mediocre crowd which monopolizes the best academic positions." He appreciated Maurras' friends, who "form an audacious *avant-garde* fighting against the scum who have corrupted everything they have touched," and praised

[4] Maurice Barrès, *Scènes et doctrines du nationalisme,* Paris, 1902, p. 123.

[5] Charles Maurras, *Enquête sur la monarchie,* Paris, 1924, p. 492.

[6] *Mes Cahiers,* xiv:136-137.

[7] Georges Sorel, "Monarchie et classe ouvrière," *Revue critique des idées et des livres* (May 1908), 1:149.

[8] *La Critica* (May 1928), 26:196.

the Action Française for its will to restore France morally by reacting against democracy.[9]

After his disillusionment with syndicalism, Sorel between 1910 and 1912 turned in the direction of the monarchist and Nationalist groups. In 1910 Maurras sent to Sorel the second edition of *Enquête sur la monarchie*, and the latter expressed his admiration in a four-page letter. In his article, "Quelques prétentions juives," Sorel held that Maurras was directing the defense of French culture. Talking to Variot, he expressed a belief that Maurras was as important to monarchy as Marx was to socialism.[10] In a shrewd assessment, Sorel had granted, "If Maurras succeeds in persuading the literate young that the democratic idea is losing its force, he will deserve to be classed among the 'maîtres de l'heure,' since his doctrine will have provoked a change in the orientation of present thought."[11]

Sorel and Maurras attempted to change this orientation by association in different projects. Through Georges Valois, Sorel attempted to found a journal, *La Cité française*, in which both the syndicalist and monarchist groups would collaborate. The project never got beyond its preliminary statement of intentions which argued against the democratic organization of society. But a similar program became the basis of Jean Variot's Nationalist review, *L'Indépendance*, the title of which Sorel himself had chosen and on whose editorial board Barrès had a seat. Sorel among others, including close friends of both Maurras and Barrès, had signed the manifesto of the new review, a bitterly antidemocratic statement which declared that "tradition, far from being a fetter, is the necessary springboard for the most daring advances."[12]

Sorel and Maurras also attempted to collaborate in the Cercle Proudhon, in the belief that syndicalists and Royalists could unite both in admiration of the "rustre heroïque des

[9] A. Lanzillo, *Giorgio Sorel*, Rome, 1910, p. 86.

[10] Jean Variot, *Propos de Georges Sorel*, Paris, 1935, p. 123.

[11] Sorel, *Matériaux d'une théorie du prolétariat*, 3rd edn., Paris, 1929, p. 18.

[12] Pierre Andreu, *Notre Maître M. Sorel*, Paris, 1953, p. 332.

Marches de Bourgogne," as Maurras called Proudhon, and in common hatred of Democracy. Maurras presided at the first meeting in December 1911, but it was a short-lived experiment. The group issued a journal, *Cahiers du cercle Proudhon*, which appeared only twice, in March-April and in May-August 1912, and which had a total of 200 subscribers and only 100 other sales in Paris. The attempt to embroider the *lys de France* and the *Sacré Coeur* on the syndicalist banner had failed.

Both Sorel and Maurras moved apart and quickly expressed their changed attitudes toward each other. Sorel wrote to Berth, September 11, 1914, "Maurras never had any serious idea of what social forces were necessary under a monarchy,"[13] and eventually dismissed him as a "café philosopher." The nationalist politicians, said Sorel, were pagans, dilettantes, and fanatical supporters of despotism. Moreover, Maurras was himself tainted with the democratic spirit, and the authors he admired—Stendhal, Balzac, Sainte Beuve—had little aristocratic distinction about them.[14] Maurras, for his part, was "appalled" (*horripilé*) by the obscurity and eccentricity of Sorel's ideas.[15]

Sorel never had the same respect for Barrès as he had had temporarily for Maurras. He was often caustic about Barrès' deficiencies. He criticized him for not being a thinker, for being inaccessible to tragic sentiments, for not knowing enough of the ancient traditions—and considered him a man who could well be an imbecile. Barrès, the educator of nationalism, the bourgeois incapable of understanding ancient greatness, completely lacked those qualities of heart necessary to be a great writer.[16] Presenting himself as the representative of the

---

[13] *ibid.*, p. 334.

[14] Sorel, *Matériaux*, p. 18.

[15] Harvard de la Montagne, *L'Action française*, September 8, 1922. Yet one nationalist, Pierre Villars, did make out a will which specified that his money was to be divided among Maurras, Sorel, and Jacques Maritain, and excluded Sorel only when the latter turned away from nationalism.

[16] *La Critica* (September 1928), 26:338; (March 1929), 27:115; (July 1929), 27:295; (January 1930), 28:44.

ancestral soul was pretentious on Barrès' part, for he was too shallow to fill this role. For only a short time were they associated, when they were among the members of the directoral committee of *L'Indépendance*. The meeting between Barrès and Sorel that had been arranged by Jean Variot was a disastrous failure.

All three writers were alike in displaying a vigor for polemics, a tendency to overstate the case, a contempt for opponents, often a vituperation which bordered on the libelous and, with Maurras and Sorel, often went beyond it, and a lack of generosity tempered only occasionally by kindness. Dimnet commented of Sorel, "I cannot remember that he ever praises or admires anybody, but a few men escape his censure."[17] All three aroused intense enthusiasm and bitter distaste and the degree of these passions is the measure of the influence of the writers on their time.

They each attempted to influence political action, were successful in some degree, and had schools or disciplines associated with them. For none of them was thought divorced from action, as Baudelaire had implied in the line that Barrès was fond of quoting: "D'un monde où l'action n'est pas la soeur du rêve. . . ."

The three writers made remarkably prophetic predictions of national socialism. The first long article that Sorel wrote for the *Cahiers de la quinzaine* of Péguy was *National Socialisms*, in which he argued that each nation had a socialism of its own, according to its particular needs.[18] Barrès had first entered the chamber in 1889 on a program of which nationalism and socialism were the chief ingredients; in his 1898 electoral program he had elaborated these ideas, proposing homes for the old retired workers, the recognition of workers' *syndicats* and their independence, and contending that *socialism* was a word in which France had put its hope. In 1890 he wrote, "Boulangism is a Socialist program, a general movement against the omnipotence of capital, in favor

[17] Ernest Dimnet, "A French Defence of Violence," *The Forum* (November 1909), 42:414.
[18] Sorel, "Socialismes nationaux," *Cahiers de la quinzaine* (April 22, 1902), 3rd Series, No. 14.

of national reconciliation and love of the disinherited.[19] Like Sorel, Barrès confessed the influence that Proudhon had had on him in his youth. The socialism of Proudhon, because it combined French national sensibility and Hegelianism, satisfied or profoundly interested Frenchmen who would never turn to German collectivism or Russian terrorism, because these two conceptions were derived from foreign races.[20] Socialism would produce both the vigorous development of national strength and the necessary effort to decentralize and federalize the government.

Maurras had argued that a Socialist, liberated from the democratic and cosmopolitan environment, could fit into nationalism like a well-made glove onto a beautiful hand. The counter-revolution in fact meant the combination of nationalism and socialism, for at the bottom of socialism there was a spirit of reaction, of conformity with the idea of traditional France against the bourgeoisie. Maurras found it natural for nationalism and socialism to combine against the revolutionary bloc, for the Socialist resolution of the problem of the working class posed by the birth of large industry meant reacting against the individualism of the Jacobins and the ideas of the Revolution.[21]

Antidemocratic, skeptical of the value of piecemeal change, attempting to influence political and social movements, appealing simultaneously to an elite and to the masses, the three writers are essential to an understanding of French political life at the beginning of the 20th century and of European political history since that time.

GEORGES SOREL (1847-1922)

Sorel is a perplexing figure in French thought, inheriting directly from Proudhon at least one great trend of thought—an intense dislike of political forms and a desire to escape decadence by vigorous moral action—while contributing to

[19] Barrès, "Les Enseignements d'une Année de Boulangisme," *Le Figaro*, February 2, 1890.
[20] *Scènes*, pp. 483-507.
[21] *L'Action française*, April 19, 1916; July 18, 1933.

other trends enthusiastically, if temporarily. If he is not, as Wyndham Lewis argued,[22] the key to all contemporary political thought, he provides a highly complex, partly reactionary and partly revolutionary, attack on political republicanism.

Surprisingly little is known of his life or inner motives, why the engineer should in 1892 suddenly resign his job, never claim his pension rights, and begin, at the age of 45, the prolific output of articles in technical, obscure, or esoteric journals, most of which had extremely limited circulations; why the moralist, who constantly praised the value of the family never formally married his wife or had children; or why the agnostic should stress the importance of religious fervor and wear the religious medal of his wife around his neck after her death. The product of a middle-class Norman Catholic family, a *rentier* leading a tranquil life in a cottage in Boulogne-sur-Seine (interrupted only by a Thursday train ride to Paris to attend the lectures of Bergson and the coteries of the magazines for which he wrote), Sorel became the theoretician of violence, but always wore in his lapel the ribbon of the Legion of Honor.

His style of writing was as curious as the pattern of his life. Proceeding by long, uninterrupted, judicious quotation, his own meaning often obscure or vague, his writing was a mixture of striking insights and unusual *aperçus*, as well as of fantastic misconceptions. His language was as ascetic and as astringent as his code of morality. His ideas were not only expressed dryly and obscurely but showed a bewildering rapidity of change. He was in turn a traditionalist in 1889, a Marxist in 1894, a Bergsonian in the same year, a Vician in 1896, a Socialist critical of Marxism in that year, a reformist syndicalist in 1898, a Dreyfusard in 1899, a revolutionary syndicalist in 1904 to 1905, a disillusioned ex-Dreyfusard in 1909, an ally of the Nationalists and monarchists in 1910, and at the time of World War I, a philosopher of morals.

He made a virtue out of his very lack of system. On April 28, 1903, he wrote, "I have never asked myself if I am con-

[22] Wyndham Lewis, *The Art of Being Ruled*, London, 1926, p. 132.

sistent in my writings. I write from day to day, following the need of the moment."[23] Consistency may be the hobgoblin of little minds, but at least it makes for comprehensibility. No one who keeps adding, as did Sorel, "Et puis, il y a autre chose," to a polemical discussion, can be a maker of systems. It is not every book on economic problems that ends as did Sorel's *Introduction à l'économie moderne*, with a disquisition on suffering. All his writings were rough drafts for a book he never wrote.

His reading was surprisingly wide—from 1884 to 1891, his borrowings from the library at Perpignan, where he was stationed as an engineer, included many works on architecture and archeology—but it was also limited. As Perrin wrote, "Often he was content with materials at second hand,"[24] taking his knowledge of ancient history from Renan or Ferrero, his knowledge of modern history from Tocqueville or Taine, and his knowledge of literature from Brunetière. Yet his reading provided the stimulant for writing on subjects as diverse as music, economics, art, and Greek philosophy.

It is ironical that the man whom his translator, T. E. Hulme, called "the most remarkable socialist since Marx" should have largely discovered socialism through his wife, who came of proletarian origins. It is even more ironical that this most erudite of French socialists, as Le Bon called him, who absorbed so readily works on social science and on philosophy both ancient and modern (including Nietzsche, Bergson, Hartmann, and William James), and who believed that the mission of the philosopher was to see and to understand the movements which seemed to him important without being obliged to take sides with the makers of the movement, should have been an advocate of direct action. And the crowning irony is that most of the valuable writing on this fierce opponent of the universities and official academies is in the form of doctoral theses.

[23] Sorel, *La Critica* (1927), 25:372.
[24] P-L-M.J. Perrin, *Les Idées sociales de Georges Sorel*, Algiers, 1925, p. 39.

Continually vacillating in his political ideas and associated with diverse groups as he was, the closest he came to exerting practical influence was on the syndicalist movement. It is a striking commentary, however, that on being asked whether he read Sorel, Victor Griffuelhes, secretary of the C.G.T., should reply, "I read Dumas." The self-confessed "old man, who, like Proudhon, obstinately remains a disinterested servant of the proletariat,"[25] was almost totally neglected by its members. A questionnaire submitted by a scholastic investigator showed that Sorel was much less widely read by the syndicalists than were Marx, Jaurès, or Tolstoy.[26]

Sorel was enthusiastic about his ideas, pouring them forth without any order, but he was modest about his own capabilities. To Jean Variot, who was recording his talk and attempting to play Eckermann, Sorel replied, "But I am not Goethe."[27] On his part there was no inevitable commitment to the struggle of the proletariat, nor devotion to the continual rebellion against the opponents of human freedom. The writer who wanted to regenerate the moral sense of man was for his chief disciple, Edouard Berth, "uniquely an isolated intellectual worker, apart from every party, every grouping, every school."[28] "Sorel, a syndicalist? He is a sectarian intoxicated with thought," declared Barrès.[29] The syndicalists, the Communists, the Action Française, Mussolini—all claimed him, but Sorel belonged to none of them. He had what Professor Shils has called "the apocalyptic outsider's view of politics."[30] Socialism was important to him as a symbol, as an invitation to a crusade, as a deeply emotional experience, as a fellowship to join in the fight against the system. He attempted to give to mankind what was meant for party.

[25] Sorel's self-portrait in the dedication of his *Matériaux*.

[26] Max Ferré, *Histoire du mouvement syndicaliste révolutionnaire chez les instituteurs*, Paris, 1955, p. 316.

[27] Jean Variot, *Propos de Georges Sorel*, p. 8.

[28] Edouard Berth, *Du "Capital" aux "Réflexions sur la violence,"* Paris, 1932, p. 175.

[29] *Mes Cahiers*, viii:31.

[30] E. A. Shils, preface to Georges Sorel, *Reflections on Violence*, Glencoe, 1950, p. 18.

MAURICE BARRÈS (1862-1923)

Barrès se retourne dix fois avant le saut.—JEAN COCTEAU

Maurice Barrès, the man from Lorraine with a Provençal heritage, the *déraciné* who came to Paris seeking a mistress, glory, notoriety, and virtue[31] and made it his base of operations for the rest of his life, while Lorraine, with which he made a *mariage de convenance*, remained little more than a *pied-à-terre* for purposes of displaying his soul, led a charmed life of his own making. "C'est un troubadour auvergnat qui s'est fait gendarme lorrain," Louis Bertrand said privately. The writer, who established his reputation by his conception of the *déraciné*, dreamed of Paris while he was still in school, sent his youthful articles to the Parisian *Jeune France*, and left for the capital as soon as he could, at the age of 20. His political career showed a similar transposition. Twice defeated at Nancy after his initial success in 1889, he adopted a constituency in Paris which he represented from 1906 until the end of his life. Barrès, contemptuous of politicians but fascinated by the game of politics, spent 21 years in the Chamber of Deputies as a bitter opponent of the political regime, ended his life with a state funeral attended by a representative of the President of the Republic, the Prime Minister, and the Minister of Education, and was laid to rest by a Marshal of France, a fellow citizen of Lorraine.

After the favorable review of his first book by Paul Bourget in *Journal des débats*, April 3, 1888, he became successful at 25, the *Eclair* paying him 400 francs for an article of 15 lines; in 1891 he was for Anatole France already "a youthful *maître*." The influence of this "prince of youth" on his younger contemporaries was remarkably strong, and individuals as diverse as Jacques Rivière, François Mauriac, Louis Aragon, Léon Blum, and Thomas Mann all testify to the power, seduction, or revelation of his work, while many succumbed to his personal charm. Edouard Herriot many times expressed gratitude for the help obtained from Barrès when his mother had been Barrès' domestic servant. As editor of *La Cocarde*,

[31] *Mes Cahiers*, I:25; II:56; IX:29.

he held the allegiance of widely divergent individuals, from legitimists to syndicalists, from Jews to anti-Semites, by sheer personal charm.[32] An anti-Semite himself, he always had Jewish admirers, and, until the Dreyfus Affair, maintained a connection with the *Revue blanche* founded by the Natanson brothers. The first article of Léon Blum in that journal on July 25, 1892 was dedicated to Barrès, and elsewhere he tells of his cruel disappointment and his break with Barrès over the latter's unwillingness to join the Dreyfusards.[33] The liberal critic Thibaudet thought Barrès one of the four great men he had met in his life.

But it was the qualities of hauteur and ambition that were dominant in his character. Called "aristo" because of his aloofness in his early days of the Quartier Latin and the Ecole de Droit, and "béotien" by Jean Moréas, he might, if it had not been for his political preoccupation, have well been the personification of the *fin-de-siècle* dilettante. Harold Nicolson significantly chose Barrès' *Le Jardin de Bérénice* as a symbol for his fictional poetic poseur, Lambert Orme, in the book *Some People*. There is a certain coldness in his work which often becomes repellent. "I do not like *Sous l'oeil des barbares*," wrote Alain-Fournier. "It chills me . . . I admire and remain cold."[34] Thibaudet has pointed out the many images of bullfighting, slaughter, hunting, and torture to be found in his writings.[35] "A brutal soul," Barrès was quick to seize on the killing of an individual as an advertising stunt for his first paper, *Les Taches d'encre*. In *Leurs figures*, his book on Panama, Baron Reinach became "a hog of the boulevards . . . who rushed about like a poisoned rat behind the paneling." His first joke in the Chamber was to propose that the still-living Jules Simon be added to the list of Republicans whose bodies were to be transferred to the Panthéon.

[32] Maurras, *Maîtres et témoins de ma vie d'esprit*, Paris, 1954, p. 26.
[33] Léon Blum, *Souvenirs sur l'affaire*, p. 87.
[34] Jacques Rivière and Alain-Fournier, *Correspondance, 1905-1914*, 2 vols., Paris, 1926, I:208.
[35] Albert Thibaudet, *La Vie de Maurice Barrès*, Paris, 1921, p. 38. Also: Bernard Fäy, *Panorama de la littérature Française*, Paris, 1925, p. 129.

He was fiercely ambitious: his first thought on seeing Hugo talking with Anatole France and Leconte de Lisle in the library of the Senate was to wish that history would include him with them as the representative of four literary ages. Gide was not unfair in stressing his desire for popularity and acclamation. Only two days after Hérédia had died on October 8, 1905, he was making a prognosis of his chances for election to the vacant seat in the French Academy,[36] which he succeeded in obtaining at 45. Steadfastly and smoothly, he organized his own success. The writer, whose dark appearance led to the rumor that he was descended from Portuguese Jews, kept a portrait of Napoleon on his mantelpiece, and was pleased on being reminded of his physical resemblance to the Prince de Condé, under whose portrait he wrote in his study.

Disdainful and contemptuous, he was always "Monsieur Barrès" in a Chamber of Deputies where the rule was to *tutoyer* each other. Shaking hands with his constituents during his electoral campaign in the Halles, he was like a King of France touching his subjects in order to cure them of scrofula.[37] Yet he was capable of generosity towards opponents, and refused to carry a grudge if conditions had changed, even with Dreyfusards.[38] He welcomed the entry of Jean Jaurès to the Chamber in an article in *Le Figaro* on January 2, 1893, and after his assassination he wrote to Mademoiselle Jaurès "The murder of your father cemented all French hearts in union," and confessed in his journal, "Adieu, Jaurès, que j'avais voulu librement aimer." After "twenty years of frightful struggle," and two proposed duels, one of which was fought, he could still feel some friendship for Francis de Pressensé. In the hour of French need, in August 1914, he was glad to shake the hand of Joseph Reinach, Jew, Dreyfusard, and nephew of Baron Reinach, because "above all, he is

[36] *Mes Cahiers*, iv:106.

[37] L. Dumont-Wilden, *Le Crépuscule des maîtres*, Brussels, 1947, p. 100.

[38] André Maurel, *Souvenirs d'un écrivain 1883-1914*, Paris, 1925, pp. 89-90.

French."[39] Clemenceau, once "a terrible man full of pride," became for him as for all France, "an incarnation of invincible hope." The former anarchist firebrand Hervé could also speak in 1914 of "mon cher Barrès."

Barrès, for all his writing on politics and his political career, was not really a political writer at all, in the sense of having a systematic approach to political problems. He was interested in an extraordinarily limited number of issues, and was incessantly repetitive, often ambivalent and equivocal about those things that did interest him. Maurras spoke of his "immobile mask," Anatole France of one of his books as "floating and indeterminate . . . an amorphous book," and M. Domenach confessed his difficulty in choosing any of his 56 works as *the* Barresian work.[40] "A great writer," Jules Renard concluded, "but what does he mean? One understands each phrase, but the total meaning is obscure."[41] Barrès himself liked to quote the remark of Novalis, "Chaos must gleam through the regular walls of order."

There was a fundamental lack of orientation in Barrès. "Life has no sense. I even believe that each day it becomes more absurd."[42] Why did he go to Paris?—for no clear or strong reason, but "with an invincible orientation like a bird." Even with what Faure-Biguet has called "his marvelous intellectual coquetry,"[43] his continuing attempt to coordinate his first conception of the *culte-du-moi*, the delicate cultivation of his own emotions, with the nationalistic tradition of "the earth and the dead," was never a wholly credible one. Indeed, both were confused, uncertain concepts. At one point he made the *culte-du-moi* the result of his childhood experience playing with bad children, at another his devotion to Lorraine the result of the loss of his mother in 1901. Anatole France, not unfairly, rebuked Barrès for his subjectivism: "We must not make life an experiment, we must live it."

[39] *Mes Cahiers*, i:297; vii:134; xi:88.
[40] Jean-Marie Domenach, *Barrès par lui-même*, Paris, 1954, p. 6.
[41] Jules Renard, *Journal 1887-1910*, 4 vols., Paris, ii:1203.
[42] Maurice Barrès, *Les Amitiés françaises*, Paris, 1911, p. 16.
[43] J-N. Faure-Biguet, *Maurice Barrès, son oeuvre*, Paris, 1924, p. 65.

Apart from his theory of nationalism, his political views were equally indeterminate. First successful as a revisionist socialist for Nancy in 1889, and sitting on the extreme left of the Chamber, Barrès was never a member of a party or group, and continually changed his electoral nomenclature while deputy for the first *arrondissement* of Paris. In the Chamber he was singularly ineffective: he spoke only 42 times, often amid a volley of interruptions. Maurras correctly maintained that "his true political career did not unfold between the walls of the Palais-Bourbon."[44]

It was as a creator of a mood of nationalism of widespread appeal to the masses, together with his plea for active leadership, that he was most significant. For Barrès himself, action was not the fullest form of realization but was desirable in order to heighten his own sensibility. Politics and Parliament became favorable settings in which to enrich himself; he confessed that one of the great passions of his life, "the most constant, the most ruinous and the most bizarre," was his taste for the Chamber. The writer who entered his study with the jest, "Maintenant, je fais ma petite musique," claimed, "I have given to the work for which I was born only the moments that I have stolen from my political task."[45]

Barrès was in fact a romantic both in attitudes and in choice of travel. He attempted to follow his image of Disraeli, "poet, dandy, ambitious, and leader of men."[46] The taste he acquired in his childhood for the novels of Sir Walter Scott fixed in his imagination the notions of the romantic hero, the mystery of the Orient, and the "Mal d'Asie." "His mind," said Anatole France, "was restless, unhealthy, perverted, and spoiled."[47] His taste in towns ran to Venice, Toledo, Sparta, Ravenna. The "amateur of souls" was hardly interested in the living; his work, as Sartre, Drieu La Rochelle, and Bordeaux have commented, was "a pathetic struggle with death."[48]

44 Maurras, *Maurice Barrès*, Paris, 1948, p. 70.
45 *Scènes*, I:6.
46 Barrès, *L'Ennemi des Lois*, Paris, 1893, pp. 167-168.
47 Anatole France, *On Life and Letters*, 4 vols., London, 1924, IV:217.
48 Henry Bordeaux, *Portraits d'hommes*, 2 vols., Paris, 1924, I:76.
Jean-Paul Sartre, *What is Literature?*, p. 131.

The sight of his heroine Bérénice, dying of fever, has an all too decadent quality about it.

His lack of contact with reality and his deficiency in relevant knowledge were often demonstrated. "Who would realize on reading this citizen of Lorraine that he is describing a metallurgical country? He has seen the *mirabelliers* and neglected the blast furnaces,"[49] commented the perceptive critic Berl. Yet Barrès did speak for science in the Chamber, and he was one of the founders of the national committee for aid to scientific research. Moreover, he was realist enough to recognize the desirability of an adequate income. "Without money," argued his hero Philippe, "how can one develop one's imagination?"

But even in literature and individuals, his taste was questionable. The Nationalist reserved his enthusiastic praise for Hérédia, Chenier, and Moréas—a Cuban and two Greeks. He dismissed Proust without reading him, and denigrated Péguy. Morès, the brutal, anti-Semitic street fighter, became for him "a heroic thinker . . . a man who gave his life to the highest form of speculations." In men as in politics, up to 1914, he was invariably on the wrong side.

CHARLES MAURRAS (1868-1952)

The private wound is deepest.—WILLIAM SHAKESPEARE

Maurras, the clearest, most consistent, and most doctrinaire of the three writers, presented the most sustained counterrevolutionary attack on the Third Republic. From the time he began writing political articles for *Le Soleil* in May 1895 (which he agreed to do after reading a passage in the *Philippics* of Demosthenes), his views rarely changed in the 20,000 articles that he wrote, and in the books which are largely compilations of them. There was a consistency in his work which that of Sorel and Barrès did not have, and one which was ambitious in its attempt to link together aesthetics and politics.

Educated and deeply influenced by two priests, both of

[49] E. Berl, *Mort de la pensée bourgeoise*, Paris, 1929, p. 28.

whom later became bishops, he underwent at 14 the decisive experience of his life, when he lost his hearing and was forced into the solitude he once called "our greatest enemy." He was forced to renounce the naval career on which his heart had been set,[50] and probably doubted forever the goodness of God. In November 1885, he left his home in Martigues in Provence for Paris, where his early years were lonely and to a large extent spent in libraries. Precocious, at 17 he was reviewing books on philosophy and economics. His affliction tended to encourage a journalistic life, sleeping in the day and working in the printing house in the evening and night. Maurras was always "un homme de cabinet,"[51] and this isolation encouraged him to be uncompromising, didactic, and authoritarian.

With his relentless, lucid logic, his humorless lack of subtlety, his dogmatic views on right and wrong, Maurras was not one to make the great refusal, or spend life without infamy and without praise. "Reaction above all" was on the masthead of the newspaper of the Action Française, and from the Dreyfus Affair on, Maurras was the standard-bearer of the attack on the Republic. He was inflexible, a ruthless antagonist—a person about whom one could not be lukewarm.[52] He took eighteen columns to reply to twenty lines of criticism by Gide of a book by Barrès. Even sympathizers who admired and revered him could not follow in the rigor of his conclusions.[53] Former colleagues and associates like Valois, Dimier, and Bernanos, who had broken with him, were bitterly castigated. Georges Valois, who had done so much to bring Sorel and Maurras together, was attacked as a Russian agent and an *agent-provocateur* for the Communist party. When Pierre Lasserre, an ally from the beginning, called Moréas "petit grand poète," Maurras broke with him and put

50 Maurras, *Tragi-comédie de ma surdité*, Aix-en-Provence, 1951.

51 Achille Segard, *Charles Maurras et les idées royalistes*, Paris, 1919, p. 84.

52 It is noticeable that both the *Oeuvres capitales* and the *Dictionnaire politique et critique* are carefully edited to exclude the violence in his writings.

53 Agathon (Henri Massis and Alfred de la Tarde), *Les Jeunes gens d'aujourd'hui*, 2nd edn., Paris, 1919, p. 16.

an end to Lasserre's column, "Chronique des Lettres," in the *Action française*. It was Barrès who spoke of his authoritarian personality, and Bernanos of his "intellectual dictatorship." He never displayed toward opponents that generosity of spirit or humanity that Vincent Auriol, President of the Republic, showed toward him in August 1951, in allowing him to be transferred from prison to the hospital of Troyes. Jaurès, for whom Barrès had warm feelings, was for Maurras "only a voice," and he refused to shake the hand of the Socialist leader when they met in a cafe.

The violence of his attacks on Bergson, "the Scottish Jew who is not even a thorough student of Aristotle and St. Thomas," when Bergson was campaigning for a seat in the Academy, led several waverers to vote for Bergson. "I do not read the *Action française*," said Gide, only half jestingly, "for fear of becoming a Republican." Maurras' violence kept him out of the Academy in 1913 and 1923, in spite of his willingness to suspend distribution of one of his books because of its "too enthusiastic preface," and it was not until 1939 that Henry Bordeaux marshaled sufficient strength for his nomination.[54]

But his life was a failure. A monarchist, he was disowned by both of his kings as "not our interpreter." The Comte de Paris said in 1912, "Maurras and Daudet are not true Royalists. . . . They do not serve monarchy; they use it for the satisfaction of their ambitions or their literary grudges."[55] Although he was a defender of the Catholic Church, his works were put on the Index, and his relations with Rome were always uncertain and unhappy in spite of his willingness to withdraw some of his early writing in *Anthinéa* and *Le Chemin de paradis*. "A very fine brain," said the Pope, "but alas, only a brain." He made the Action Française the home of French lost causes.

The writer who so staunchly believed himself to be the champion of classicism was often appreciative of romanticism

[54] Henry Bordeaux, *Charles Maurras et l'Académie française*, Paris, 1955.

[55] L. Dumont-Wilden, *op.cit.*, p. 173.

in literature. This fierce denigrator of romanticism in literature and politics, the Mediterranean voyager who declaimed Lucretius in his cabin at one in the morning was also the poet whose work was strongly influenced by Verlaine, Baudelaire, and romantic themes,[56] and the man who in 1897 made a special trip to the mouth of the Arno to the spot where Byron had lit Shelley's pyre. In his sweeping indictment of the Third Republic Maurras linked politics, religion, and aesthetics, and his own life showed that he always related them. Putting his lips to the columns of Propylea became a symbolic gesture: "I am a Roman by all the positive power of my being." "The philosophic and aesthetic theories of *Anthinéa* form the true foundation of my politics."[57]

The Nationalist obsessed with xenophobia, partly caused by the table manners of an English lady on board ship, was strongly influenced by and inordinately praised Jean Moréas, the Greek poet whose real name was Papadiamentopoulos. A vigorous anti-Semite, his first work was published by Calmann-Lévy, and his first vote was cast for Naquet, a Jewish Boulangist. Convinced of the need for decentralization and of the value of Mistral and Provençal culture, he joined the Société des Felibres in Paris "to promote the love of Provence," but was expelled for too much vigor. The man whose life was spent attempting to mold the country to his pattern ended it sentenced to a prison term and "national degradation." The man who prided himself on his appreciation of reality was deluded into thinking that a few companions— Ernest Raynaud, Raymond de La Tailhède, Maurice Du Plessys—in the café Vachette opposite the Odéon theatre constituted the Ecole Romane, a significant literary group.

Though he acknowledged the influence of many, he was the pupil of none. If he accepted Bonald's idea of unity and continuity, he rejected his theory of divine right. If he shared de Maistre's belief in a "political science" and in the need for a leader, he rejected his religious emphasis. If he turned

[56] L. S. Roudiez, "The Early Poetic Activities of Charles Maurras," *The French Review* (January 1951), 24:197-208.

[57] *La Revue d'action française* (1901), as cited in Achille Segard, *op.cit.*, p. 70.

to Comte for certainty after Kant had left him a sceptic, and if he approved Comte's positivism, defense of society and stress on the social order, he rejected his ideas on spiritual power and the three laws. From Taine, Le Play, Fustel de Coulanges, Saint-Beuve, Maurras took what he needed.

His own intellectual influence was extensive. He won over a substantial part of the Ecole de Médecine, Ecole de Droit, and a significant number of literary and scientific figures. In 1925 the undergraduates of Louvain voted him the person who had most influenced them intellectually. In 1928, T. S. Eliot confessed that "most of the concepts which might have attracted me in Fascism I seem already to have found, in the work of Charles Maurras."[58] His apartment in the Rue de Verneuil was a meeting place for intellectuals of the Right: Leon de Montesquiou, Bainville, Lucien Moreau, Bernard de Vessins, Louis Dimier, Robert de Boisfleury, Pugo, Lasserre, Daudet. He gave to the Right a "method and an object."[59] But what Thierry Maulnier called his political aristocratism"[60] did not extend beyond intellectuals to the crowd or to practical activity. In politics he was always to be the *eminence grise* of a coterie. The Action Française was never able to get a single deputy elected under its own name. It was through the uncompromising political intransigence of Maurras that the political thought of the extreme Right became more and more detached from the practice of politics in the Third Republic.[61]

[58] T. S. Eliot, "The Literature of Fascism," *Criterion* (December 1928), 8:288.

[59] Henri Massis, *Charles Maurras et notre temps*, 1:280.

[60] Thierry Maulnier, "Charles Maurras est mort," *La Table ronde* No. 61 (January 1953), p. 170.

[61] Raymond Aron, *Espoir et peur du siècle*, Paris, 1957, pp. 18-19.

CHAPTER IV

ATTACK ON DEMOCRACY

IN EARLY 20th century France, democracy as a way of life implied a society which cherished values of tolerance rather than fanaticism, compromise rather than rigidity, persuasion rather than force, diversity rather than conformity, discussion rather than dogmatism. Democracy as a system of government implied the consent of the governed, the possibility of an individual's participating in the process of government, and the government's taking account of the wishes of those governed. This implied, therefore, an electoral system in which all would be free to participate, a refusal to recognize that any individual or group was indispensable to the governmental process, and the essential right of an opposition to exist.

Barrès, Maurras, and Sorel were not prepared to accept these essential characteristics of democracy; they all disputed the desirability of an electoral system and postulated the desirability as well as the inevitability of a rigid elite.

Barrès had no organized or methodological approach to the basic problems of society, nor did he deal with theoretical questions in any systematic way. Rather, by a process partly of intuition and partly of sensitivity, he touched on a number of defects he observed in a democratic system, although he was primarily concerned with the specific problems of the Republic, its political institutions, and its politicians.

It is paradoxical that the chief defect that Barrès, the aesthete who stressed the desirability of refined, emotional, individual sensations, should have seen in democracy was that of individualism. In a manner reminiscent of de Maistre, he asked, "The Rights of Man? What Man? Where does he live?"[1] For Barrès, the thoughts of an individual were the product of and determined by his time and place, and were not of his own making. The individual was limited and circumscribed. Individual experience was only part of the whole

[1] *Mes Cahiers*, ii:83.

tradition of society which, made up of the sum of individual experiences, alone truly represented "the idea." Presumably, Barrès would have resolved the contradiction between the right of individual sensitivity and the individual's dependence on society by means of the elite which he considered inevitable.

With Sorel and Maurras there was a more unequivocal attack on democracy than was to be found in Barrès. Pirou, one of the biographers of Sorel, argued that "antidemocracy was the immovable point about which his doctrine turned."[2] And indeed, his hatred of democracy was such that at the end of his life he confessed, "May I before dying, live to see the humiliation of the bourgeois democracies full of pride and and today cynically triumphant."[3] He wrote to Delesalle on August 18, 1918 that it was because of his hatred of democrats that he had so much sympathy for Lenin and his colleagues.

Sorel found all the deficiencies of 20th century democratic philosophy present in the 18th century: materialistic philosophy, pantheistic religion, cynicism, immorality, optimism. This supposed century of light was above all "the era of superficiality," the *Encyclopédie* no more than "bric-a-brac written in folio." The 18th century had transformed everything into agreeable subjects of conversation; literature had degenerated into journalism. The educational reforms of Condorcet would produce "enlightened men," men free of all chains, all authority, all traditions. "The meanest village meeting would seem like a branch of the salon of Mme Geoffrin."[4]

Sorel was more concerned with the deleterious moral effects of democracy and with its specious ideological premises than with democracy as a system of political institutions. "When one speaks of democracy," he wrote, "it is necessary to be concerned less with political institutions than with the effect on the popular masses."[5] The entry of the mass into politics and the increase in literacy brought a number of dan-

[2] Gaetan Pirou, *Georges Sorel*, Paris, 1927.
[3] *Reflections on Violence* (ed. E. Shils), p. 311.
[4] *Les Illusions du progrès*, p. 58.
[5] *Matériaux*, p. 72.

gers to any desirable political system. Sorel was alarmed by the passion with which the public was interested in events, by the influence that opinion exercised on governments, and by the dissemination of the press and its consequent hold over the masses.

Sorel attacked the ideological premises on which democracy rested, including its rationalism, its abstract nature, its pacific nature, its optimism and belief in progress, its hedonism—and also the results of the system. He regarded democracy as false science, as *scientisme*, the result of a rationalism too abstract, too universalist, too unitary, too unrelated to facts. Ideological constructions were necessary, but they were also the most frequent causes of error. Rationalism did not sufficiently take account of the constant changes and transformations in life, and did not appreciate living reality. He criticized Descartes for having seemingly given the answer to everything through his oversimplified rationalism, a philosophy which was essentially one for the habitués of salons, which was resolutely optimistic, which pleased a society eager to amuse itself, and which led to a senseless confidence in the decisions of enlightened people. Sorel was opposed to the excessive rationalism that, for Comte, would lead to the adoration of the Earth, Space, Humanity. Comte could just as well propose for adoration the steamship, photographic plates, and the Bibliothèque Nationale.[6]

Moreover, democratic theories implied abstraction, and that produced two problems. One was that abstraction was used to dupe the people. It was the feeling of the lack of reality of democratic philosophy that led Sorel to doubt that democracy had any real principles at all. Democracy had a credo as abstract and as unintelligible as that of any religion; its trinity—Liberty, Equality, Fraternity—presented as many mysteries as the Apocalypse.[7] He compared it unfavorably to syndicalism, which was a reflection of reality, a theoretical

---

[6] Georges Sorel, "La Crise morale et religieuse," *Le Mouvement socialiste* (July 15, 1907), 22:13.

[7] Sorel, "Y-a-t'il de l'utopie dans le Marxisme?" *Revue de métaphysique et de morale* (March 1899), 7:154.

interpretation of working-class struggles and a basic concern for the producer. The decrees of democracy, like those of popes, based on revelation, were foreign to the nature of experimenmental science. Democracy therefore would favor the theoretician rather than the practical experimenter; for Sorel it was not surprising that the Physiocrats were much less famous than the Philosophes.

The second problem was that a bourgeois democracy, through the most charlatan methods, used the superstitious respect that people instinctively had for science both to heighten its own prestige and to attempt to transform the least literate individual into a mandarin. Sorel was as distrustful of Christian democracy as of all other kinds; for him it was a farce designed to dupe the simple for the benefit of an oligarchy.

An essential element of the strong current of rationalism on which modern democracy floated was the idea of progress— a bourgeois doctrine and a democratic dogma. The idea was harmful because it permitted the consumption of available goods, without thought for the difficulties of the future. For democrats and Cartesians, "progress consists not in the accumulation of the means of techniques, nor even in scientific knowledge, but in the adornment of the mind."[8] But true progress, which was neglected by democrats, took place in the technique of production. It was fortunate for modern democracies that the benefits from the riches drawn from nature enabled it to survive its faults.

The idea of progress in a democracy meant optimism about man and society, and the optimist in politics "is an inconstant and even dangerous man, because he takes no account of the great difficulties presented by his projects."[9] By pretending that problems have solutions, the optimist attempted to make the masses believe that unrealizable things were possible, in order to control them more easily. Sorel, like Nietzsche, saw optimism, rationalism, utilitarianism, and democracy, its po-

[8] *Les Illusions du Progrès*, p. 51.

[9] Sorel, *Reflections on Violence*, New York, 1941, p. 9. Henceforth, all references will be to this edition, unless otherwise stated.

67

litical contemporary, as nothing but symptoms of declining strength, senility, and exhaustion.

The significance of Sorel's criticism was that he found contemporary ethical ideas in great disorder; the old idea of ethics as an imitation of moral theology was no longer valid, but a social ethic had not yet replaced it.[10] In the forwarding of this social ethic, Sorel believed that Aristotle and Marx were to be allies in the attack on Descartes and Kant. Democracy, with its exciting sentiments, cupidity, hatred, puerile dreams of happiness, vulgarity, and lack both of personal dignity and of appreciation of the dignity of work, had not succeeded in developing a theory of a General Will conforming to reason, following the theory of Rousseau. Democracy, inheriting the defects of the aristocracy, was decadent in spirit, not revolutionary. Lacking in organization and directed by instincts of destruction, it was a school of servility, denunciation, and demoralization. The contemporary Republican democratic philosophy of *Solidarité* was more exactly one of hypocritical cowardice. Sorel warned that the greatest danger menacing the working-class movement would be its imitation of democracy.

Maurras was as complete an antidemocrat as Sorel. He confessed he took his opinions of democracy from Renan, who took them from Comte, who took them from de Maistre and de Bonald, who took them from the great traditions of the human mind.[11] For him, democracy was not simply decadent but also poisonous, evil, and fatal. Having neither body nor soul, its essence was a denial or neglect of the eternal laws. Maurras attacked not simply the defects but the essence of the democratic and parliamentary regime. Liberalism, democracy, universal suffrage were equally abhorrent, the result of Protestant and revolutionary individualism, of Rousseau. To Maurras, the chain was completed; democracy was libertarian, individualist, revolutionary, Kantian, Jean-Jacquist, and Lutheran. The individual had become the center to which every-

[10] Sorel, *D'Aristote à Marx* (L'Ancienne et la nouvelle métaphysique), Paris, p. 260.
[11] Charles Maurras, *Les Princes des nuées*, Paris, 1933, p. 59.

thing was to be subordinated, and individuals left to themselves made a society of barbarians.

Democracy was a natural state in primitive societies, very poor and very simple civilizations where the division of labor had not introduced great complexities. It was the politics of Robinson Crusoe, conceived and forged entirely in terms of isolated man. The democratic convention was the extreme refuge of savage states or states fallen into barbarism.[12] Maurras held the democratic and Republican doctrines to be visionary and unrealistic. The democratic idea was in disagreement with nature, because it submitted the best to the worst, the superior to the inferior, quality to numbers. It inspired laws that were disastrous, destructive to the natural tendencies of customs, to spontaneous instincts, and to the development of progress. Social hierarchies and even the principle of hierarchy itself were overturned. Hereditary distinctions were excluded to such a degree that, outside of a revolution, the superior man could only reach the top slowly.

Democracy was unrealistic in that it refused to recognize that society arose not from a contract of wills but from a fact of nature. Maurras took from Comte the analogy of the lack of freedom in mathematics and in society, an argument which would be unanswerable if the end of society were the creation of definitive behavioral patterns. Law for Maurras was not arbitrary, but was determined from an examination of natural situations; it was the expression of the relation of things and not, as the Declaration of the Rights of Man had said, of the General Will.

Moreover, democracy, together with concepts like liberty, equality, justice, the natural goodness of man, was a *nuée*, a false idea which would prove to be fatal, leading to anarchy and disorder. Democracy destroyed values and honors, could not maintain harmony in community interests, and set up false values. Curiosity and tolerance were two basic characteristics of democracy, and this meant that all objects would be subjected to examination by the same standard and assigned a uniform value.

[12] *L'Action française*, August 14, 1915.

Democracy meant a regime of profit and immediate pleasures, forgetful of the past and negligent of the future.[13] It was characterized by disunited individuals who were ruled by the caprice of money. Full of envy, division, and hate, a democratic regime was a permanent conspiracy against the public welfare. Another source of danger arose because democracies were founded on the will and social comforts of the individual in the present. This meant that the dimensions of time were neglected, and that the lessons of the past, providing useful precedents and warnings, were unheeded. Only provision for the future would control consumption, would stimulate production, and would encourage moderation, initiative, prudence, and precaution.

Those defenders of democracy who did not altogether lack sense and intelligence were pure mystics; their opinions were upheld only by a mixture of reveries and truly subjective impulses. The democratic theories of Renouvier and other Kantians were "creations of pure mythology, anthropomorphic shadows."[14] Views of this kind were in manifest and complete disagreement with all the theorems of positive politics. Science was an adversary of democracy, for the latter would not admit a science of politics.[15] Democracy instead evoked the concept of pure ethics at the moment when it should have studied the relations of facts and of their combinations. The insidious revolutionary spirit never failed to introduce the moral concept at the precise point where ethics had nothing to do with the matter.

Democracy was not only undesirable in itself, but also for France in particular. Most governments and peoples put their material interests first. France alone put general causes before its particular profit and made war for an idea. Taine was wrong to call the democratic spirit a classical one. In reality it was foreign, Protestant or Jewish, Semitic or German. The democratic and parliamentary idea came, as Mon-

[13] Maurras, *L'Allée des philosophes*, Paris, 1924, p. 28.

[14] Maurras, "Les Droits de l'homme et la philosophie naturelle au xixième Siècle," *La Revue hebdomadaire* (November 1899), 12:522.

[15] Maurras, *De Démos à César*, 2 vols., Paris, 1930, 1:115.

tesquieu said, out of the forests of Germany.[16] The idea was dangerous for France because the obsolete forms of democratic rights struggled against the realities of national rights. What Michelet, "theologian of the rights of the multitude and of that popular instinct which seemed infallible to him," exalted were two passions, not native to France: the disparagement of order and the passion for equality.

Democracy was both inefficient and harmful. It was inefficient in that forgetfulness was the rule and management was paralyzed. Its timidity, unpredictability, violence, and turbulence, its delay in making decisions, its absence of all authority, and its inferior personnel would lead democracy to anarchy or to state socialism. Democracy took care of the physical necessities of the mass of the population less than any other regime. It impoverished and enfeebled communities. Maurras refused to recognize the United States as a democracy because in it reality it was governed by captains of industry, a mobile feudal group, after having been governed by a theocratic and rural patriarchy. Neither were England or Germany democratic, for in both countries the rulers were either members of or brought into the aristocracy. Democracy was harmful in its ability to destroy other systems or ideas. What rendered socialism anarchical and revolutionary was not its Socialist aspect, but the democratic poison it contained. "Inorganic, individualistic, inert or revolutionary, democracy kills what is living in socialism."[17]

THE NEED FOR AN ELITE

A democratic system includes in its underlying assumptions the views that no man is indispensable, that political positions are occupied on the basis of competence or aptitude, that careers are open to talents, and that talents are widespread. Sorel, Barrès, and Maurras denied these premises, treated the elite as a reality of political life, and postulated the existence of a minority naturally capable and inevitably

[16] Maurras, *Réflexions sur l'ordre en France*, Paris, 1927, p. 36.
[17] Maurras, *Pour un jeune français*, Paris, 1949, p. 159.

71

destined to rule. Each of them confessed that he was writing for the few, for the minority that would heed his warnings and would be prepared to take up the responsibility that rightfully belonged to it.

"It is reserved for certain members of the elite to explain what is fundamental in the emotional life of an epoch and to describe it," said Sorel.[18] The object of Barrès was to touch "a small public, the princes of youth," those who could develop the *culte-du-moi*, their own sensibility. Maurras, possibly speaking of himself, wrote that a single person, well equipped and well placed, could, if he had ability, dominate millions of others and determine their destiny.[19] There were active and passive Frenchmen, and the passive, although eminently respectable, were useless to a revolutionary movement like the Action Française. Maurras was not concerned with converting the whole electorate, but only with convincing a minority, energetic enough to found a monarchical regime. An elite could not appeal to numbers; a true aristocracy did not strengthen its regime on the infamous liberties of the publican. The general interests of the French nation were far too complicated to be equally and clearly within the understanding of all alike.

Sorel agreed with part of this analysis. The masses, he argued, held to their traditions. Not only was the mass of the population unable to appreciate or to understand political phenomena, they were incapable of initiating change. The struggle for the conquest of power was made in the name of the masses by innovating groups holding ideas contrary to those that were generally accepted. The innovators were an elite who could succeed only by boldness; they were a minority, but if they had a faith, they could sometimes triumph by taking advantage of favorable opportunities.[20]

Sorel applied the concept of the elite to all fields. In war, an elite of soldiers, officers, and generals decided victories. In production, American capitalists—a minority with indom-

18 *Sorel, D'Aristote à Marx*, p. 150.
19 Maurras, *Mademoiselle Monk*, Paris, 1923, p. 50.
20 Sorel, *Le Procès de Socrate*, Paris, 1889, p. 205.

itable energy, audacity, and a cold calculation of interests—were the captains of industry, controlling the industrial riches. In ideology, it was the superior individuals who understood what was fundamental in the emotional life of a period. In revolution, it was always the minority who, with much guile, utilized a momentary discontent of the people against the old authorities. In religion, it was the elite of the monks which gave to Catholicism its ability to encounter all obstacles and its absolute confidence in victory.

A democratic system was no exception to this general pattern, and Sorel regarded it as a kind of aristocratic dictatorship. It rested on the existence of a solid hierarchy, an oligarchy of professional people, intellectuals, and politicians.[21] When one thought of the Third Estate, it was always necessary to think of the bourgeois elite of officials and lawyers which succeeded in governing France almost completely, and which had given it such a strong statist tradition.

Maurras similarly could find no example in history of a positive and creative action initiated by a majority. The normal procedure was the opposite. Will, decision, enterprise came from small numbers; it was minorities that possessed virtue, audacity, power. A religion, an education were necessary not for the people but for its leaders and advisers. It was wrong that everyone should be concerned with politics, because in a world of inequality, gifted people were in a minority. However, this gifted minority was likely to be an hereditary elite, and with such an elite, a prosperous republic would still be possible. Maurras saw the Third Republic as under the influence of people lacking in direction, deficient in culture, and wanting in dignity. Moreover, while all prosperous republics had been governed by a jealously closed aristocracy, in contemporary France there was a further danger because the leading oligarchies were antinational and wide open to foreigners.[22]

Barrès treated the concept of the elite in a somewhat different way. He saw the human species as composed of a rather

[21] *Les Illusions du progrès*, p. 272.
[22] *L'Action française*, March 17, 1914.

limited elite, an elite made up above all of the dead, Athenian, Roman, and French, while the rest of mankind remained in a state of barbarism, of savage nature, and, although benefiting from the work of the elite, ignoring and even detesting it. Humanity moved through its elite. Barrès confessed, "I wish to be of that elite, of that small number."[23] He admired the man of Brumaire and the five or six heroes, "men who knew how to walk on the waves and were not engulfed, because they had confidence in themselves."[24]

But it was on the nature of the elite that the writers differed. Sorel, argued the Nationalist Lasserre, invented working-class imperialism and conceived syndicalism as "an instrument of aristocratic selection among the workers."[25] Barrès and Maurras differed on the necessity of monarchy, but agreed on the value of hereditary rulers. In his reply to the questionnaire of Maurras on monarchy, Barrès argued that an aristocracy, indispensable if monarchy were to exist, was lacking in France, and therefore the revival of monarchy was impossible.[26] A people or a religion which lacked an aristocracy no longer had a model, a direction toward which to aim in order to perfect itself. Rich people did not know toward what to climb. France needed, urged Barrès, a traditional cadre which would permit the French mind to develop and flourish happily, to impose a necessary but not too rigid discipline. Louis XIV as well as Robespierre had been responsible for destroying the nobles who would have been the political leaders of the country.

Maurras agreed on the desirability of an aristocracy. The unity of France resulted from a small number of families devoting themselves over a long period to the permanent interests of France. It was through these families—generations of dukes of France—happy, doing good, used to the exercise of supreme power that Capet had succeeded where Bonaparte

[23] *Mes Cahiers*, IV:155.

[24] Barrès, "Napoléon, professeur d'énergie," *Le Journal*, April 14, 1893, as cited in J-N. Faure Biguet, *op.cit.*, p. 17.

[25] Pierre Lasserre, "Georges Sorel, théoricien de l'impérialisme," *Revue des deux mondes* (September 1, 1927), 41:163.

[26] *Enquête sur la monarchie*, p. 135.

had failed, since Bonaparte did not have behind him what had supported Capet. It was the decay of aristocracy that meant the impossibility of a prosperous, powerful, viable Republic. But Maurras disagreed with Barrès that the monarchy had been partly responsible for this decay and that the monarchy itself was not indispensable for the re-creation of such an aristocracy.

Elitist theorists, as Friedrich has shown,[27] often assume what they need to prove, that there is in a society a coherent group, possessing distinguishing characteristics. Maurras, Barrès, and Sorel were all guilty of this, and tended to attribute to the individual or social group they supported most or all of those characteristics that Mosca in his *The Ruling Class*[28] said were necessary for the members of an elite. Moreover, their theories of the elite were rigid in a way in which that of Pareto was not. With the latter, the emphasis was on the circulation of the elite, the inevitable changes that take place in the types of individuals who will be dominant, and the relatively free circulation up and down the social hierarchy. With Maurras, Barrès, and Sorel there was a much more pronounced emphasis on limitation, both of numbers and of flexibility. In their discussion of the limited group that would be capable of wielding either political or economic power and correcting the deficiencies of the regime, all three writers took for granted a fixed internal or external hierarchy of peoples or nations. They all agreed with Pareto that an attempt by a new elite to supplant the existing one would introduce tension and probably force. They agreed also that emotion, myth, charisma, the sudden leap were essentials that would be involved in the change. Yet essentially their view of the elite was an aristocratic one, an application of Bergson's concept of the outstanding individual to the needs of monarchy, dictatorship, or heroic action.

[27] Carl J. Friedrich, *The New Belief in the Common Man*, Boston, 1942, p. 251.

[28] The characteristics include capacity for hard work, ambition, no extreme sensitivity or goodness, perspicacity, an intuition of individual and mass psychology, strength of will and self-confidence, and the luck that results from having been born in the right bed.

Democratic theorists have been slow to admit the existence of an elite, but both historical insight and empirical research have made it acceptable. The democratic theory of an elite, however, differs in several important ways from the theories suggested by Maurras, Barrès, and Sorel. First, it is a pluralistic conception rather than a unitary one, an admission that power is used only to a limited degree and that it is always subject to other powers used by other individuals or groups in society. Once a notion of equilibrium of political powers, it is now willing to recognize constant oscillation in the expression of these powers. Secondly, even if the theory is willing to admit that the power of decision-making is still limited to relatively few, it also qualifies this proposition by specifying that this limited number will be subject to constant change. And thirdly, there is the final assumption that ultimate power remains in the hands of the people. The concept of the sovereignty of the electorate may be a vague one, and may leave many problems unresolved, but at least it does introduce the vital element of responsibility of government into the political system.

THE ATTACK ON THE ELECTORAL SYSTEM

If the writers regarded an elite as essential, it was not surprising that they should whole-heartedly challenge the desirability of an electoral system, regard it as an inefficient, incompetent, and weak political institution, or think that its consequences were disastrous.

Sorel looked on the electoral system as incompetent and subject to chance. Elections were like dishonest roulette where the banker and the players tried to cheat each other.[29] They meant compromise, the sale of favors, the buying of the press. To politicians, the electoral advantages resulting from a conciliation of interests were worth more than a very large bribe. Sorel found a great resemblance between the activity of an electoral democracy and the Stock Exchange.

[29] *Le Procès de Socrate*, pp. 182-186.

For Maurras the inefficiency and incompetence of the system lay in the fact that the inferior elements of the population were allowed to choose the superior. For the "people," Maurras had contempt; he regarded electoral bodies as inorganic collectivities, with unlimited faculties of forgetfulness and no faculties of reflection.[30] Those exercising power found themselves at the mercy of ignorance disguised as public opinion, played on by the press and the financial system. It was necessary to relieve the incompetent citizens from the heavy weight of responsibilities with which they had been overwhelmed in order to dupe them more easily. Although Maurras nowhere criticized the method by which a pope or members of the French Academy are chosen, he regarded the electoral principle as enfeebling or destroying authority, in contrast with the hereditary principle, which led to tranquillity, order, and stability. The case Maurras made against the electoral system is the case always made against Jacobinism, that the electorate was usurping the place of government. Moreover, the larger the number of people concerned with governing, the more it seemed to him that government was being affected by formulas and generalizations, and becoming more unrealistic.

Maurras regarded the electoral regime as weak because it was based on individualism, because it was open to foreign influence, because it resulted in a failure to consider the general interest of France, and because it led to a class of professional politicians. Psychologically, the regime could be defined as the intense antagonism of eleven million egos or delegates of egos.[31] This meant that organizations and parties depending on the electoral process had neither will nor unity. Individual interests were put ahead of the general interests of the French nation, which were far too complicated to be equally and clearly within the understanding of all alike. It was unrealistic to treat each elector, as Sangnier did, as if he had the soul of a saint or a king, or to presume the equality of electors and the uniformity of functions. Maurras believed

[30] Maurras, *La Contre-révolution spontanée*, Paris, 1943, p. 112.
[31] *Enquête sur la monarchie*, p. lxxxvii.

that if people were allowed the vote and the choice of a leader, they would assuredly elect the man "whose nose pleases them, and who will have no more brain than a calabash."[32]

For Maurras this was disastrous, because the great offices of state—the ministries for Foreign Affairs, War, Navy, Justice —ought not to have been dependent on election, especially when the electoral mechanism upheld the domination of foreign influence through the four *Etats Confédérés*. Under a nondemocratic regime, opinion was only one of the powers in the state, and the state was capable of resisting opinion and resolving problems which affected the public interest in spite of public sentiment to the contrary. A state definitely enchained to the caprices of opinion led to suicide.[33] A political system based on election produced agitation, chronic revolution, and constitutional anarchy. This was demonstrated when the Second Empire, born of plebiscitary and democratic origins and dependent on popularity, had found itself condemned to economic and foreign adventure.

An electoral regime, moreover, produced a powerful group of politicians, a plebs, half-bourgeois, half-proletarian, that controlled elections. The evils were that eminent representatives could never be obtained, while those who were elected dreamed only of popularity in order to be re-elected. They did whatever flattered the eye, with no thought for the future. "Electoral parasites," deputies traveled first class when unseen, third class when nearing their constituency.

Sorel and Barrès agreed with Maurras on the mediocrity of deputies—an evil arising from the system. Sorel held that in all states where elections existed, men of ability were turned down in favor of politicians and the *déclassés*, although even this exclusion of the capable was, for him, less of an evil than government by intellectuals. Democrats were wrong, he thought, to ask for free secondary education. They were wrong to think that France would be a hundred times happier and stronger when it would have a greater number

[32] Maurras, *Mes Idées politiques*, Paris, 1937, p. 165.
[33] *Les Princes des nuées*, p. 192.

78

of candidates for elective functions capable of dazzling the workers by their facility of speech.[34]

For Barrès, the deputies of the Third Republic were undistinguished, possessing a mediocrity which allowed them not to offend their electors. "With us," he said, "the deputies never forget that they are future candidates; they are all concerned with satisfying their constituency electoral committees rather than with serving their country."[35] In fact, all their behavior could be understood by this desire to remain candidates. Barrès wrote of the fictional tutor and adversary, M. Bouteiller, professor and deputy from Nancy (a figure that was based on Barrès' own teacher), that he "had too much sense to give money to a Parisian newspaper which had no local influence and which would compete with and irritate the Nancy newspapers."[36]

Both Maurras and Sorel regarded electoral reforms as useless and illusionary, Sorel saying that no reform in the method of voting could change a result which depended on the fundamental structure of contemporary society.[37] He suggested that proportional representation would serve only to develop the party spirit; Maurras thought that since the majority system oppressed minorities, proportional representation would reverse the evil, not suppress it, and the majority would be suppressed by a minority. The referendum at best was only a negative remedy. It could prevent certain stupidities and misfortunes. It could not create an active organ of government, because of the essential lack of direction in the system.[38]

All three writers attacked democracy because of its individualism, its incompetence, its electoral process, and its lack of direction. Sorel attacked it for its premises of rationalism and inevitable progress, and for its lack of absolute standards. Maurras attacked it as essentially unnatural. Barrès attacked

[34] Sorel, *Introduction à l'économie moderne*, 2nd edn., Paris, 1922, p. 208.

[35] Barrès, *Leurs Figures*, Paris, 1902, p. 19.

[36] Barrès, *Les Déracinés*, 2 vols., Paris, 1897, II:129.

[37] Sorel, *La Révolution Dreyfusienne*, 2nd edn., Paris, 1911, p. 72.

[38] *L'Action française*, April 16, 1913.

it for its lack of stimulation to excite enthusiasm, glory, and adventure. In these attacks there are two fundamental mistakes, one concerning the premises of democracy and the other concerning individualism.

The first results from Sorel's having taken an extremist argument as a typical one. The view of a limited number of 18th century Philosophes on the inevitability of progress is not one that a 20th century democrat would uphold. Even if he were optimistic, he would not claim progress to be either inevitable or automatic, but instead would devote his efforts to its promotion. In Sorel's analysis of the rationalistic basis of democracy (which reappears in Chapter vii), he fell into that pitfall described by Graham Wallas as a false dichotomy between reason and impulse since reflection consists of processes which are largely subconscious. But above all, Sorel's assumption that democracy could have no fundamental ethical beliefs and that it had no final end was based upon his misunderstanding of the character of the tolerance that is essential to democracy. A democratic society is characterized by its toleration of dissent, but this does not imply an inability to hold an absolute ethic of right or wrong, a lack of judgment and of values, or a refusal to preserve its existence. Whatever characteristics a democratic system may have, suicide is not one of them.

The second mistake arises from the false antithesis of the individual and the state. There was in Maurras and Barrès, and to a lesser degree in Sorel, the tendency to see social relationships in these stark terms, and to ignore those other organizations and voluntary associations to which men belong and to which they may owe their strongest allegiance. It may be going too far to suggest that Maurras and Barrès merged state and society, as later totalitarians did, but certainly they identified the state with the nation, argued that no freedom existed except within the state, and that democracy meant liberty against the state and a limitation of the latter. Maurras and Barrès were typical of that tendency of Nationalists in general who, as defenders of a specific social group, the nation, are even more clearly disposed than conservatives to sacrifice

80

individual values in the interests of society.[39] By this false antithesis between the isolated individual and the supreme state, the three writers' picture of the relationships among the individual, group, and government became necessarily an incorrect one.

Since the French Revolution, the mass has entered politics. In the period under discussion, the significance of this factor had been increased by a more highly developed industrial system, the beginning of universal education, and the growth of working-class movements. In this context the writers postulated their antidemocratic theories. These theories were not only antiplutocratic but, with Maurras and Barrès, antiproletarian as well, and the combination of these two antipathies created a new dilemma. The ruling group needed mass support in order to survive, but the mass was incompetent. It is no coincidence that Maurras called the mob feminine and argued that it must be mastered, or that all three writers agreed that only a limited group could understand contemporary conditions and be capable of ruling. It is this dilemma —the power of the mass and the writers' fear of it, and their conception of the practical interests of the country—that caused the three to attack the Revolution so bitterly.

[39] Frederick M. Watkins, *The Political Tradition of the West*, Cambridge, 1957, p. 281.

CHAPTER V

ATTACK ON THE REVOLUTION

AMONG the myths on which the French political system operates is that of the Revolution as a basic watershed of French political belief. The classic interpretation of this myth of the Revolution is the division of France into two blocs: one, the party of progress and intellect, supporting the crusade against the past on behalf of equality, reason, and liberty; the other, the party of tradition and privilege, refusing to be relegated to oblivion, and basing itself on the values of the family, religion, and authority.[1] Both the Left and the Right—Clemenceau as well as Taine—have made use of the idea of the existence of two "blocs." It is clearly true, as Aron argues, that the "unity of the Left" is less a reflection than a distortion of the reality of French politics and that the Republican unity shown during the Boulanger and Dreyfus crises are the exceptions rather than the rule. It is also clear, however, that a crisis would, because of the very existence of the myth, produce the needed unity. Political thinkers and politicians operate on the basis of its existence. "You accept the Republic of course," said Léon Bourgeois to a right-wing group, "but do you accept the Revolution?"[2] Of our three writers, Maurras and Sorel were completely opposed to the Revolution, while Barrès, treasuring its Bonapartist element, declared in a debate in the Chamber, "Many of us . . . are not perhaps the pupils of Gambetta, but we are the responsible sons of the Revolution,"[3] and was prepared to give it qualified support.

Barrès, with his conservative approach to history, was prepared to accept the fact of the Revolution and the political regimes that had resulted from it because the Revolution had taken its place in history, and history was essentially a

[1] Raymond Aron, *The Opium of the Intellectuals*, London, 1957, pp. 5-9.
[2] Albert Thibaudet, *Les Idées politiques de la France*, p. 225.
[3] *Journal Officiel*, January 29, 1891, p. 155.

continual process.[4] One could not make a distinction between the soul of France before the Revolution and afterwards. Moreover, not only was Barrès prepared to accept the present; he was also ready to admit the faults of the past.

Barrès implied that the Revolution could be justified. The Revolution had not been made by assault of the revolutionaries, but was the result of the behavior of the rulers at Versailles. "France was dead in 1789, it was not dead of 1789 nor of 1793."[5] Barrès even approved of the "sinister slaughterers of '93, not for their acts, but for their *élan*. They were not moderates." In a curious passage, he invoked the image of Rousseau. "O mon cher Rousseau, mon Jean Jacques, vous l'Homme du monde que j'ai le plus aimé et celebré sous vingt pseudonymes, vous un autre moi-même."[6] But in talking of the deficiencies of the Revolution, his views were diametrically opposed to those of Rousseau. The Revolution had based society on natural rights, that is, on logic; its philosophers and lawyers had declared that all men were the same everywhere and that they had rights as men, an argument that was not acceptable to Barrès. "Our task is to ruin the religion of the Revolution and to serve the Church," he wrote.[7] The task was even more imperative because the Revolution had upset traditional values. The very legend of the Revolution had destroyed the legends of the provinces, the corporations, the families.

Unlike Barrès, Maurras was both uncompromisingly opposed to the Revolution and reluctant to admit any deficiencies in the *ancien régime* that might have been responsible for producing it. Ideologically incorrect, the product of foreign ideas, for Maurras the Revolution had been wrongfully named French.[8] The Revolution came from the Bible of the Reformation, the statutes of the Republic of Geneva, the Calvinist theologians, the old individualist ferment of the Germany

---

[4] *Mes Cahiers*, iii:107, 176; iv:180.
[5] *Mes Cahiers*, v:60; ii:202.
[6] Maurice Barrès, *Le Jardin de Bérénice*, Paris, 1921, p. 141.
[7] *Mes Cahiers*, ix:319.
[8] *L'Action française*, April 30, 1908.

ATTACK ON THE REVOLUTION

for which the trilingual Swiss served as European interpreters; the revolutionary ideas were anything but natural to France. Since Maurras believed that almost the whole French Revolution came from Rousseau, he repeatedly attacked "the Genevan vagabond, a homeless individual." Optimistic and sensitive, the miserable Rousseau was a man of folly, savagery, ignorance, singularity, solitude, pride, and revolt, nourished on a Biblical upbringing. Rousseau had broken with the whole of civilization, with the general principles of the ancient City, mediaeval organization, and modern Europe.[9] It is not surprising that Maurras joined with Barrès in objecting strenuously to the bicentennial celebration of Rousseau's birth in 1912.

For Maurras, one could not talk of defending one part of the Revolution and opposing another, one could not at the same time love the Revolution and hate its excesses.[10] There was no Jacobin revolution to distinguish from a French one; all of the Revolution was anti-French and was marked by insurrection of the individual (liberalism), which led to tyranny of the state (democracy). Maurras followed Taine in arguing that 1789 and 1793 proceeded from the same spirit, represented the same personnel, the same tactics, the same events. The two men supported the doctrine of the "revolutionary bloc" for reasons completely opposite to those of Clemenceau, who had used the slogan as a rallying cry for support of the Revolution and for the Republic. Maurras, from the opposite point of view, said there was only one true schism in all the history of France, and that was the Revolution. He condemned the Revolution because its success meant the end of France.

The Revolution, the most enormous stupidity France had committed, had changed the natural course and the normal rhythm of the life of the country. It had disorganized the nation, reduced the people to a state of atomistic division and of individual rivalries.[11] The heirs of 1789 had destroyed

[9] Charles Maurras, *Réflexions sur l'ordre en France*, p. 21.
[10] *Réflexions sur la Révolution de 1789*, Paris, 1948, p. 83.
[11] Charles Maurras and Lucien Moreau, "L'Action française," *Le Correspondant* (June 10, 1908), 231:973.

the domestic, local, economic, and religious organs of French power. Maurras regarded the legend of the volunteers of 1792, the fable of Valmy, as poisonous, and the Revolution an event from which the decadence of the middle class dated.[12] The night of August 4th ruined the collective liberties, local liberties, professional liberties that had made France powerful and glorious.

Maurras always made a curious division between what was caused by the Revolution and what could be attributed to France. The victories of the Revolution—Valmy, Jemmapes, Fleurus, Hohenlinden, Marengo, Wagram—were won by France, while the defeats were due to the Revolution. What had flourished on the Rhine from 1792 to 1814 was the work of two centuries of French influence, and not the result of the Revolution.

The effect of the Revolution was pernicious. It had led to individualism, the destruction of families, local powers, and other social authorities, the utilization of religion for the profit of the state. Furthermore, it had divided the country into departments, which set up a false barrier to population and interests.[13] The ideas stemming from the Revolution— democracy, liberal Protestantism, and romanticism—degraded the three fundamental characteristics of French civilization: monarchy, Catholic sentiment, and the classical spirit.

The spirit of 1789 was individualistic and pacific, but it led to 25 years of war and to the alliance of the most powerful nations against France. The Revolution had had a greater effect than previous crises, and reduced France to the level of a second-rank power at a time when Italian and German unity had been created, and those nations were of increasing importance. Supporting the view of Bonald, Maurras believed that if it were through France that the Revolution had begun in the world, it would also be through France that the counter-revolution must begin.[14]

[12] L'Etang de Berre, Paris, 1915, p. 130.
[13] Réflexions sur la révolution, p. 139.
[14] La Contre-révolution spontanée, p. 35.

His opposition to the Revolution was a total one, for he believed everything about it was either unrealistic or unsuccessful: it had attempted to destroy great fortunes, but there had been no decrease in them; it had tried to abolish organizations standing between the employer and the employee, but had resulted in the rise of trade unions and considerable violence; it called for a democratic fusion of classes, but had led to class war; it advocated the abolition of differences between nations, but had led to the most violent nationalist enmities. Maurras rejected 150 years of French history, refusing to acknowledge that the Civil Code, the administrative and electoral apparatus, had created permanent habits of thought and action, and denying that Jacobin and Napoleonic centralization was the continuation of a trend begun under the monarchy.

Sorel, while maintaining the myth of revolution and of the use of violence, was totally opposed to the Revolution and its outcome. Taine had "taught us all about the false great men who led the great European upheaval," he wrote.[15] Sorel spoke of the "Jacobin anarchists," "the perfect pedant" Robespierre, the "hallucinators of '93." Fundamentally intellectual and middle class, democratic ideology was a degenerate daughter of the bourgeois ideology of '89. Sorel believed that the Revolution had caused the growth of state power and had increased the activities of politicians, and that this might mean greater, not less, servitude than that under the Old Regime.

IDEOLOGY OF THE REVOLUTION

The three writers were hostile to the chief principles of the Revolution, liberty, equality, and fraternity, and the individualism on which they were based.

Liberty.—Maurras regarded the principle of liberty as false and unrealistic, as undesirable in its method because it put discussion first, and as unfortunate in its resulting disorganization and enfeeblement of individuals. Liberty for all, "the Nuée of Nuées," was a false metaphysical principle, contrary

15 Georges Sorel, *Le Procès de Socrate*, p. 204.

to nature. It prevented the submission of the citizen, not only to the laws of the state, but to the profound laws of nature and of reason. One of these laws, born from the fact that men were unequal, was that liberty was the privilege of the few. It was meaningless if it was to be exercised by all. Since "we are born slaves of a thousand fatalities,"[16] liberty must be limited to a small number of essentials, beyond which the rule of the strongest legitimately applied. To guarantee the liberty of each meant the servitude of all.

The idea of liberty was unrealistic because it was based not only on the theory of individualism, but also on that of the sovereignty of individuals, which Maurras, following Comte, regarded as "an ignoble lie or oppressive mystification."[17] Admitting that the individual existed and could create, Maurras objected to the emphasis on his primacy; in a case of conflict, society should always be placed first. If it was the individual who created, it was the community that maintained and perpetuated. Maurras felt that the individual had more obligations to society than it could have to him. Social man had no natural rights, only duties. Moreover, Maurras regarded societies as composed of families, not of single human beings. A society could no more be broken up into the individuals that composed it than a geometrical surface could be broken up into straight lines, or a straight line into points. Maurras attacked the idea of the individual as an isolated being. He recognized that the working-class movement of the 19th century was essentially a reaction against this isolation, which had been imposed by the Revolution and maintained by Bonapartism and by bourgeois liberalism, the successor to Jacobinism.[18] In fact, the whole of 19th century history was a series of reactions against the individualist and centralist tendencies bequeathed by Rousseau and Napoleon.

The exercise of liberty was disastrous in all fields. It was wrong to believe that at the bottom of each individual's

[16] Maurras, "L'Evolution des idées sociales," *La Réforme sociale* (February 1, 1891), 21:201.
[17] *L'Action française*, November 4, 1909.
[18] *Mes Idées politiques*, p. 244.

sensibility there existed the principle of unity and order. Barbarism began when the perceptive individual, preferring his own judgment to what was reasonable, began to decide for himself. If good and evil became the result of individual judgment, anarchy would ensue. In all fields the principle of free examination meant chaos: a liberal was nothing but a disorganized mind. Religious liberty meant that everything was challenged and that any truth would be put in peril because of individual doubt. Individualism in religion had resulted in the Reformation. Individualism in politics had resulted in the Revolution. Political and social liberty led to enfeeblement of the individual, to tyranny over those not belonging to the majority party, and to anarchy, for it would destroy the ties of family and tradition, upset the state and destroy patriotism.[19] Economic liberty meant individual competition and the liberty to die of hunger. Liberty of thought really meant libertine thought, as the 17th century had argued. Liberty in art resulted in romanticism.

True liberty for Maurras meant something quite different. It needed authority; it was for Maurras, as he claimed it was for "cet illustre Hobbes," a share of power. It was the product of certainty. Just as there were fixed rules in mechanics, finance, astronomy, figures, or pure numbers, so in social affairs there were rules of habit and discipline based on reason, intelligence, and true understanding. For problems of inheritance there was a head of family, for communal or provincial problems there were social authorities, for religious problems there were spiritual laws and an official hierarchy, for syndical and professional problems there were rules of corporations and trades.

In society, a system with fixed rules of this kind would entail hierarchy and stratification, a Platonic pattern, with each individual gaining his own happiness from within himself and from the proper exercise of his function. It was because of his devotion to real liberty, Maurras said, that he entirely repudiated all liberalism, just as it was from respect for and

[19] Maurras, *La Démocratie religieuse*, Paris, 1921, pp. 395-396.

love of the people that he would fight democracy. Petty individual liberties were not important compared with maintaining the independence of the country and preserving its customs and traditions. Those liberties which favored the national effort were to be encouraged, those which contradicted it were to be watched or suppressed.[20] In particular, control was necessary over the four *Etats Confédérés*—the masons, the Protestants, the Jews, the *métèques*—who were destroying society and true liberty.

Equality.—The Revolution and liberalism, on which it was based, also implied to Maurras the equal political value of individuals. But reason could not accept as natural or biologically true the democratic premise that the value of all members of society was equal. A society could tend to equality, but, from the biological point of view, equality existed only in the cemetery. Equality did not and could not happen of itself, it had to be made. When the law proclaimed equality it lied, for in any society an unequal division of liberties was inevitable, and this precluded the idea of equality.

As one rose in the biological scale, the inequalities present became more numerous and deeper.[21] Organization meant differentiation, which involved useful inequalities; to democratize would be to equalize, which would mean methodical disorganization—one could not organize democracy, and one could not democratize organization. Though Maurras warned specifically against the danger of accepting too readily the analogy between the organism in nature and in politics and criticized the excessive use of such an analogy, in fact he equated natural with political inequality and pointed out the inevitable political disadvantages resulting from the attempt to overturn the natural order. The idea of equality meant surrendering power to the herd, to inferior classes, to incompetence. Democrats argued on the basis of equality for "one man, one vote," but those who opposed this demand and by invoking quality[22] demanded categories of suffrage, represen-

[20] *Gazette de France*, September 4, 1901.
[21] *Gazette de France*, May 1, 1899.
[22] *L'Action française*, May 3, 1913.

tation of families and of social and local bodies, were arguing on more natural grounds.

Equality, moreover, meant weakness, both because it led to internal difficulties and because it was another instance of the penetration of foreign, unhealthy ideas. The existence of a society whose members were practically equal meant that industry and the arts would be retarded. The obsession with and desire for equality established a political spirit directly contrary to the vital needs of a country; it destroyed military discipline, and since the people had need of an army, it led to national abasement. The choice was clear: either political inequality, or the death of the country; inequality, or decadence and anarchy. Moreover, the choice was essential, since egalitarian ideas were foreign and unhealthy, came originally from Israel, and had been reintroduced in the 16th century when the Reformation, multiplying the number of Bibles and making everyone use them, propagated the egalitarian mysticism of the prophets.[23] But even this spiritual equality was false. The Church admitted neither equality of human rewards nor the equal distribution of the divine graces, since unequal souls received unequal supernatural favors.

Just as Maurras believed equality to be an essential element of democracy, and just as he regarded rights as equal only when they corresponded to naturally unequal situations, so did Sorel see the idea of equality, conceived as approximate identity, as belonging, not to socialism, but rather to pure democracy, to radical and Jacobin stupidity—an ideal altogether foreign to socialism.[24] Equality was the chief cause of degradation of citizens, because it was a product of jealousy and of the sophism of generalizing the particular. It was necessary to restrict equality, as did Aristotle, to a small caste,[25] for democracy, which was founded on abstract equality, would result in anarchy.

Fraternity and Justice.—Barrès thought anarchy would result if justice were preferred to society. Referring to the

23 *Gazette de France,* January 23, 1900.
24 Sorel, "Superstition Socialiste," *Le Devenir social* (November 1895), 3:729-764.
25 *Le Procès de Socrate,* p. 174.

Dreyfus Affair, he argued that the French Kantian intellectuals had spoken of sacrificing everything to justice, and would willingly have preferred the destruction of society to the upholding of an injustice. "Speak of Justice when one man condemns another! Let us be content to speak of social preservation."[26] Justice, he thought, was not of this world; in its name revolutions were made, leaving ruins, not heaven, on earth.

The idea of metaphysical justice was equally abhorrent to Maurras, for it was unnatural and essentially Jewish. The first condition of life was not justice, but ability to exist. Then came the capability of possessing the independence and liberty of action without which justice was only a dream. Since this liberty of action was likely to be attained by only a few and since the idea of metaphysical justice was therefore likely to provoke disorder, the consequence was that true justice lay in order and inequality.

True justice was also opposed to the idea of fraternity, "this bad imitation of the evangelical precept of charity,"[27] which, anti-French in nature, was the foundation of the contemporary cosmopolitan regime. Fraternity was meaningless, because the law of life was self-satisfaction, not love for others. Nature had implanted the violent passions of anger and hate in the political animal; the idea of fraternity, by ignoring the existence of these emotions in international relations, would lead to their breaking out internally, and embroiling France in civil war.

SOVEREIGNTY OF THE PEOPLE

The idea of the sovereignty of the people was rejected by all the writers as a fiction, but one that had had disastrous consequences. Sorel, suggesting that the fiction of the sovereignty of the people was the favorite element of democratic theory,[28] thought that such a fiction could lead to anarchy. If government depended on the popular will or on parliamentary rule, this would mean the domination of the ignorant

[26] *Mes Cahiers*, i:263; ii:106.
[27] Maurras, "L'Evolution des idées sociales," p. 200.
[28] *Matériaux*, p. 118.

over the wise and the bad over the good, and would result in demoralization and social disintegration. The decadence of the French bureaucracy had begun on the day when it was subordinated to the parliamentarians—everything bowed before the majesty of the national sovereignty, a title the deputies had been invested with as representatives of the people. Moreover, the ideas of the people themselves could not be trusted since they were played on by the press, ideological inheritor of the 18th century.

Maurras argued that the founders of modern democracy, Protestants like Rousseau, Catholics like Lamennais, had thought of the sovereignty of the people as a divine right. He agreed with Barrès that numbers had taken the place of the king. Even the concept of the General Will, once a vague metaphysical entity, had been reduced to that of precise and particular wills, and rule by the majority. And the principle of majority rule was ridiculous in origin, incompetent in practice, and pernicious in its effects.[29]

It was ridiculous in origin because it took for granted the political equality of individuals and equality of capacity, and these ideas he had already attacked as unnatural and false. Politics was too intricate and complex a subject to be abandoned to the caprice of everyone.

Majority rule was incompetent because it was the regime of those least qualified and least interested in national life, the most inert and the least human. Democratic intellectuals thought that action must be preceded by infinite discussions between the least competent persons: lawyers without cases, professors without students, doctors without patients. The great misfortune of the times was that it was supposed to be necessary that the citizen have a deliberate opinion on the state, and where opinion governed, no one governed. There was no instance of a "people" ever having "wished" or "done" anything in the precise sense of these words. Public opinion, which changed from day to day, was the vaguest and the most fleeting, the most badly defined of the fashions. In such a

[29] *La Démocratie religieuse*, p. 397.

situation nothing was fixed and durable.[30] State affairs would be delivered to the hazard of chance or would decline into insolvency, and the state would become enslaved to unforeseen events and changes of opinion. If it was true that on certain subjects the crowd was a child and public opinion a minor, the forgeries in the Dreyfus Affair were permissible and legitimate, and the act of Colonel Henry useful.[31]

The sovereignty of the people as expressed by majority rule was pernicious both because it meant that there was no thought for the general welfare and because the true "Kings of the Republic" were the Jews, Protestants, masons, and *métèques*. The destiny of the country where the crowd ruled was internal strife, producing agreements detrimental to the life and property of the state.[32] Each person thought only of his individual interest, and the sum of individual interests did not add up at all to the general interest of the French nation. Private and party interests superseded interest in the general welfare or in the country as a whole. The idea of Nation ought to replace that of People. Whereas "People" implied the changeable and insignificant desires of mortals, "Nation" was a superior entity which endured spiritually and materially.[33] Only if this change were made would the influence on the people of the foreigners, the true kings, be counteracted.

Maurras was the standard-bearer of the 20th century counter-revolution in France, and his annotated volumes, *Dictionnaire politique et critique*, a serious attempt at a counter-*Encyclopaedia*. "In the name of reason and of nature, conforming to the ancient laws of the universe, for the sake of order, for the existence and progress of a menaced civilization, all hopes float on the ship of the counter-revolution."[34] For Maurras, the counter-revolution had become as radical, as

[30] Maurras, *Quand les français ne s'aimaient pas*, Paris, 1916.
[31] *Gazette de France*, September 6, 1898.
[32] Maurras, *Anthinéa*, Paris, 1919, p. 275.
[33] Maurras, "De l'Autorité légitime: le Droit national et le droit démocratique," *La Revue Universelle* (June 1924), 17:666.
[34] Maurras, *L'Avenir de l'intelligence*, Paris, 1918, p. 104.

destructive, as brilliant, and as luminous as the Revolution had been at a previous time. He supported all the antidemocratic and antirepublican tendencies of the day: the attack on the revolutionary system in the name of true liberty, requiring the revival of the power of the family; the attack on economic liberty in the name of the liberty of the *syndicat,* requiring the revival of professional groups; the attack on political liberty in the name of independence, requiring governmental liberty to act; the attack on municipal centralization in the name of local liberty, requiring the reawakening of the commune; the attack on the departments in the name of regional liberty, requiring the reanimation of the province.

Maurras claimed that all counter-revolutionary theories had as their fundamental theses necessity, drawn from the essence of things and not from the will of men; authority, not liberty; hierarchy, not equality; family, not the individual; duty, not the rights of man.[35] In his own day, the Dreyfus Affair had produced the first article of the counter-revolutionary creed of the Action Française;[36] namely, that there were duties which did not oblige Frenchmen to regard all judicial decisions as infallible and eternal, duties which forbade believing in judicial error without strong reasons, duties which were good for the social system.

Maurras was the archetype of the modern reactionary who does not derive his ideas from or base them on the premise of God. It was significant to him that the three men most divided on religion, Comte, Bonald, and Le Play, were agreed on opposition to the first principles of the Revolution.[37] "His ambition," said a critic, "was to be the Phidias of a social Parthenon founded on logic, geometry, the tested canons of architecture."[38] Maurras resolved that reason would provide the basis for his creed because he believed that there was nothing less individualist than reason. Reason was concerned with the general, not with the particular or the indi-

[35] *La Contre-révolution spontanée,* p. 45.
[36] Charles Maurras and Lucien Moreau, *op.cit.,* p. 966.
[37] *L'Etang de Berre,* p. 51.
[38] R. Kemp, "Charles Maurras, Prince des Nuées" (November 20, 1952), p. 5.

vidual, and therefore could not be a revolutionary force. It would furnish for him, as for the Athenians, the foundation of order and stability. But Maurras was nowhere able or willing to explain the dilemma of how the counter-revolution on which he set his hopes could respect the law of continuity that had been violated by the Revolution. It is an indication of the irresponsibility of much of the criticism of the Right that, because it was totally opposed to the current institutions, it had to work outside of, and not through, them.

The extreme conservative, as MacIver has suggested,[39] insists on the paramount need of law and order, but what he really believes in is his own law and order. When his dislike of the existing regime is strong enough, he is prepared to rebel. Sorel reached this conclusion through his conviction that a new kind of law and ethics was urgently needed. Barrès reached it through his realization that a new *mystique*, one of nationalism, had to be created, and that the leader of the counter-revolution would have to depend on mass support. Maurras reached the same conclusion because of his rejection of the whole ideology of the Revolution. One of the basic legacies of the Revolution is the concept of the sovereignty of the people, and in France this has led to the sovereignty of the electoral assembly, as representatives of the people. Since Maurras claimed that electoral assemblies were incapable of leading, or of dealing with crises, and since the necessary institution of strong executive power was absent, he was eager to overturn the regime and restore what he considered to be the true political equilibrium.

At the time of the Dreyfus Affair there were two principal right-wing groups, Déroulède's Ligue des Patriotes, which Barrès claimed had a membership of 100,000, including 25 members of the French Academy, and Lemaître's Ligue de la Patrie Française, with a membership of 15,000, with other minor and short-lived bodies like Guérin's Anti-Semitic League. But it was the Action Française movement, subsidized in part by Lemaître's friend Mme de Loynes, which became the

[39] Robert M. MacIver, *The Web of Government*, New York, 1947, p. 277.

focal point for extreme right-wing opposition, going beyond the intellectual traditionalism of Brunetière and Bourget. Vaugeois, initial leading figure in the movement in 1899, at first thought it would be a legal movement within the Republic, and the policy statement on November 15, 1899 for which he was largely responsible, was a nonmonarchical one. It is a commentary on the dominance of Maurras over the movement that it quickly came to realize the necessity for a *coup d'état*, and to believe in monarchy.

The first issue of the *Action française* journal appeared on August 1, 1899; on March 21, 1908 it became a daily. The organization had its own review, the *Revue critique des idées et des livres*, its own publishing house, the Nouvelle Librairie Nationale, and weekly study groups. It had its affiliated organizations like the Jeunes Filles Royalistes, and its strong-arm men, the Camelots du Roi. With the latter, the movement took to the streets, and from 1908 until 1914, there were continual incidents. The breaking of statues of Dreyfusards, the public slapping of Briand, the attempted assassination of Dreyfus in 1908, the attack on a professor of the Sorbonne for his criticism of Joan of Arc in 1909, the incitement to murder Caillaux in 1914, all belied the pretense of the movement. Maurras argued that the violence of revolutionaries was put at the service of disorder, not of order, at the service of theft, not of property, at the service of anarchy, not of authority, at the service of the enemies of France, not of the country. Yet Péguy was not the only one to register pain that the Action Française movement, professing to restore the ancient dignities of the race, resorted to so much derision, sarcasm, and injury. The distressing paradox was that a movement based on the value of order should be so full of invective.

Though Maurras' movement had a considerable effect on the Parisian university youth, its political impact was almost nonexistent. None of the Royalist senators or deputies joined the group, nor did Barrès. The leaders of the Church were wary. They had not forgotten, even if Maurras had, that it was the monarchy that had expelled the Jesuits in 1767. The movement held itself aloof from the right-wing combination of ex-Boulangists, clericals, and Méline Progressists formed in 1902. Maurras, unable and unwilling to take advantage of monarchical feeling except on his own terms, refused to ally himself either with the ex-ralliés, largely legitimist and aristocratically liberal, or with the Progressists, who had moved further to the right with the Dreyfus Affair. During the Boulanger crisis the Orleanists were at best reluctant allies of the general. The warning by the Comte de Paris that it was imprudent to remind people incessantly of monarchy and that monarchists should fight for conservative ideas on conservative ground was disregarded by his too-enthusiastic supporter, Maurras.

Julien Benda pointed out that the real danger to the regime was always Caesarism or Boulangism. The truth of this observation was shown in 1905 when Déroulède, returning to France after having been exiled, was welcomed by a crowd of 300,000. It was Barrès who sensed the wave of the future, linking the old Bonapartist ideas—its authoritarianism, its magnetic leader, its mass appeal, its appeal to the love of glory—with the growing antiparliamentarianism, the strident militarism, and the political anti-Semitism. Barrès' national republicanism was more appealing than Maurras' monarchy.

But in all this the eyes of the counter-revolutionaries, as both Halévy and Brogan have suggested, were on the wrong revolution, on the political noise of France, rather than the industrial hum of England. They were too eager to see the red carnation of Boulanger triumph over the red flag, and not sufficiently interested in real, fundamental changes in social life.

CHAPTER VI
ATTACK ON DECADENCE

ALL three writers were concerned about the decadence of France, the weaknesses in the system, and the decline of what they considered to be the appropriate traditional values. The manifestations of decadence they saw prevented France from maintaining her historic status as a first-class power and from being the political and cultural leader in the hierarchy of nations. It was this concern about the declining place of their country among the powers of the world and the awareness of France's internal weakness that made the writers prophetic of those in other countries whose reaction to a similar problem was to be a violent one, dangerous to the peace of the world.

Sorel, Barrès, and Maurras were all aware of the diminished glory of the country, and in this each paid almost as much attention to the literary as to the physical attributes of France. "We must serve France and defend a Latin culture of which we are the extreme bastions,"[1] said Barrès. From the European point of view, argued Maurras, "every Frenchman is a politician."

All three writers were disappointed with the existing political institutions and with the politicians running them, whom they considered to be betrayers of the best interests of France. The three condemned the overcentralization of the country, which had had unfortunate effects. But each of the writers stressed a different aspect of the problem of France's decadence. Barrès and Sorel emphasized the negative characteristics of the Republic, its lack of doctrine, energy, and heroic qualities. Maurras and Barrès emphasized the foreign elements, personal and ideological, which in the cultural, economic, political, and financial worlds, were rotting the very fiber of France.

Sorel was a moralist who emphasized the need for *élan* and denounced the dullness, lack of heroism, pacific nature, and

---

[1] *Mes Cahiers*, III:145.

unity of the country. He was also a technician who criticized the Republic's fatal tendency to consume rather than produce. The moralist and the technician were interconnected because the laxity of morals was harmful to the activities of production. Sorel crossed the normally accepted barriers between Left and Right. He was representative of the Left in regarding decadence as an outcome of rigid stability, denying the desirability of a state of equilibrium, and arguing that the proletariat had a unique mission to perform in the regeneration of society. He was representative of the Right in his belief that energetic action as such would create a more desirable moral state, in his attacks on rationalism and intellectualism, on individualism and on bourgeois plutocracy, and in his partly paradoxical belief in rural values.

Barrès disagreed with Sorel over the desirability of an unstable society. With his acute sensitivity to human failings and desires, he was the first person in modern literature to stress the elements of decadence resulting from the instability of society and the psychological problems of modern citizenship. Change, centralization, and abstract ideology had resulted not only in stifling the life of the provinces, but in an uprootedness of individuals which had left them shiftless, helpless, and rudderless. The result had been, as Simone Weil at a later date was to express it, "a lack of participation in the life of a community which preserves . . . certain particular treasures of the past, and certain particular expectations for the future."[2] Decadence, for Barrès, was the result of this alienation of man from the traditions of his society and his culture.

But if the conservative Barrès urged stability, Maurras, the counter-revolutionary, desired not stability—despite his avowal of this aim—but radicalism in reverse, with the restoration of the past, a past which he idealized to the point of incomprehensibility. To the fact that revolution too can have its traditions, as France had had since 1789, he was completely opposed. For Maurras, the Revolution and the Third Republic

[2] Simone Weil, *The Need for Roots*, Boston, 1955, p. 43.

neglected true values, attacked the natural authorities of society, and overthrew tradition. In the ceaseless war he waged on the Third Republic, there were a bitterness and antagonism which prevented any kind of compromise. Indeed, there was in Maurras more hate for the present than love for the past. The writer who stressed so incessantly the need for unity was himself a prime divisive force in France, an irreconcilable opponent of those who exercised power.

The response of the three writers to the decadence that they observed was to look for elements of certainty with which to erect barriers against universal chaos. The anti-democrat can never tolerate the conditional or the tentative and is always interested in definitive solutions, in certainty, in the finite. The antidemocrat will always mistake flexibility for anarchy. Sorel spoke for the other two when he talked of a democratic parliamentary regime as a regime "where everything is provisional . . . where the revision of laws is perpetually on the order of the day."[3] For all three writers, a desirable moral state of society could never be attained through expediency instead of assured principles or through stratagems rather than integrity.

Sorel, Maurras, and Barrès were all agreed on the necessity of accepting traditions, on the danger of squandering of resources through consumption, and on the need for vigorous action, but each emphasized his own starting premise for the attack on decadence. With Sorel, who had criticized the Socratic philosophy for its absence of moral certitude[4] and indicated the Marxian fear of a completely rigid and closed system,[5] it was the desirability of recognized moral rules. With Barrès, it was the search for a discipline of tradition which the individual would willingly embrace, and which would provide the necessary foundation for the exercise of individual sensibility. With Maurras, it was the return to the spirit and ideal of classicism, the static and perfect order, hierarchical, authoritarian, untainted by any foreign element.

[3] Georges Sorel, "De l'Eglise et de l'état," *Cahiers de la quinzaine* (October 1901), 3rd Series, No. 3.
[4] *Le Procès de Socrate*, p. 92.
[5] Sorel, preface to Arturo Labriola, *Karl Marx, l'économiste, le socialiste*, Paris, 1910.

ABSENCE OF TRADITIONS

Between the years 1910 and 1912, the three writers were associated together in a demand for a revival of traditions that were lacking under the Republic. To uphold traditions is to approve certain institutions, certain sentiments and ideas of value which have been the result of the historical experience of a community and which that community wishes to maintain. However, a believer in tradition is not necessarily a supporter of traditionalism, which is partly a psychological characteristic of human behavior and partly a political phenomenon. As a psychological characteristic, traditionalism means a clinging to the old ways of life and an acceptance of the value of the past simply because it is the past.[6] As a political phenomenon, traditionalism in France implies a return to the political past, a reaction favorable to the values and often the institutions of the *ancien régime*, and therefore desirous of destroying the ideology, heritage, and institutions of the Revolution. Not all traditions will thus become part of a traditionalist attitude. Since the 19th century there have been the two traditions of the *ancien régime* and of the Revolution, and acceptance of the latter does not denote traditionalism. It was in this sense that Sorel denied being a traditionalist if this meant supporting monarchical or Catholic institutions and marching beside Maurras to achieve these institutions.[7] And it is in this sense also that Maurras and Barrès were traditionalists in their desire to reconstruct political and social institutions, in their stress on the absolute dependence of the individual on society, in their use of the symbols of the earth, the dead, the glory of France, and in their denunciation of innovation. But all three writers were aware of the absence of desirable traditions, those traditions which might act as a substitute for or an appendage to religion in the attempt to give meaning to human existence. Unfortunately, all three writers were apt to forget that tradi-

[6] Karl Mannheim, *Essays on Sociology and Social Psychology*, London, 1953, p. 95.

[7] Edouard Dolléans, "Le Visage de Georges Sorel," *Revue d'histoire économique et sociale* (1940-1947), 26:107.

tion, as Raymond Aron once wrote, is a fact of which one must take account, not a value before which one must incline.

Sorel saw the absence or neglect of traditions as a threat to French society, and drew historical parallels to show the danger. The lack of a conservative spirit had led to a rapid decadence in Hellenic culture.[8] The philosophers of that culture, foreign to Attica, had had no fatherland, and so they had declared that their fatherland was the world. Just like the heterae, they had no hearth, no national culture, no tombs of ancient ancestors to guard, no relics to protect against the barbarians. In opposition to the Socratics and the Stoics, it was Aristophanes who, by singing the glory of ancestors and recalling the heroism of the past, was accomplishing a great and holy mission. Rome, too, had shown that only a people with profound respect for traditions could have a great legal system.

It was the absence of this profound respect for traditions that was disturbing to Sorel in the contemporary scene. The Republic, with its vices of envy, greed, ignorance, skepticism, and license, was leading to the destruction of the family, the marriage sacrament, and religious sanctity. The French bourgeoisie was producing this destruction because it attached no importance to the things that could neither amuse it nor serve it for exercising its command. It was to the masses, who were conservative by nature, that Sorel looked for defense of the traditional concepts of morality and law against the relativism of the bourgeoisie.[9]

For Sorel there was no question more interesting than that of the transmission of a heritage from one era to another, and he agreed with Marx that socialism must be careful not to compromise the acquisitions of the capitalist era. All revolutions conserved many things of the past: a heritage, a body of writings and sacred histories, a severe discipline of manners and a way of utilizing books, traditions, and practical ethics.[10]

8 Sorel, "Les Intellectuels à Athènes," *Le Mouvement socialiste* (September 15, 1908), 24:234-235.

9 *D'Aristote à Marx*, p. 100.

10 Sorel, *Le Système historique de Renan*, Paris, 1906, pp. 467-468.

France was living on what remained of the *ancien régime* in democratic France; a century of revolutions and of the representative system had not succeeded in breaking down all that the old royalty had created. French democracy had not abandoned itself to instincts of spoliation because it found the invocation of the glory of ancestors too useful.

"We live on the resources accumulated by our fathers," Sorel had said in a speech in 1899,[11] and in 1910 he was again urging the value of traditions. Sorel helped draft the declaration of the new journal, *l'Indépendance*, addressed to men who "disgusted by the silly pride of democracy, by humanitarian nonsense, by foreign fashions, wanted to make the French spirit independent." *L'Indépendance* resolved to attain this end by following the noble routes opened by the masters of national thought, declaring that tradition was a springboard rather than a fetter.

Much of this decadence and neglect of traditions was due to intellectuals, whose chief role was to destroy the authority which was the basis of the *ancien régime*. An intellectual like Condorcet, in his educational reforms, did not propose to produce agriculturists, industrialists, engineers, geometricians, or wise men, but wanted to produce "enlightened men," men free of all chains, all authority, all old habits.[12] Intellectuals destroyed tradition, and thus singularly favored the triumph of the bourgeoisie.

Maurras made many of the same criticisms of the neglect of traditions as Sorel, and agreed that the democratic Republic had profited from the start given it by eternal France; it profited from the genius of military men, whom it had not honored.[13] But democracy and the Republic were detrimental to tradition and to all the desirable, time-hallowed values: hierarchy, authority, discipline, order, peace, family, property. Democracy, venerating anarchy as its true mode of expression, excluded both the idea of time and that of public spirit. To Maurras, who was Burkean in his view that although the

11 Sorel, "L'Ethique du socialisme," in Georges Sorel et al., *Morale sociale*, Paris, 1909.
12 *Les Illusions du progrès*, p. 55.
13 *Enquête sur la monarchie*, p. l.

individual passes the nation endures, this was disastrous. Whereas the wisdom of the community was concerned with the public good—collective unity, family, state, race, and nation—the democrat and the revolutionary thought of private happiness and satisfaction—in other words, insurrection.

Maurras regarded the Republic as inimical to the natural authorities of the nation, and the Revolution as a break with national traditions. The Republic, by the spirit of its founders and its logicians, admitted neither army, nor family, nor classes, nor savings, nor property, nor order, nor fatherland—nothing which was national or social.[14] The Revolution had proclaimed the reign of popular assemblies; France now regarded them with limitless contempt. The Revolution had established the departments; France now spoke only in terms of provinces. The Revolution had abolished the guilds; France now was syndicalist.

In their solicitude for desirable traditions, Sorel was primarily concerned with the search for and the maintenance of an appropriate code of ethics and juridical sentiments and Maurras with the revival of the classical spirit founded, as he saw it, on authority, hierarchy, and inequality. But it was Barrès, with his desire for a firm foundation on which an individual could develop his sensibility, who stressed most strongly the idea of dependence on traditions.

BARRÈS: ABSENCE OF EXALTATION

In his articles on Baudelaire in his early journal, *Les Taches d'encre*, Barrès had recognized the existence of a specifically Baudelairean psychology and language concerned solely with the search for sensations and with their analysis.[15] Barrès himself began his literary career and quickly achieved fame by advocating the desirability of such a search and analysis through the *culte-du-moi*, the method by which each individual developed himself.

Barrès had declared that "our malaise comes from the fact

[14] *L'Allée des Philosophes*, p. 28.
[15] R. Nugent, "Baudelaire and the Criticism of Decadence," *Philological Quarterly* (April 1957), 36:234-243.

that we live in a social order imposed by the dead, not chosen for us. The dead poison us."[16] In his first trilogy, *Sous l'oeil des barbares, Un Homme libre,* and *Le Jardin de Bérénice,* Barrès heralded a restless, experimental individualism. "I wish that each morning life would appear new to me and all things start afresh," he wrote.[17] Since life had no sense, and the universe and existence were senseless tumults, since all certainty had vanished and religion and national sentiment were fragile things from which to derive rules of behavior, since he encountered philosophic skepticism and cynicism everywhere, the ego became the only tangible reality and manifested itself through the cultivation of the largest number of exalted, rare, complicated, subtle emotions. From Loyola he took the idea of subjecting himself to a train of images. Reflection was unimportant compared with the omniscience and the omnipotence produced by the subconscious.

Cultivation of the ego, the heightening of sensibility, meant feeling differently from others. The *barbare* was not the barbarian, or the philistine of Matthew Arnold, but simply the "non-ego." The first concern of the individual, therefore, was to be surrounded by high walls, and to seek his own development. "What I have followed everywhere, in my enthusiasm for Lorraine and France together, in traveling, in seeking power, is an immense increase of my personality."[18] Everything became a method by which his soul could be nourished —parliament, electoral activities, politics in general, Spain, religion, all played their part in this. His voyages—in later life he or his memory was honored by Metz, Sainte-Odile, Pau, Toledo, Marseilles, Beirut, Alexandria—were made primarily, not to understand, but to enlarge, his ego. Toledo was less a town than a significant site for the development of the soul. Spain and Italy were places of savagery and passion.

This undisciplined exaltation was the key to the individualism of Barrès. "I am a garden where emotions flourish. I am

[16] Maurice Barrès, *Sous l'oeil des barbares,* Paris, 1892, p. 141.
[17] Barrès, *Un Homme libre,* Paris, 1905, p. 237.
[18] *Mes Cahiers,* v:77.

lost in vagabondage, not knowing by what principle to direct my life."[19] He confessed that he would not have spent the nights of his 20th year reading poetry if it had not been capable of stirring him emotionally. He approved of the fact that a Renan, a Stendhal, was concerned only with his internal development. They were voluptuaries in the noble sense of the word. "For Barrès," said Bourget in his preface to *The Disciple*, "nothing is true, nothing is false, nothing is moral, nothing is immoral." Even a friendly critic like Pierre Lasserre recognized that the *culte-du-moi*, "this formula of disinterestedness and idealism, this repudiation of the utilitarian spirit . . . contains a certain perfume of anarchy."[20] Maurras too admitted that "he was the hero of the most beautiful adventures of the soul."[21]

But the ironist and dilettante pupil of Renan became the nationalist, traditionalist, antidemocratic pupil of Taine, with his ideas of uprootedness, decentralization, respect for national traditions, passion for energy, and acceptance of discipline. The place where he was most likely to realize himself changed from Venice to France, and in particular, to Lorraine. Tradition became the certitude with which to escape from nihilism, death, destruction, and decomposition.

Yet there was no real change in the basic attitude of Barrès. In his early book, *Un Homme libre*, which remained "my central expression," the individual ego was completely fed and supported by society. Individuals were only fragments of a more complete system that was the race, itself a fragment of God. Barrès admired Tiepolo as the conscious center of his race, for he found the Venetian painter typical, as was Barrès' own fictional hero, of his whole race. In the third book of Barrès' first trilogy, *Le Jardin de Bérénice*, he had said, "Our meditations, like our sufferings, are the result of our desire for something that can complete us."[22] His heroine,

[19] Barrès, *Le Jardin de Bérénice* (Definitive Edition), Paris, 1921, p. 76.
[20] Pierre Lasserre, *Faust en France*, Paris, 1929, p. 117.
[21] *Enquête sur la monarchie*, p. 490.
[22] *Le Jardin de Bérénice*, p. 65.

Bérénice herself, was symbolic of Barrès' belief that the self can be enriched by communion with the unconscious primitive soul of the people because it is in the people that the human substance and the creative energy, the sap of the world, the unconscious, are revealed.

Barrès changed his front, but never his ground. To seek his own good, to nourish his imagination, his sensibility, his soul, he imposed a discipline on himself, a discipline of tradition and of the dead, a Tainean acceptance of the necessities of life. But, commented M. Parodi, "under the appearance of a nationalist terminology, it is always, in truth, pure anarchic individualism and moral nihilism that are expressed in his work."[23] The soul of France was the soul of Barrès externalized. His nationalism was only the expression, the clamor, of ideas held from his birth.

Barrès argued that tradition allowed the extension and development of individuality and also admitted the individual into something larger than himself. "There is at the bottom of ourselves a constant neurotic point . . . it does not simply provoke the sensations of an ephemeral individual but also stirs the whole race."[24] The tradition of a country did not consist of a series of fleshless affirmations that could be catalogued, but was a way of feeling life rather than judging it. There were no personal ideas; ideas, even the most rare, judgments, even the most abstract, metaphysical sophisms, even the most infatuating, were ways of feeling in a general way. Reason, that enchanted queen, obliged men to follow in the footsteps of their predecessors.[25] "There are no personal ideas . . . we are the prolongation and the continuation of our fathers and mothers," wrote Barrès. Individuals were not masters of the thoughts born in them. Thoughts were reactions, movements of the organism in a given milieu. They were not born of intelligence, but were ways of reacting that were common to all those in the same milieu.

[23] D. Parodi, "La Doctrine politique et sociale de M. Maurice Barrès," p. 24.

[24] *Scènes*, p. 10.

[25] Barrès, *Amori et dolori sacrum*, Paris, 1903, p. 277.

In a revealing passage, Barrès attempted to link his conception of individuality with that of tradition:

"I am not a social utilitarian . . . what is useful for the life of the individual is to increase the number of his dreams. . . . I am not preoccupied above all to save society . . . or to trace a rule of moral conduct for men. That would be good, but it is not my message. I am preoccupied with understanding, with feeling the world, with making it understood and felt, acting on the thought of man, and do this by defending the Church."[26]

It was tradition that gave Sturel, the character who most closely resembled Barrès himself, a motive for acting and provided direction to his internal drives. Individuals, moreover, were glad to accept the fact of this determinism, the yoke of necessity, the yoke of the past. The word "discipline" was one of the favorite words of Barrès, important for the individual, for Lorraine, for France. Everyone felt the necessity of discipline whether he was attached to syndicalism, nationalism, Catholicism, or monarchy because, he argued, acceptance of a discipline was less difficult than complete liberty. Barrès was remarkably prophetic in his awareness of the willingness of men to merge their individuality in the whole society. Between the Grand Inquisitor of Dostoevsky and totalitarian movements, Barrès stands equidistant in time, and provides the link between thought and action. In 1889 Barrès had felt it was important that each individual choose his own discipline, and that it would be abominable if he submitted to a discipline he had not chosen. At the end of his life, in 1922, he was writing that a discipline was necessary for man; it did not suffice to know the laws that ruled things and the material universe, it was also necessary to know the law that ruled the individual, the moral law. Though Barrès spoke of the *Social Contract* as "imbecilic because it is a dialectical construction about an abstract man," at times he approached Rousseauistic ideas, in talking of "being a slave

26 *Mes Cahiers*, ix:24.

of my earthly and family formation," and of "the slavery I have slowly learned to love."[27]

An essential part of Barrès' deterministic pattern of tradition and discipline was acceptance and individual self-limitation. In his *Du Sang, de la volupté, et de la mort*, he had seen in the Christ of Leonardo's *Last Supper* in Milan, the supreme word of a complete knowledge and meditation on reality, which was acceptance. In *Les Déracinés*, it was the powerful speech of Taine about his plane tree that emphasized the most sublime philosophy, the acceptance of necessities. The tree was a repeated symbol for tradition and continuity in the works of Barrès. Just as the tree without denying itself, without abandoning itself, had drawn the most from the conditions furnished by reality, so man, by accepting inherited philosophies, gave substance to the works of ancestors.

But it was also necessary to concentrate on a limited end. The master rule was to limit desires, as Renan had done, and to turn activity towards a precise and single end. It is curious to find Barrès, the individual so complex and of such diverse emotions, at the end of his life arguing that the great thing in life was to unify oneself, to be entirely employed in the same way, not to be dispersed in efforts that contradicted, annulled themselves, and were troublesome.[28] For the duality always remained in Barrès between his need for tradition in a French setting and his love for Asia, "le vaste flot de l'Asie," and its divinities of a brutal, animal nature.

For Barrès the best example of the danger caused by the lack of tradition and discipline was the *déraciné*, or uprooted individual. The tragedy of the *déraciné* was that he had lost all the traditions in which the experience of the race was conserved. From both an individual and a national point of view, a young person isolated from his nation was hardly worth more than a word isolated from the text; he was a young beast without a lair. *La patrie* was always stronger in the soul of an *enraciné* than in that of a *déraciné*. The *déraciné*, once

<hr>

[27] *Mes Cahiers*, xiv:52; ix:319; vi:266.

[28] Barrès, "La Vie Exemplaire de Paul Bourget," *Revue hebdomadaire* (December 15, 1923), 32.12:266-271.

he left his homeland, was no more than an individual, for to be uprooted is to have no place in the world. Barrès was one of the first to introduce the theme of individual loneliness which Durkheim was later to call *anomie*.

This *déracinement*, moreover, was dangerous for France. Barrès had noticed, and was distressed at the fact, that in the suburbs of Paris, the population was anarchic and their names indicated they came from all the provinces of France. Anyone who had lived there for twenty years was regarded as belonging to an old family.

Organic metaphors are always treacherous, and Barrès' analogy between the *déraciné* who has left his homeland and a plant that has been uprooted is, as André Gide has shown,[29] both imprecise and false. The human being who "cuts off roots" can survive in a way that might be impossible horticulturally. Also, the view that the animal or plant prospers only in its place of origin denies the possibility of transplantation, which has proved to be successful organically. Moreover, the tendency to equate a healthy growth with a natural one may be restrictive in obliging adherence to one given pattern. It is not easy to know exactly who is a *raciné* for Barrès. He himself was content to study the soul of Lorraine either in Paris, on his constant travels, or on his annual but brief pilgrimage to his birthplace. The concept of *raciné* in fact seems at times to mean little more than one who agrees with the Barresian political views. Lemaître was one of those whom he had called "petits français," but when the literary critic took the antirevisionist side in the Dreyfus Affair, "I felt he was a *raciné*."[30]

Tradition was doubly desirable. It was a means of protection against the brutal pressures of life, a means of individual exaltation, and also a basis for organizing French energy in order to accomplish French destiny.

The necessity of exaltation within a traditional framework was a national as well as an individual phenomenon. Like other Nationalists, one of the primary aims of Barrès was to

29 André Gide, *Incidences*, Paris, 1924, p. 56. Also, *Prétextes*, Paris, 1913.
30 *Mes Cahiers*, II:145.

reassert the position of France in world politics. Barrès, like his character Sturel, had felt that French nationality, the substance supporting him and without which he was nothing, was in the process of diminishing and disappearing. The fact that French energy was at a low point in an epoch of deep depression determined his role. It was necessary for France to recapture, protect, augment the energy inherited from its ancestors. France would save itself only by a fever; "our whole national history says it."[31] The patriot must be prepared to defend those hereditary reserves that everyone falls back on in order to find his direction. In all this, the old enemy was not forgotten. Part of the hereditary reserves was the fund of subconscious sentiment which provided the resistance to Germany.

One of the essential characteristics of conservative thinking is the manner in which it clings to the immediate, the actual, the concrete.[32] Reacting against the abstract ideology of democracy, Barrès attempted to found his traditionalism on concrete places and people, though his "points of spirituality and of fixity" changed from time to time. It was on seeing *la colline inspirée* that Barrès understood "my country and my race, and saw my true post, the end of my efforts, my predestination."[33] Included in his summits of the embodiment of the French spirit were the mountain of Sion-Vaudémont, the ruined stones from the Chateau of Vaudémont, Sainte-Odile and the Puy de Dôme. What Barrès, the advocate of energy, action, and sensations, liked in the past was, he said, "its sadness, its silence, and above all, its fixity."[34]

It was in Lorraine, and especially in its dead, that he found his tradition. "My ideas are not mine; I found them, breathed them from birth in the ideas of Lorraine."[35] At the end of his life he wrote that of all the ideas to which he had devoted himself none was more deeply rooted than the sense of his dependence on his family and Lorraine.[36] In *Mes Cahiers,*

---

[31] *Scènes*, p. 274.   [32] Mannheim, *op.cit.*, p. 102.
[33] *Amori et dolori sacrum*, p. 281.
[34] *Mes Cahiers*, iii:287.   [35] *Mes Cahiers*, xi:395.
[36] Barrès, preface to J-B.A. Barrès, *Souvenirs d'un Officier de la Grande Armée*, Paris, 1923, p. iv.

in the *Scènes et doctrines du nationalisme*, and particularly in the chapter, "Le 2 Novembre en Lorraine," in *Amori et dolori sacrum*, and in his long description of the journey along the valley of the Moselle in *L'Appel au soldat*, Barrès was continuously searching for the heritage of Lorraine. At Metz, he admired the old names on the shops, the simple polite manners, and the virtues of humility and dignity which were in accordance with the heritage of the inhabitants.

Lorraine patriotism was manifested for both emotional and material reasons. Barrès said that Lorraine was not essentially "our countryside, works of art, customs, resources, dishes, not even our history . . . but it was a special way of feeling."[37] But it was also true that Lorraine adhered to France solely to obtain order and peace. "Our patriotism has nothing idealistic, philosophic about it; our fathers were very realistic."[38] Moreover, the idea of Lorraine was useful to Barrès himself. Lorraine, from which something mystical arose to guide and rule, from which Barrès sought "the law of my development," was also a mirror in which he contemplated himself, a concept which accorded with his nature, his habits, and his works. As more than one critic has suggested, if Lorraine did not create Barrès, he created it.

Barrès was also extraordinarily preoccupied with the idea of death and decomposition, both physical and national. It is with the idea of the "earth and the dead" that his traditionalism is most closely associated, although possibly it was not an original idea. Henri Peyre has suggested that in this, as in some other matters, he may have been influenced by Louis Ménard, since Barrès republished Ménard's article, "Le Jour des morts," originally written in 1889 for *La Critique philosophique*, in his own journal, *La Cocarde*, on the 2nd and 3rd November 1894.[39] Lorraine, in fact, became a matter of sentiment to him only after his parents died: "I created Lorraine on the tomb of my father." His mother, too, was an important influence in the formation of Barrès' cult of the

---

37 *Mes Cahiers*, IX:121.
38 *Scènes*, p. 84; *Un Homme libre*, p. 133.
39 Henri Peyre, *Louis Ménard*, New Haven, 1932, p. 522.

earth and the dead. She had gone to the cemetery and his father's tomb to re-read an article on Picquart that Barrès had written during the Rennes trial of Dreyfus. He confided that when he walked behind the bodies of his parents to the cemetery, the bells of his parish suddenly began to speak to him publicly of his dependence on his native soil of Lorraine.

From the dead he gained discipline, genius, courage, and knowledge. He made one of his characters, Saint-Phlin, explain that in cemeteries he saw the tree of life and its roots stir up the soul. The earth gave him the *racinement* which was essential to preserve tradition and encourage development. Each act which "denies our earth and our dead means a lie which sterilizes us."[40] A race which thought of itself, affirmed its existence in honoring its dead, for great works had been accomplished by generations of unknowns, the labor of ancestors. Many generations rested in the Lorraine cemetery, but the results of their activity persisted.[41]

Barrès called himself "an advocate of the dead" who had loved cemeteries in Venice, in Toledo, in Sparta, in Persia, but above all in Lorraine. He took refuge in them, defended them, and allowed himself to be governed by them. The heritage from the past had to be preserved and passed on to others. "The soul which today lives in me is made of thousands of dead, and that sum, increased by the best of myself, will survive me when I am dead and forgotten." An individual was a moment in the development of his race, an instant in a long culture, "one movement in a thousand of a force which preceded me and will survive me." The essential part of an individual was that part of eternity deposited in him. An individual found his true essence in the family, the race, the nation, in the thousands of years nullified by the tomb. Barrès said he defended "not the past, but what is eternal."[42]

Maurras said of Barrès that "he was a decisive return to the old taste, to the natural and traditional taste, to the

[40] *Amori et dolori sacrum*, p. 279.
[41] Barrès, *Colette Baudoche*, Paris, 1923, p. 150.
[42] *Mes Cahiers*, xiii:25.

eternal taste of France . . . [against] impressionism, naturalism, and all the other forms of degenerate romanticism."[43] But in January 1899, at a meeting at which Barrès and others argued for "the respect for traditions," when Lavisse asked, "What traditions?" no one would answer.[44] Certainly Barrès' conception was less rigid than that of Maurras, for "there are many reasons and many traditions in France, because France comes from Pascal and Rousseau."[45] The contradiction between Barrès' alternative proposals of austerity and exaltation, the love for Sparta but also for the Orient, remained. His love for the austere was shown by Lorraine. He recognized that neither the land, nor the physiognomy of the people, nor the young girls were attractive; the land was never vibrant, the nights rarely sentimental. Barrès preached the doctrine of discipline, sacrifice, and austerity, but not for himself. In his voyages, his romantic adventures, his cult of egoism, his constant interest in action and combat, he was the eager seeker after sensation who would not submit to the self-limitation he advocated elsewhere.

It is surprising that one who wrote so continuously and so emotionally of tradition should know so little of it. He read little—his books, said the Tharauds,[46] formed a company of the dumb which he left in silence—and of 17th century literature, knew only Pascal well. In related cultural fields of music and architecture, he had little knowledge. Strongly influenced by Pascal in his ideas on nationalism and obedience to laws, Barrès adopted Pascal's analysis of custom as second nature as a justification for traditions as such, oversimplifying Pascal in the process.[47]

Barrès' curious mixture of the ideas of individualism and tradition, of aloofness and participation—a product both of

---

[43] Charles Maurras, *Gazette de France*, April 1905, as cited in R. Gillouin, *M. Barrès*, Paris, 1907, p. 58.

[44] Pierre Moreau, *Maurice Barrès*, Paris, 1946, p. 109.

[45] *Mes Cahiers*, II:157.

[46] Jérôme and Jean Tharaud, *Mes Années chez Barrès*, Paris, 1926, p. 98.

[47] R. Virtanen, "Barrès and Pascal," *Publications of the Modern Language Association of America* (September 1947), 62:823.

his own personality and of the state of the country—was an influential one. With its concentration on traditional modes of behavior, on the heroic figure, the need for energy, the spirit of *élan*, it provided a remarkable parallel to Sorel's ideas for ending the spirit of decadence.

SOREL: ABSENCE OF ETHICS AND LAW

On May 6, 1907, Sorel wrote to Croce that "the genesis of moral ideas is the passion of my life."[48] Since a religious belief was not acceptable to Sorel, and since he believed it was a law of human nature to want something indemonstrable in which to believe, he was concerned with the search for fundamental principles. His life therefore was spent in the search for and the preservation of a social ethic—those ethical ideas and juridical principles which would express the sentiments and the ideals of the community, and to which its members would subscribe. "Our business," he said, "is not to know which morality is better, but to determine whether there exists a mechanism capable of guaranteeing the development of morals."[49] He found this mechanism in the working-class movement, which could ensure that the essential values of individual and social vitality, devotion to labor, and therefore personal freedom and creativity, were maintained.

From his early book, *Le Procès de Socrate*, on, Sorel warned of the dangers that would confront civilization if it were indifferent to law and ethics, for the result would be decadence. Law and ethics were of the greatest importance both for social reforms, which would be based on them, and, more particularly, for individual conduct. Law was concerned with external relations, ethics with the internal development of the individual. Law always related to economic facts and to the existing social structure. That explained why all modern legislation was founded on the presupposition that it was necessary, by all means, to accelerate production.[50] Sorel thought

48 *La Critica* (March 1928), 26:100.
49 Sorel, *L'Avenir socialiste des syndicats,* Paris, 1898, p. 127.
50 Sorel, "Les Aspects juridiques du socialisme," *La Revue socialiste* (October 1900), 32:414.

that the influence of Italy on all phases of law—the Roman code of law, canon law, criminal practice, and now revolutionary syndicalism—was beneficial because of its relation to reality.[51]

Ethics was concerned with individual conduct, and therefore could remain more independent of the economic environment than could law. Ethics required something mysterious, or at least foreign to social institutions, something in fact analogous to religion.[52] In a manner similar to that of Barrès, Sorel suggested that, in true ethics, it was a question not of concepts, but of profound states of the soul. The ethics of the Greeks was deficient in that it refused to take account of the reality and importance of consciousness.[53] What was important was not merely to search for and find precepts and examples, but to animate conduct conforming to the precepts and examples. The important thing in life was to know how to take account of one's own conduct. The final end of a social movement existed only in terms of one's internal life. Socialism would be realized only to the extent that socialist conduct was followed; in the last analysis, socialism was a metaphysics of manners.[54]

In order to determine what were beneficial standards of morality and juridical principles, it was necessary to define "law" exactly. The bourgeoisie was incapable both of providing a satisfactory definition and of ending the degeneration of the existing social system because its members flitted with great facility from one political or social conception to another. They were victims in law, as in literature and music, of the inconstancy of fashion. Contributing to this inconstancy was the democratic electoral system, and Sorel attributed the principal cause of the juridical decay of modern nations to the activities of legislative bodies. These bodies acted in un-

[51] Sorel, "Pro e contro il socialismo," *Le Devenir social* (October 1897), 3:880.
[52] Sorel, "La Crise morale et religieuse," *Le Mouvement socialiste* (July 15, 1907), 22:27.
[53] *Le Procès de Socrate*, p. 299.
[54] Sorel, "Pour Proudhon," *"Pages libres"* (June 8, 1901), 23:503-505.

systematic fashion, and there could not be a science of law where everything depended on chance.[55]

The bourgeoisie could not provide the necessary code of law and ethics not only because of this inconstancy, but also because of its essential superficiality and its concern with immediate problems. Among these problems was that of the influence of commercial ideas on law: the complicity of the courts in misdeeds committed by adventurers rich enough to buy statesmen produced a real decomposition of law and a consequent skepticism toward it.[56]

In general, the elaboration of juridical conceptions would include three considerations: the desire to assure more just laws to the largest number of people, the protest of the oppressed invoking his title of man against political authority, and the hope of rendering future generations more happy and, from the moral point of view, more enlightened. But the juridical ideas of the bourgeoisie had to be discarded. Ideas like natural justice and natural rights were meaningless. Ideas like the right to existence or the right to work treated the worker as an absolutely passive being, but the cooperative relations of production had to be taken into account. In particular, the idea of work must have as important a place in the proletarian code as property had in the bourgeois. Above all, the juridical system must express the manifestation of the proletariat to revolt.

There was in Sorel's idea of juridical sentiments a degree of similarity to Mosca's idea of juridical defense, those social mechanisms which regulate moral behavior. Since man was not good, social organization provided for the reciprocal restraint of people by one another. Rule by law was established, restrictions put on those exercising power, and individuals obtained protection against the exercise of that power. But whereas Mosca argued for a balance of social groups to attain the equilibrium of power which would provide a frame-

[55] Sorel, "La Crise de la pensée catholique," *Revue de métaphysique et de morale* (1902), 10:530.
[56] Sorel, "Le Prétendu socialisme juridique," *Le Mouvement socialiste* (April 1907), 21:328.

work for the rule of law, Sorel tipped the scales to one side, in favor of the proletariat.

Only the proletariat could produce the necessary code, because only in the proletariat did one find the necessary qualities: sentiment for law, dignity, frugality, and honesty, and respect for work, love, and the family. The task of Marxism, Sorel urged, was to regenerate the juridical studies that were in the process of decomposition, and to formulate a socialist ethics. In 1898, he was lamenting the absence of directions in morals and religion which was one of the weaknesses of modern socialism. In 1909, one of the criticisms he made of Marxism was that it provided no juridical criticism of private property.[57] Above all, the historical mission of socialism was to produce juridical and ethical conceptions properly belonging to it.

The way in which the necessary sentiments that would form the basis for this new morality would be developed was through the struggle for liberation. In this struggle man was free, heroic, and dignified. An epic state of mind would be produced. Man was free in the sense that he acted without reflection; the moral decision was instantaneous, coming out of the depths of man like an instinct.[58] During the struggle, the maximum tension existed in society, and therefore also the noblest and most dignified feelings.

This plea for free autonomous development of man and the maximization of heroic feeling was coupled with a rigid code of personal conduct, in which the chief emphasis was on the family and on marriage. In an obviously autobiographical passage, Sorel spoke of the happy man who has met the devoted woman, energetic and proud.[59] Woman in modern society he regarded as the great educator, not only of children, but of man himself.[60] Sorel attacked the quality of homosexuality in Greek thought, the poetic theory of Socrates on unisexual love, and the communism of Plato which was fatally pederastic. One of his major charges against the Socratics was the

57 Sorel, *La Décomposition du Marxisme*, 3rd edn., Paris, 1925, p. 37.
58 *Reflections on Violence*, p. 242.
59 Sorel, "J-J. Rousseau," *Le Mouvement socialiste* (June 1907), 21:513.
60 Sorel, "Morale et socialisme," *Le Mouvement socialiste* (March 1, 1899), 1:210-211.

contempt with which they treated women. It was necessary that man respect woman, if he wanted to acquire the necessary qualities to participate in the mission of the proletariat. Sorel regretted the decisions of the German Social Democratic party regarding women. In wishing them to be in the workshop, the Social Democrats, under the specious pretext of preparing a superior future relationship between the sexes, was leading to the ruin of the family.[61]

Unlike the bourgeois family, which was formed by the union of a profession and a dowry, the proletarian family was a moral union, and therefore free. The family was founded on a religious principle and was the chief source of French moral ideas; the home was the symbol of tradition, unity, and society. Sorel thought that the aberrations of neo-Malthusians deserved the severest condemnations, while divorce added to the ruin of the dignity of the family. He applauded the way in which conjugal fidelity had been celebrated by Homer and Aeschylus. The true values of virtue were to be found in the family: the respect for the human being, sexual fidelity, devotion to the feeble. Love meant devotion and chastity. The juridical conscience could not be purified in a country where the respect for chastity had not become an important part of manners. The world would become more just only to the degree that it became more chaste.

It was with this new code, a combination of morality, desirable juridical sentiments, emphasis on labor and the *élan* and heroism that could be based on it, that Sorel believed an end would be put to decadence. And it was the workers' groups which, for moral and industrial reasons, and by reason of their opposition to the bourgeois and intellectual environment, would be the instruments to this end. By remaining loyal to their proletarian character, the workers would create a more desirable society.

In this plea for a moral revolution, Sorel traveled much of the same ground that one of his contemporaries did. "The social revolution is moral or it is nothing," Péguy had printed

[61] Sorel, "Les Polémiques pour l'interprétation du Marxisme," *Revue internationale de sociologie* (May 1900), 8:355.

on the flyleaf of his *Cahiers*, and Sorel, a close friend at the time, had agreed. Like Péguy, Sorel talked of the value of the family, the workshop, the local community, and shared Péguy's dislike of intellectualism, the party system, and the process by which religion had become mechanical, political, and devoid of emotional life. If Sorel refused to share Péguy's dislike of modern industry and its techniques, it was a measure of his greater appreciation of industrial and social life.

It must be admitted that there is both obscurity and some contradiction in Sorel's writings on ethics and law, yet the general tenor is clear and the inherent logic consistent. Man must live by certain values. For Sorel these values could not be established by religion, in spite of its useful mystical elements, nor could they, in contemporary France, be embodied or protected by any other class but the proletariat. The proletariat, by its *élan*, its energy, its heroism, must be the instrument through which the traditions and values of society could be upheld. This combination of the revolutionary and the conservative, the combination of Marx and La Tour du Pin, made him the most perplexing French writer since Proudhon. But his stress on the need to expend energy to obtain the correct values was an improvement on both Marx and La Tour du Pin. It was an improvement on the naïve socialist belief that goodness would automatically be the outcome of a change in economic conditions. And also it was more realistic to deny that the old privileged group would be the means of preservation. Sorel's idea of the purity of morals as an aspect of the sublime in life, and his ultimate belief in goodness is a refreshing and more attractive alternative both to the exhilaration of Barrès, and the order of Maurras.

MAURRAS: ABSENCE OF CLASSICISM

To Maurras the indication that the system was decadent was that civilization was being threatened. He regarded civilization as transmitted capital, the result of the transmission of material and spiritual reserves, memory, and tradition. Tradition was what had endured, and must always be greater and

more important than the individual. There could be no society
without tradition, or men without society. To support Dreyfus
and the individual against society was to imperil the ethics
and politics of former centuries and to destroy peace, the
defense and security of the nation.[62] Tradition was what had
endured, but it did not mean the transmission of everything.
It could not include revolutionary, humanitarian, or romantic
ideas. Distinction must be drawn between those ideas of an
inferior nature, of animal instinct, and those which were produced by intelligence. Tradition was the transmission only of
the beautiful and the true.[63]

At this point Maurras linked together his ideas of aesthetics
and politics. Order in the state was akin to beauty in the arts.
The laws of beauty were like the laws of life, inspiring him
with a horror of all disorder and anarchy. The good lay not
in things but in the relation of things, not in the number
but in the composition, not in quantity but in quality; it lay
in the holy notion of limits. It was in Greece that Maurras
found his model of the well-ordered system. For a Greek,
beauty was identical with the idea of order; it was composition, hierarchy, gradation. Form was more important than
emotion. The nationalist Maurras explained that his love was
not for the Greeks, but for the works of the Greeks. "It is not
because it is Greek that we go to beauty, but because it is
beautiful that we run to Greece." What Maurras took from
Greece were the ideas of a rule, of perfection, of heroic activity.

But this analysis is open to objection on two counts. The
first is that the Maurrasian view of Greek history was limited
to the Periclean century. When he talked of the Athenian
heritage, "this priceless good,"[64] and of Attica, the model for
the world, he referred to only a short period in history. Moreover, it was a period which, in its democratic and libertarian
behavior and ideas, was the exact antithesis of everything
that Maurras was advocating for France. The second objection
is that even in the most static of societies, political laws can

[62] Charles Maurras and Lucien Moreau, "L'Action française," p. 967.
[63] Maurras, *L'Ordre et le désordre*, Paris, 1948, p. 14.
[64] *Anthinéa*, p. 86.

121

have little reference to those of aesthetics. To equate political order with beauty, the institution of monarchy with quality, and nationalism with the real is to raise prejudice to the level of a science.

France, claimed Maurras, had become the legitimate inheritor of the Greek and Roman worlds—the inheritance that had been laid aside since the Revolution. The whole of Europe was barbarous by comparison, and when French influence diminished, universal barbarism increased. French literature, like France, was a work of art, and an aristocratic art in that it emanated from the noblest traditions of the human race and from the continued efforts of a long historic elite. It was necessary to preserve these traditions and the world's high regard for France. Maurras warned that it was when Rome ceased to believe itself absolutely superior to the barbarians that it began to yield to their invasion and that it became barbaric itself.[65]

Classicism was the essence of France's inheritance of the best of civilization, and the classical spirit to Maurras was the essence of the best of humanity. A spirit of authority and tradition, it was both "the tradition of the human species and that of our particular ethnic group."[66] To call classical the spirit of the Revolution was to strip a word of its natural sense and to substitute ambiguities, since democrats by conviction detested history, tradition, the past.

France was in peril because classicism was being replaced by romanticism. Even for people to whose political opinions Maurras was not totally opposed, romanticism was unwise. Commenting on Barrès' *L'Appel au soldat*, Maurras wrote that he could observe that Boulanger was sacrificing his glory, his party, his country, his fortune, and even his life, to the will of love. Romanticism in politics for Maurras meant liberalism and anarchy, stemming partly from the influence of English and German literature. Democracy and Protestantism were both barbarisms connected with other barbarisms like roman-

[65] Maurras, "Pour les Langues Romanes," *Soleil* (August 23, 1895). As cited in L.S. Roudiez, *Maurras jusqu'à l'action française*, Paris, 1957.

[66] Maurras, *Prologue d'un essai sur la critique*, Paris, 1932, p. 92.

ticism and "Hugocracy" in the 19th century.[67] French literary history closely resembled its political history. The defects of romanticism, present in so much French literature, were similar to those of democracy—egotism, foreign origin and perversions, independence and anarchy, a fundamental lack of reality. Sensibility inspired the direction of romanticism and led to anarchy, for the ego was made the center of the world, and the ego meant individualism, tumult, and the constraint of reason. Moreover, it was a feminine, not a masculine, quality.

Romanticism meant an end of French traditions, and a taste for what was foreign, as was shown by the books that it produced. *La Nouvelle Héloïse* was written by a Swiss, *De l'Allemagne* by a Swiss woman of Prussian origin, *Lélia* by a descendant of de Saxe. Written by foreigners, romantic works showed traces of the strange, the novel. Traditional values were being threatened by this barbarian invasion in literature, in political ideas, and in personnel. While Le Play and Spencer had used the idea of the barbarian to signify the savage or the infantile, Maurras used it to denote all to which he was opposed. The family was being menaced by class struggles and parliamentary intrigues, traditional culture was being menaced by the Protestant and Jewish spirit. To the Oriental, German-Judaic dream, individual, liberal, and mystical, "we oppose Western thought, traditional, classic, scientific, and social thought; to subversive Nuées are opposed Hellenic-Latin civilization, French order."[68]

But Maurras, as Basil de Selincourt said,[69] was a restrictionist whose love of the classical was the love of an achievement, not of the achieving power. He inverted the maxim of Hobbes: for him, happiness came from having prospered, not in prospering. He limited civilization to a small minority of races and to a small minority within each of these races. It is indeed putting a high price on one's opinions to relegate

[67] Maurras, *La Critique des lettres*, Paris, n.d., p. 69.
[68] *La Démocratie religieuse*, p. 320.
[69] Basil de Selincourt, "A French Romantic," *The English Secret and Other Essays*, London, 1923, p. 26.

123

the vast majority of the world to an inferior status of barbarism. Moreover, even his criticisms of romanticism were
unjustified. Romanticism at its height was both monarchist
and antirevolutionary. It is difficult to see, as Lucas suggested,
what was anarchistic about Alfred de Vigny, Sir Walter Scott,
Rossetti, Disraeli, or Walter Pater.[70] Even Barrès would not
agree that romanticism was either un-French or unhealthy,
and he counted both "classical and romantic fathers" in his
inheritance. "Romanticism does not come from Germany. It is
French . . . Saint-Just and Chateaubriand, two illustrations
of romanticism of action and dreams, are sons of Rousseau."[71]

Barrès, always loving and admiring the great romantic
books, was even willing to believe that a sentiment called
romantic, if it led to a superior degree of culture, took on a
classical character.[72] It is noticeable that in contrast to Maurras, what Barrès admired in Greece was not Athens, but
Sparta. For Barrès, Athens compared very unfavorably with
Provence. The Acropolis was a "deserted house," and the
Athens of the fifth century an open-air museum, a cold tomb.[73]
But he realized in 1901 that for Maurras, Athens was less a
divine ruin, less one of the three great historical periods of
the world than a source of energy and a useful symbol. Yet
Maurras himself was not always the classicist he claimed to
be. In Florence, he had moments of nihilism, in Paris in his
early years he had been attracted to and influenced by the
symbolists, in his homeland of Provence, he wrote with deep
feeling of the Swamp of Marthe, and even in Greece, his
enthusiasm for the country was disproportionate.

"Classicism" and "romanticism" are terms which have slain
their tens of thousand critics. Neither term can be properly
defined, for, as Anatole France said of the latter, the ideas
they represent are multifarious and contradictory. But the
interrelationship between literary classicism and political reaction has been of some significance in recent thought, and it

[70] F. L. Lucas, *The Decline and Fall of the Romantic Ideal*, Cambridge, 1936, p. 6.
[71] *Mes Cahiers*, XII:187.
[72] Barrès, *Adieu à Moréas*, Paris, 1910, p. 11.
[73] Maurice Barrès, *En Provence*, Paris, 1930, p. 106.

is no coincidence that in Pierre Lasserre's influential book, *Le Romantisme français*, the contemporary reference is to counter-revolution rather than to classicism. Henri Peyre has pointed out that whereas the classicism of the 17th century implied acceptance of its time and its milieu, the late 19th and early 20th century neo-classicism refused to do so, and in fact used the 17th century to attack contemporary life.[74]

Maurras was the dominant figure in this neo-classicism, and could claim T. E. Hulme, Ezra Pound, and T. S. Eliot among his intellectual disciples. His attitude was largely an expression of bewilderment before the problems of modern life, in which traditional authority had lost its effect, whether the authority was political groups, symbols or ideas, or canons of form and stylistic rules. It was an affirmation of the desirability of order, universality, permanence, and the static in both politics and art.

From the counter-revolutionary point of view all these necessary values were being overthrown or discarded through the influence of Rousseau. Through him came the belief in natural goodness, in humanism, in optimism, in progress, the belief in the value of internal authority, and the challenge to external authority. Against these, Maurras urged the necessity for known and accepted rules, for form in literature and for authority in politics.

The vehemence of Maurras' struggle for his traditional classical values led him to prison on three occasions, to violence of word and of deed, and to political isolation. Tolerance, warmth, humanity were qualities absent in him. If, as de Tocqueville said, in politics a community of hatred is almost always the foundation of friendships, Maurras in his relation to the Action Française movement was no exception.

A society is regarded as decadent by those who believe both that its heritage is not being preserved, and that nothing of value is being substituted. The attitude of the critics is one of repugnance, antipathy, and rejection. Such an attitude was a common experience in the Third Republic, especially

[74] Henri Peyre, *Le Classicisme français*, p. 216.

between the years of 1885 and 1899, which nationalists called the "gelatinous" period of the Republic. Literature aptly commented on the lack of prestige of the regime. Proust's Swann would turn down an invitation from the President of the Republic to dine at a fashionable house. His Mme de Villeparisis declined in the kaleidoscopic social hierarchy because of her love affair with a Republican minister. The fashionableness of anarchy in the 1890's was another indication of the belief in the degeneration of the country. Barrès' own book, *L'Ennemi des lois*, followed closely the trend which included Paul Adam's eulogy of the anarchist-terrorist Ravachol, Jean Grave's *La Revolte*, and a number of reviews dedicated to praising the "brave gestures" of the anarchists.

Barrès, Maurras, and Sorel made devastating attacks on what they considered to be a stultifying regime. But the attacks were being made in an era which can justly lay claim to being one of the greatest in French history, and a rival to the great 17th century of which all three writers were so proud. One can understand their attacks on political ineptitude (discussed in Chapter ix), but it is remarkable that they could dismiss with scorn a period in which Gide and Proust, Ravel and Debussy, Van Gogh and Picasso, Stravinsky and Diaghilev were only the most notable of a great cultural ferment. The cultural conservatism and the distaste for innovation of the three writers made them insensitive to the glories of their own era.

CHAPTER VII
INTELLECTUALS AND THE NEED
FOR ACTION

HOSE who read a great many books," said Anatole France, "are like eaters of hashish . . . books are the opium of the West. We are being devoured by them. A day will come when we shall all be librarians, and that will be the end."[1] There was at the end of the 19th century a climate of opinion which refused to allow itself to be so devoured and was reacting against the tyranny of words. It was a climate in which Bergson and Nietzsche were the principal intellectual influences, and from which Sorel was to draw much in his attack on intellectuals and intellectualism. Barrès, but not Maurras, would support such an attack, and all three, in the attempt to turn back the tide of decadence, would propose the necessity for heroic action and even violence.

SOREL AND THE ATTACK ON INTELLECTUALS

No matter how the political and social views of Sorel varied, his attack on intellectuals and intellectualism was a constant one. Intellectualism he equated with extreme rationalism, which he had attacked as incapable of understanding the complexity of phenomena, and which therefore was based on the conception that science could produce solutions to all problems.[2] History showed that rationalism had led to deplorable results. Through Greek rationalism, philosophy had become dogmatic, incapable of directing experimental research, and responsible for the lack of success in the common arts and mechanics. Greek rationalism was responsible for artificial abstractions, verbal analogies, words that ruled things. The deductive spirit of Greek science and geometry was in absolute opposition to the inventive spirit.[3] Its monist

[1] Anatole France, *On Life and Letters*, i:xii.
[2] *Reflections on Violence*, p. 154.
[3] Georges Sorel (pseudonym J. David), "L'Idéalisme de M. Brunetière," *Le Devenir social* (June 1896), 2:505.

127

superstition had become the vice of most classical philosophers.

In similar fashion, Sorel objected to the popularity and underlying premises of neo-Kantism. He disliked its popularity because Kant and his disciples had introduced into philosophy "a horrible chatter that had noticeably confused problems,"[4] and had thereby greatly contributed to its discrediting. He opposed its subjective and purely moral premises since these were in opposition to the objective certainty of science.[5]

Another objection he raised to rationalism was that of its inevitable optimism. Sorel criticized the optimism of the Sophists which led them both to regard the spectacle of the world as a very interesting panorama, and to conclude that everything had been made for amusement. Pessimism was the indispensable stimulant to creative energy, and every great movement, religious and political, had had a pessimistic conception of life as its basis.

In the contemporary world one could hope to find at most "incomplete developments," traces of fragmentary movements. Even then, observations had to be limited to the economic field. Intellectualism could never fully understand living reality, because it assumed an "invariant structure," a logical movement toward some definite end. In every complex body of knowledge it was possible to distinguish a clear and an obscure region, of which the latter was perhaps the more important. Intellectuals could not deal with the obscure part, the more important part of relationships. In morality, they could deal with problems of justice but not with relations between the sexes; in legislation, with the problem of duties but not of the family; in economics, with the problem of exchange but not of production. A very false idea of revolutions would be obtained if one supposed them made for the reasons that philosophers often attributed to their makers.[6] It was

[4] Sorel, "Vues sur les problèmes de la philosophie," *Revue de métaphysique et de morale* (1910), 18:611.

[5] Sorel, "La Science dans l'éducation," *Le Devenir social* (February 1896), 2:138.

[6] *Les Illusions du progrès*, p. 135.

unfortunate that the social reformers of the 19th century had been dominated by intellectualist conceptions and that for them pure logic had had the value of a social science. The clear, the simple, the distinct—in all these Sorel saw the same metaphysical illusion. Bergson, who was not so deluded, but who, on the contrary, had put mystery in the center of his philosophical preoccupations, was the vigorous tree in the center of the isolated steppes of modern philosophy. Scientific investigation had its honored place, but science was not the only method of knowledge.

The 19th century applications of so-called natural rights had not been happy. Social utopias constituted the clearest manifestation of the aberrations to which the theory of natural rights logically led. However, socialism was not a social science, nor was the revolution a scientific process.[7] Indeed, those revolutions inspired by idealism had been ferocious; the Terror in France had been the work of obstinate theoreticians. Sorel was true to his own maxim: "One dreads bringing too great a rigor into language because it would be in contradiction with the fluid character of reality and the language would be deceptive."[8]

Since intellectualism was incapable of understanding the real world, it was not possible to provide an intelligible exposition of the passage from principles to action without the use of myth. The myth could not be refuted, it was an appeal to a "deeper consciousness." It meant freedom from the "superstition of the book." Though Sorel anticipated the idea of myth in several of his books, in *Le Procès de Socrate, La Ruine du monde antique, Le Système historique de Renan,* and in his *Introduction à l'économie moderne,* and applied it to the demon of Socrates, the hysteria of Mahomet, the stigmata of Francis, and even the resurrection of Christ, it was not until the *Reflections on Violence* that he gave a full explanation of what he meant, and defined it as the image held by the participants in a movement of impending action in which their cause will triumph. Sorel paid tribute to those

[7] Sorel, "La Crise du socialisme," *Revue politique et parlementaire* (December 1898), 18:598-612.
[8] *Matériaux,* p. 58.

thinkers who had speculated on the general idea of the myth. In *Le Procès de Socrate* he had found Plato to be superior to Aristotle by virtue of the former's appreciation of the value of myths and by the use he made of mythical expositions. He regarded Platonic myths neither as fables, nor as purely poetic inventions for amusement, nor mystic reveries, but as serious and scientific. He praised Vico's *ricorso*, a poetically creative state characterized by the construction of myths.

Through the teaching of Bergson, he understood that movement explained itself above all by means of images.[9] No philosophic system owed its success to the logical value of its arguments alone. Probably Marx had put forward the conception of a catastrophe only as a myth, illustrating in a very clear way the ideas of class struggles and social revolution.[10]

For Sorel, myths were not descriptions of things, but expressions of the determination to act. It was not reason that had guided and that continued to guide crowds in their passionate actions, but kinds of schematical ideological projections. Active groups were motivated by emotional appeals, which played an important but nonlogical role in history. A myth could not be refuted, since it was fundamentally identical with the convictions of a group, being the expression of these convictions in the language of the movement. In this way, the Knights of the Middle Ages had gone in search of the Holy Grail, and the soldiers of the Convention tramped through Europe. All the major historical movements propelling action had had myths—early Christianity, the Reformation, the French Revolution, militant Catholicism—and the next would be revolutionary syndicalism. While the effect of utopias had always been to direct men's minds toward reforms which could be brought about by patching up existing systems, contemporary myths led men to prepare themselves for a combat that would destroy the existing state of things.[11] Historically, ideologies had been only translation into an abstract form of the myths which impelled to the final destruc-

9 *La Décomposition du Marxisme*, p. 60.
10 *Introduction à l'économie moderne*, p. 396.
11 *Reflections on Violence*, p. 33.

tion. In contemporary France syndicalism was such an ideology, and the idea of the general strike, because it made the concept of socialism more heroic, should be looked upon as having incalculable value, even though, like all myths, it might never come about. The general strike had a character of infinity because it put to one side all discussion of definite reasons and confronted man with a catastrophe.

The manner in which Sorel used the idea of the myth, with its emphasis on the General Strike and on violence, is indicative of the correctness of Cassirer's view that the myth reaches its full force when man faces an unusual and dangerous situation, that 20th century myths have been a recourse to desperate means, and that myth is not only far remote from empirical reality but is, in a sense, in flagrant contradiction to it.[12] Moreover, Sorel's view of intellectualism was always an extremist one. It was an excessive rationalism which neglected the place of emotions or of instincts in the human situation, which regarded progress as inevitable, which lacked appreciation of reality, and which was exclusively optimistic. It was in fact the same kind of extremist 18th century belief— that all problems could be solved by some simple, uniform method—which had led Graham Wallas in 1908 to warn against the tendency to exaggerate the intellectuality of mankind. Yet the warning Sorel gave of the dangers of excessive rationalism was a salutary one, and it is remarkable that he anticipated, 50 years before it arose, the opposition to what is now called scientism and historicism.

If Sorel was philosophically opposed to intellectualism, he was opposed to intellectuals for a variety of reasons. They were superficial, they were interested only in material benefits or in capturing power, they thought only of their personal interests and never of the general interest, they misunderstood the nature of science, they were interested in politics and in the strengthening of state power, their ideas were basically negative ones, they were attached to the bourgeoisie and to the petty-bourgeoisie and were opposed to the

[12] Ernst Cassirer, *The Myth of the State*, New York, 1955, pp. 55, 349-350.

best interests of the proletariat, they were incapable of leadership, they thought an end was definite and foreseeable and that solutions could be found to all problems, they thought of themselves as a sacerdotal caste destined, by their superior culture, to impose a new order on the world.

Sorel's personal expressions of distaste for intellectuals, as shown in *Reflections on Violence* and *La Révolution Dreyfusienne*, often bordered on the libelous. When "Agathon's" book, *L'Esprit de la nouvelle Sorbonne*, with its attack on the Sorbonne appeared, Sorel gave it a laudatory review under the title "Lyripipii Sorbonici moralisationes."[13] Sorel expanded his attack on intellectuals to cover the whole of recorded history. His first book, *Le Procès de Socrate*, was a bitter attack on Socrates and his disciples. Socrates had created the most deplorable confusion between law, ethics and science, and had introduced probabilism into ethics and lack of certainty into politics. His school was to be condemned for its optimism, for its desire to strengthen the state and to transform it into a church, and for its lack of attention to the problem of work. Socrates' chief disciple, Plato, was condemned because of the central place he had given to the philosopher in the ideal city state. In a later work, *Le Système historique de Renan*, Sorel attacked the philosopher-king, Marcus Aurelius, who had attempted to persecute Christians, failed, and thus demonstrated the impotence of official wisdom. Although Christianity had triumphed and had introduced the notion of the sublime, it too would have succumbed because of its theologians and doctors, if it had not been for the mystics.

In the 17th century the humanists, descendants of the Renaissance with its pagan love of life, had replaced the pessimism that had fostered the moral value of Christianity. The Protestants had attempted to conserve the old characteristics of religion, but Protestantism had been vanquished in its turn by intellectualism. In the 18th century, a stupid century,[14] the Philosophes, from Diderot to Voltaire, were "immoral

13 *L'Indépendance*, April 15, 1911.
14 Sorel, *La Ruine du monde antique*, Paris, 1924, p. 229.

buffoons of a degenerate aristocracy."[15] Only Rousseau escaped partially from this scathing criticism, and that was because he had upheld the dignity of workers. In the 19th century, Sorel criticized the Utopians, Fourier and Saint-Simon, for their desire to impose a strong state, Comte for the authoritarian attitude expressed in his assertion, "There is no liberty of conscience in geometry," which he made analogous to relations in society, and Renan for his intellectual dilettantism, which led to the exploitation of producers.

This historical analysis was significant for Sorel. He argued that one could not read the history of Christianity of the third century without thinking of the present and wondering if the alliance of French intellectuals with politicians could not have consequences very similar to those produced in the third century,[16] with its spectacle of corrupted philosophers and intellectuals who followed their personal interests and allied with those who exploited public credulity. Intellectuals were interested only in material benefits and personal advantages, and would be prepared to sacrifice the general interest to that end. Each of them aspired, like Caesar, to be first in a little group.[17] Unlike workers, they had no spirit of solidarity, they did not form a bloc; they had professional, not class interests.

Intellectuals were not thinkers, but men who had adopted the profession of thinking and who expected an aristocratic salary because of the nobility of that profession. It was because of this desire to maintain the level of their salary that so many intellectuals tried to prevent women from becoming members of the liberal professions, since they believed that a profession quickly lost its prestige when women entered it. They made the exploitation of thought and of politics their profession; they had no regard for ideas as such, but appreciated them only for their value in capturing power.[18] They had no industrial aptitude, but tried to persuade the workers that it was in the workers' interest for them to exercise power.

[15] *Les Illusions du progrès*, p. 133.
[16] Sorel, *Le Système historique de Renan*, Paris, 1906, p. 333.
[17] *Matériaux*, pp. 97-98.
[18] *La Révolution Dreyfusienne*, p. 30.

The Socratics had asked that government belong to the intellectuals,[19] but could one imagine a more horrible government than that of academicians? It was because of their exploitation of politics that they were capable of adopting attitudes so unexpected and so disturbing to public order. The creative hatred, the ferocious jealousy of the poor intellectual who hoped to send the rich speculator to the guillotine was an evil passion without socialist sentiment. Since rich men had ceased providing their revenues, poor intellectuals had pursued them with fanatical and ferocious hate.[20] Moreover, if intellectuals strove for the conquest of power, they could not want the disappearance of the state, since they would want to use it for their own benefit. Modern intellectuals were like the Socratics and like Calvin who supervised, directed, oppressed public opinion; opponents would be reduced to silence as disturbers of order. The end of intellectual projects like that of Saint-Simonism would be to transform industry according to a unitary, Napoleonic plan.

Intellectuals had more effect as a harmful than a helpful force. History had many examples to bear this out, and the abuse of sophisms that had corrupted socialism was not one of the least examples showing the danger of professional intellectuals. The incommensurable stupidity of M. Homais was the natural product of the influence of the man of letters on the French bourgeoisie for almost a half century.[21] Intellectuals were not competent to understand great historical movements in general, and their theories had little relevance to the working-class movement in particular. In fact, there was only an artificial link between socialist theories and the proletarian movement, since the theories were already old and decrepit.[22]

Sorel was concerned both with attacking the supposed superiority of intellectuals and their hold over the proletarian movement, and also with asserting the ability of the workers

19 *Le Procès de Socrate*, pp. 7-8, 183, 237-238.
20 *La Ruine du monde antique*, p. 273.
21 *Les Illusions du progrès*, p. 134.
22 Sorel, "Les Syndicats industriels et leur signification," *La Revue socialiste* (August 1902), 36:174.

to take charge of their own movement. The role of the intellectuals was at best an auxiliary one. Some of them, badly paid, discontented, or unemployed, became members of the "intellectual proletariat," but attached themselves to the petty-bourgeoisie, and tried to turn socialism into reaction and utopian socialism. The proletariat, despised by the petty-bourgeoisie, could hope for nothing from the poets, philosophers, and professional do-gooders who lived at its expense and who were interested not in the dictatorship of the proletariat but in the representative dictatorship of the proletariat. Since intellectuals would suffer professionally from a proletarian revolution, those who "had embraced the profession of thinking for the proletariat"[23] must therefore be acting in their own interests. Sorel agreed with Kautsky that "the interests of the proletariat are diametrically opposed to those of the Intelligentsia."

Sorel thought his greatest claim to originality was in having maintained that the proletariat could emancipate itself without the help of middle-class intellectuals. The makers of machines did not need the guidance of theoreticians; the workers had to rely on themselves to ameliorate their conditions of life.[24] The idea of the superiority of intellectuals was false. Qualities of leadership were not exceptional, and were often found among manual workers, perhaps more often than among intellectuals. If the worker accepted control by the intellectuals, he would always remain incapable of governing himself. Theories were born of bourgeois reflection; the task of the proletariat was to march forward without imposing upon itself any ideal plan. "I do not believe," Sorel said, "that one stirs up the masses with writings. . . . It is necessary to galvanize people by an untiring drive, by a struggle that goes beyond manifestos, by the formation of a real army.[25]

Like Sorel, Barrès was opposed to the idea that intellectualism could provide an understanding of life, partly because intellect played but a small part in human action, and partly

[23] *Reflections on Violence*, pp. 37, 151.
[24] *Matériaux*, pp. 65, 307.
[25] Jean Variot, *Propos de Georges Sorel*, p. 124.

because people were not even masters of the thoughts born in them. The thoughts were inevitably determined by a person's given milieu. In the *Culte du moi* trilogy, Barrès argued that communication takes place mainly through vibrations, by manifestations of sentiment rather than by a process of ratiocination. In the *Romans d'énergie nationale* trilogy, he asserted that communion with the earth and the dead, the family, the province, and the nation would provide a substitute for reason. There was no liberty to think, for one could live only according to one's ancestors.

Barrès has the dubious distinction of having first used the word "intellectual" as a term of opprobrium. For Barrès, an intellectual was an individual who was deluded by the idea that society must be founded on logic, and who failed to recognize that it rested on prior necessities perhaps foreign to individual reason. Chief among these prior necessities were the ideas of the strengthening of France and restoration to it of the territories lost in 1870. Intellectuals thought of France not for its own sake, but as a means of serving something else.

THE NEED FOR ACTION

Maurras and Barrès joined with Sorel in his insistence on the need for action and in advocacy of the heroic figure who was so lacking in the Republic. Change had to take place through the hero, either as the embodiment of true values, or as the leader of the attack on the contemporary institutions.

The death of French energy, Barrès argued, meant the decadence of the country.[26] The regeneration of its energy, especially as expressed by the hero, would be the means of renaissance for the regime. Barrès was concerned therefore with the hero both in fiction and in history. The artist was great, he said, as he possessed an idea of the hero. In fiction, his leading characters were all concerned with aspiring to heroism and the affirmation of their will. Barrès' leading figure, Sturel, in *Les Déracinés*, was seeking internal animation

[26] Maurice Barrès, *Taine et Renan*, ed. V. Girard, Paris, 1922, p. 103.

THE NEED FOR ACTION

through expenditure of energy, presentiment of danger, knowledge of risk, ability to face the unforeseen and to support misfortune. In history, Barrès talked of the common traits of all the heroes of France, from Vercingétorix to Boulanger and Marchand. "It is possible that in all places Nature is beautiful, but I recognize its temples only on the tombs of great men."[27] The tomb of Napoleon, the professor of energy, was not, for young men, a place of peace; it was the meeting place of all the audacious energies, wills, and appetites. Barrès confessed to loving the man of the 18th Brumaire and along with him, five or six heroes, men who knew how to walk on the waves and, because they had confidence in themselves,[28] were not engulfed.

He was constantly stressing the need for *élan*. It was, in fact, "less by their doctrines than by their *élan* that men lead us."[29] It was this more or less tense energy that accounted for the value of an individual or race. In the past, the *élan* had been expressed in different ways. In the atmosphere of the *Last Supper* of da Vinci, one could see the internal life attaining its greatest intensity, and the human spirit embracing all aspects of reality. In Michelangelo, Barrès saw the effervescence of the man wanting to be God. The Sistine Chapel was one of the immortal reservoirs of energy. Barrès always looked back to the bravery and heroism of the Middle Ages, chronicled in legends, epics, and history. One of the useful ways in which the *élan* could be developed was through "intercessors," intermediaries between nature and the Infinite. Among these intercessors were Constant and Saint-Beuve, two saints of sensibility who were of great assistance in self-analysis.

In contemporary society, it was socialism that was being organized to utilize the considerable force it had accumulated.[30] Barrès' interest in socialism, in spite of his electoral

[27] *Mes Cahiers*, iii:213.
[28] Maurice Barrès, "Napoléon, professeur d'énergie," *Le Journal*, April 14, 1893.
[29] *Amori et dolori sacrum*, p. 64.
[30] Barrès, *Toute Licence sauf contre l'amour*, Paris, 1892, p. 62.

programs, was less an absorption with economic problems than a passion for self-development. His collaboration in the Socialist movement was one of communion with the soul of the masses, a stimulation of his *élan*.

Barrès was even willing to allow that cosmopolitans might have as much ability as Catholics to give expression to this *élan*. He regarded Marie Bashkirtseff as a representative of the eternal force which made heroes emerge in each generation.[31]

But the real contemporary means of inspiring action was the man on horseback, Boulanger. In him, the French people would be able to envision the modern army, penetrated by the spirit of all classes—an army in which nonprofessional soldiers could play such a large part. Boulanger, in contrast with the old legalist in the Elysée who was incapable of an appeal that could touch the masses, had a brilliance which was always appealing to a warlike nation and was capable of summoning French reserves of energy. It was disillusioning for Barrès later to admit that Boulanger had been for 30 years an official, for three years an agitator, and for one year a melancholic.

In Barrès' demand for action, hate, an emotion that was dominant in the soul, might be a more important sentiment than love in that it could propel the greatest amount of energy in a single direction. The most intense and beautiful hatred was produced by civil wars, and the best of civil wars took place in the corridors of the Palais Bourbon.[32]

Yet Barrès, with his taste for combat—seeing the struggle of Jacob against the angel as one of the most beautiful warlike images, and Jacob as embodying the heart of life—and continually deploring the lack of energy, never reconciled this feeling for action with his attraction to symbols of death and decadence. The writer who so stressed action and *élan* also thought that the most beautiful thing in the world was "a man, falling to pieces." With such complexity of motivation,

[31] Barrès, *Trois Stations de psychothérapie*, Paris, 1891, p. 68.
[32] Barrès, *Du Sang, de la volupté et de la mort*, Paris, 1910, p. 130.

a temper of moderation becomes impossible, and the emphasis is inevitably placed on destruction.

For Sorel as well as Barrès, the problem was how to produce a renaissance of energy in a society dominated by politicians as empty of ideas as of grandeur of soul, by rhetoricians and money-dealers, a society—interested neither in the sublime nor in eternal glory but only in enduring. Sublimity was dead in the middle class and therefore the bourgeoisie was doomed not to possess any ethic at all. Sorel, who in 1914 had written to Croce that the great problem was to live without religion, was, as his disciple Berth suggested, haunted by the sublime. To introduce the sublime into society meant action, the necessity for tension, the desirability of struggle, the need for the heroic. Movement was the essence of emotional life, and it was in terms of movement that one could speak of creative consciousness. Conscious action was vital because "movements toward greatness are always forced and movements toward decadence always natural."[33] It was unwise to neglect the enormous power of mediocrity in history.

Sorel again drew historical parallels to illustrate his argument. In *Le Procès de Socrate*, he expressed admiration for Xenophon, the man who was an example of heroic behavior and who attacked Socrates, the adversary of the heroes of Marathon. The Socratics were responsible for the fall of Athens because they had destroyed the heroic conception that gave the city its moral basis. "Let us salute the revolutionaries as the Greeks saluted the Spartan heroes who defended Thermopylae and helped to preserve the civilization of the ancient world," urged Sorel.[34] If Christianity had become the master of the Roman world, it was due to the intransigence of those leaders who, like Tertullian, would not admit any conciliation or accept any lessening of antagonism between the Church and the State. Similarly, Calvinism was to be admired. It showed that the enthusiasm accompanying "the will to salvation" would provide the courageous man with sufficient satisfaction to maintain his spirit.

[33] *La Critica* (January 25, 1911), 26:343; (November 14, 1914), 27:114.
[34] *Reflections on Violence*, p. 99.

This desirable enthusiasm and spirit was lacking in the French contemporary scene. The bourgeoisie had risen as the auxiliary of the crown, and had benefited from the struggle between the monarchy and the Fronde. A class that had risen in this way could not act as a class of actual rulers would.[35] It was concerned only with the immediate interests of its members. It had lost all idea of the mission of the state or of its own mission as the leading class. Its cowardice showed that it was condemned to death. Only two events could prevent the stultifying of the middle class: a great foreign war which might renew the energy that was lacking, and which in any case would doubtless bring into power men with the will to govern, or a great extension of proletarian violence. Since Sorel thought the first was unlikely, it was necessary to have the latter. Employers as well as workers would benefit from the struggle, because the knowledge of the revolutionary tendencies of the proletariat would act on the bourgeoisie as a moral force capable of arousing it from the lethargy to which its too easy prosperity had led it.[36]

Sorel attacked not only the refusal to fight but the very idea of pacifism. It was war above all that explained the juridical genius of Rome. In France the solidity of the Republican regime was due not to reason or some law of progress but to the wars of the Revolution and the Empire which had filled the French soul with an enthusiasm analogous to that provoked by religion. Sorel approved Proudhon's justification of force, agreeing that war makes man greater.[37] He criticized the prevailing British pacifist feeling which was closely associated with the intellectual decadence there. The trouble was that they did not take war seriously; in the Boer War, they went to war as if they were gentlemen going to a football game.

Sorel was disturbed not only by the pacific nature of the bourgeoisie but also by its preoccupation with the future. Even more unfortunate was middle-class influence on Social-

[35] Les Illusions du progrès, p. 80.
[36] Reflections, pp. 82-83; Matériaux, p. 412.
[37] Sorel, "Essai sur la philosophie de Proudhon," Revue philosophique (July 1892), 34:45.

ists, who were led to think about future society and to plan utopias. But utopianism was illusionary; to know the present was to be practical. The desired final state was secondary; what was essential was the knowledge of how to act.[38] The question was no longer what society should be like, but what the proletariat could accomplish in the actual class struggle. And for Sorel, it was only the syndicalist movement that studied the Socialist movement from the point of view of the present, not from that of the future.

Sorel ridiculed the "worldly socialism" of the Dreyfusard financiers, the mutualist organizations that fostered social peace, acquired a stake in society, and had a body of officials acting in a bourgeois spirit, consumers' cooperatives which, like all democratic societies, were incompetent, dishonest, and self-seeking, and trade unions that were interested only in arbitration.[39]

Sorel thought Marx was wrong to believe that a democratic regime made revolution more accessible because under it the class struggle became easier to understand. In fact, the exact opposite was the truth, and the workers were led to a trade union mentality. Sorel attacked reformism and rejected social legislation, the eight-hour day, profit-sharing schemes, workers' insurance, and cooperative schemes. All promoters of social reforms were victims of illusions; to believe in reform of bourgeois society was to affirm the principle of private property. Social legislation was useful only if it assisted the progress of revolutionary syndicalism. Sorel broke with his friend and colleague, Lagardelle, because the latter had tried to convince himself that they had been associated together in order to surpass, not to destroy, democracy. To preserve democracy would be to perpetuate the omnipotent politician.[40]

The bourgeois conception of life was incapable of giving rise to the vital noble instincts, to heroism, and the sublime,

[38] Sorel, "L'Ethique du socialisme," p. 135.

[39] Sorel, "Notes additionelles à l'avenir socialiste des syndicats," *Le Mouvement socialiste* (September 1, 1905), 17:10; *Matériaux*, pp. 111, 154; *Reflections on violence*, p. 63; *Les Illusions du progrès*, p. 211.

[40] Letter to Croce, January 25, 1911, in *La Critica* (September 1928), 26:345.

which rested on a pessimistic conception of life. Whereas optimism led to the glorification of passion, the sanctification of cynical individualism, to utilitarianism, a school of moral skepticism, and the formation of utopias, pessimism, with its strong ethics, was necessary for creative activity and the march to deliverance. Sorel's pessimism was not the result of a theory of the world based on original sin, nor was it the romantic pessimism expressed in elegant posturing. Pessimism was valuable as a guide to action: on the one hand because it took account of the obstacles that stood in the way of the satisfaction of human wants, and on the other because of its appreciation of the natural feebleness of man. Sorel's pessimism was in reality the outcome of his belief that the transformation of society was an heroic task requiring heroic qualities. Sorel preferred Corneille to Voltaire because the former created tragic plots whereas the latter, in harmony with his century, knew only success and optimism.

The hidden unity in the theory of Sorel, argued Johannet,[41] was the idea of heroism. It was the pole around which his meditations turned. Sorel's theory seems an excellent illustration of Bergson's belief that heroism is a return to movement and emanates from an emotion akin to the creative act. Yet Sorel made clear his difference on this point from Bergson. In a letter to Berth in February 1911, Sorel said he had never supposed an *élan vital*, a popular instinct leading humanity toward superior social forms; he had demonstrated that almost all the views proposed by Bergson in reality had their origin in political and economic phenomena.[42]

Although Sorel was always certain of the need for the heroic, he was curiously changeable about the means of deliverance. He had criticized Christianity for its influence on military decadence through the vulgarization of the idea that victory depended on moral, not material, causes.[43] But in 1889 he asserted that the Bible would be the means of regeneration, that it was the only book that would instruct the

---

[41] René Johannet, *Itinéraires d'intellectuels*, Paris, 1921, p. 193.

[42] Quoted in Pierre Andreu, "Bergson et Sorel," *Les Etudes Bergsoniennes* (1952), 3:57-58.

[43] *La Ruine du monde antique*, p. 42.

people and initiate them to heroic life. Sorel always paid tribute to the effect of religion on action, as in 1909 when he approved both William James's bemoaning of the feeble part played by heroism in life, and James's demand of religion that it excite heroism.[44] Nor in 1898 could Sorel offer a very heroic solution. The most effective guarantees one could institute against despotism, he wrote in that year,[45] were those provided by working-class associations: cooperatives, *syndicats*, mutual societies. Temporarily he thought that the bourgeoisie might regenerate society, but he quickly turned to the myth of the proletarian revolution, and of the general strike. The renewal of the vital energy would come from the proletariat. It would, unaided by theoreticians or intellectuals, create its own institutions and fight its own class struggles. It was not simply a matter of asking favors, but of profiting from bourgeois cowardice in order to impose the will of the proletarians. The militants of the proletariat were without doubt mystics, if one meant by that disinterested individuals, ready to sacrifice their lives.[46]

With faith in its mission, the proletariat, making use of fighting where necessary, would dedicate itself to the noble role of producer, careful of technical and moral progress, leading society in the direction of economic progress, and directing the free workshop. Sorel, in this argument, was challenging the belief in the natural superiority of the upper class and its automatic assumption that it should rule.

But myth and reality became confused for Sorel. The ideas of a people, he argued, always corresponded to the conditions of existence of a very limited group. During the Napoleonic wars very few soldiers became generals, but all acted as if they had the baton of the marshal in their knapsacks; there were not many Americans who became millionnaires, and yet all American life operated as if each citizen was destined to become head of a great enterprise.[47]

[44] Sorel, "La Religion d'aujourd'hui," *Revue de métaphysique et de morale* (1909), 17:257.
[45] Sorel, "La Crise du socialisme," p. 609.
[46] *Matériaux*, p. 356.
[47] *Le Système historique de Renan*, pp. 142-143.

But if, as Sorel argued, an elite is both inevitable in human history and desirable for the successful capture of power, it is difficult to see how the whole proletariat could possess these noble qualities attributed to a minority, unless Sorel, like Barrès, was basically concerned with the heightening of sensibility and the moral qualities of that minority alone. It is in fact noticeable that the qualities Sorel chose—daring, energy, strength—are the martial qualities of the aristocracy. The Sorelian hero, chaste and sober producer, admirer of industrial technique and of law, a kind of ascetic worker, inheritor of the virtues of artisans, soldiers, and monks,[48] is a figure somewhat withdrawn from reality. Both he and Barrès, in attacking uniformity, were in effect like John Stuart Mill, pleading for uniqueness.

Moreover, it is difficult to see how anyone who stressed as much as did Sorel the necessity for juridical principles which could only be the outcome of stability could combine this with the desirability for *élan*, movement, and revolution. What would be the purpose of all the violence and activity if it were not to engender a system of rules; what would be the purpose of the myth stimulating action unless it were action for the mere sake of action?

For Maurras, force was not, as for Sorel, a method of spiritual or moral development; it was simply a means of attaining power. "We did not have to await the ardent oration of Gohier nor even the curious meditations that Sorel entitled *Reflections on Violence* to say and write, perhaps the first of our generation, that it might be necessary to use violence."[49] Maurras was aware that he could not capture power by constitutional means. The Action Française was neither an electoral bureau, nor a group of spectators, nor a simple party or political opposition, nor a philosophic school to change ideas and manners. It was a conspiracy to prepare a state of mind through which to make a *coup de force*, a coup directed against the regime that had killed France. The true

48 René Salome, "Le Lyrisme de M. Georges Sorel," *Revue des Jeunes* (January 25, 1923), 13:162.
49 *L'Action française*, September 21, 1912.

object of the movement was the establishment of the monarchy, the act of instituting the royalty, the royalization, the monarchization of the country.

Maurras, impressed on this occasion by a British example, believed himself to be writing for Monk, the Monk who awaited the suitable opportunity that would allow him to arise and make himself the servant of the needs of his country.[50] A study of the needs of France and of its confused aspirations dictated, authorized, and made legitimate the use of force in the making of the monarchy. Any Republican, who had lost his faith in the Republic could be Monk: it might be the Minister of the Interior, a prefect of police, or a questor of the Chamber. The task was to prepare and organize a *coup de force* together with the formation and diffusion of a state of mind that would allow that coup to succeed.

Maurras was the defender of order, but only of the right kind of order. His opponents, "those who opposed our street fights,"[51] took for order what was really their stagnant ideas, and the periodical recourse to the "electoral fair."

There was between the extreme Left and Right a remarkable reliance on the conception of the *élan vital*,[52] and on the idea of violence as the only cure for the evils of a bourgeois civilization. This was the result of a fusion of ideas between the syndicalists, providing a theoretical justification for their small movement, their lack of funds, their minority control, and the Right, with its stress on French strength, on an offensive spirit, and on hierarchical authority and quality. Sorel anticipated the later criticism of the Cartesian world which pointed out that not only was it a mechanical world in which all wants were finitely determined but also a static one. Therefore, since the norm was inertia, the need was for action and heroes. Sorel, argued Guy-Grand, attempted to give to activ-

[50] *Enquête sur la monarchie*, pp. 487-488, 596.
[51] *La Contre-révolution spontanée*, p. 118.
[52] J. Bowditch, "The Concept of the Elan Vital," *Modern France*, ed. E. M. Earle, pp. 32-43.

ity a metaphysical value analogous to intuition,[53] but in fact it has not and cannot have such a moral value.

The argument of Sorel, Barrès, and Maurras aptly illustrates what Isaiah Berlin has shown to be the essence of 20th century political thought—finding the process, natural or artificial, whereby the problems are made to vanish altogether.[54] The process attempts to alter the outlook giving rise to the problem, rather than accept the premise of 19th century thought that social and political problems exist and that they can be solved only by the conscious application of truths on which all can agree. Philosophies of life of the kind that Sorel, Barrès, and Maurras expounded claim that they indicate the limitations of bourgeois rationalism which is threatening to obscure and devitalize everything that is alive in the world. These philosophies may be useful as a check on absolute rationalism, but, as Mannheim has suggested,[55] they constitute a latent opposition to the rationalist world, exalting the idea of "becoming" in the abstract, but severing all connections with the world that is actually coming into existence. The three writers may have suggested that they had a more intimate view of the nature of reality than that possessed by democratic thinkers, but neither the logic of their theories nor the political conclusions they drew from them justify such an opinion.

[53] Georges Guy-Grand, *Le Procès de la démocratie*, Paris, 1911, p. 211.
[54] Isaiah Berlin, "Political Ideas in the Twentieth Century," *Foreign Affairs* (April 1950), 28:351-385.
[55] Karl Mannheim, *Essays on Sociology and Social Psychology*, p. 162.

CHAPTER VIII

THE DIVIDED REPUBLIC

ONE OF THE DILEMMAS of any constitutional government is that laws make clear what one cannot do, but not what one should do. Since there is no single end for society to pursue, and since a democratic system by its essence involves the conditional and tentative, such a system means avoidance of commitment beyond that of the preservation of freedom. Maurras saw the dilemma of liberalism inherent in this fact: the one thing it could not tolerate was the repudiation of liberty itself. It did not therefore know what to do either about religious bodies or about economic questions which might interfere with that liberty.

All three writers were concerned about the lack of vitality of principle and of inspiration behind the Republic and the lack of orientation in the country. Barrès argued that the country did not want a king or an emperor or a parliamentary republic or socialism. "What did it want? It did not know."[1] In a situation of this kind, where agreement on policy was lacking and where the leaders of the country were incompetent, there could be no firm attachment to the regime. The lack of policy was largely the result of the fact that, for anyone who had a real desire to succeed, it was essential to become a moderate. The politicians were afraid to open their mail, the newspapers of their *arrondissement*, and the letters of their political committees. They were afraid of alienating a single person in the corridors or differentiating themselves from one another by taking a position at the tribune. Barrès' fictional M. Bouteiller himself confessed, "The regime lasts only because of the fear of war."[2] Energetic young men were disgusted at the stupid ends to which their activity was supposed to be directed.[3] The effect of this lack of purpose on the country was, as Barrès, in *Les Déracinés*, showed in his portrayal of the seven youths from Lorraine, that all were

[1] *Mes Cahiers*, ix:361.　　　　　[2] *Les Déracinés*, ii:25.
[3] *Toute licence sauf contre l'amour*, p. 60.

147

in the process of becoming anarchists and of advocating disorder. Out of the inchoate revolt against these conditions, against the lack of government in a country which wanted to feel itself governed, a movement like Boulangism was born. For Maurras, since democracy was unreal and visionary, it could not have any coherent policy. This was the result of deficiencies both in the governmental and parliamentary institutions. Logically, the Republic could only be negative in operation because by definition it meant the exclusion of a hereditary leader, and it had no other chief. With the government divided and segmented, France lacked a tradition and a leader, the former nourished by the wisdom of the past and the latter thinking of the future of the country. The Republic could therefore have no doctrine of its own. The choice France had to make was clear: liberty or a leader, equality or order.[4]

The writers agreed that a common doctrine was lacking, but were not altogether in accordance either on the prognosis or on the cure. They agreed that the country was overcentralized and needed decentralizing (though their analyses and remedies were somewhat vague), that the educational system was deficient (though again, the proposals for change varied), but they differed widely on the need for unity.

UNITY OR SCISSION

The problem of how to obtain a stable, coherent system unified by general acceptance is one that has constantly troubled political thinkers from Plato on. It is a problem that has become even more important in an industrial society with a mobile population. Though Mr. Friedrich has argued[5] that agreement on fundamentals is not a necessary condition of either representative government or democratic or constitutional government, it is difficult to see how any political system can operate successfully where irreconcilable ideological differences are present. It was the presence of these irrecon-

4 L'Action française, April 18, 1913.
5 Carl J. Friedrich, The New Belief in the Common Man, passim.

cilable differences, religious, political, and social, in the Third Republic that made its history so difficult, so perplexing, and so interesting.

The attitude of the right to differences which exist is always to attempt to remove them. It will stress unity rather than diversity, the national factor rather than individual interests, and will issue an appeal to all men of good will to rally together. It will criticize those features of the political and social system which encourage division, in particular, the party system. It will oppose the idea of class struggle, and will talk instead of cooperation or collaboration among classes. It refuses to allow that legitimate differences of opinion may present problems difficult to solve or that there might be more than one point of view. It emphasizes conformity, unity, and authority, the subordination of the individual to the whole society. It tends to emphasize the concrete rather than the abstract, the enduring rather than the changeable, the organic social unit rather than agglomerations.[6]

Barrès and Maurras were the chief exponents of these rightist doctrines in France, although the problem was made more complex there by the fact that since August 1792, official religion had also been associated with that point of view, as a guardian of order against the people.

The profound evil, said Barrès, lay in the absence of the needed conformity in society. This was due partly to the fact that France was divided and troubled by a thousand particular wills, by a thousand individual imaginations. Partly it was due to "the lack of a common knowledge of our end, our resources, our central core."[7] The Dreyfus Affair had added to the division of the country and to the troubling of the national mentality. Barrès approved the formula of Déroulède, "There is only probability that Dreyfus is innocent, but it is absolutely certain that France is innocent."[8] He therefore ranged himself against Dreyfus, agreeing with the opinion of the men whom he believed society had desig-

[6] Karl Mannheim, *Essays on Sociology and Social Psychology*, pp. 113-114.
[7] *Scènes*, p. 80. [8] *ibid.*, p. 29.

nated to be competent, and disagreeing with those he re-garded as incompetent, the intellectuals, the "stage anarchists," the metaphysicians of sociology—the Affair was an orgy of metaphysicians—a band of fools who treated French generals as idiots, French social institutions as absurd, and French traditions as unhealthy.

Barrès looked for the sentiment or the common interests that would unite the country he found so "divided and head-less," and found them in the idea of a unified group and a strong leader. He stressed the myth of national concentration that would many times in the future become the basis of appeal to the country both in France and elsewhere, as the only method of solution to political problems. The desire for unity, what he called the universal dream, not only satisfied the moral needs and the desires of the thoughtful, but also was satisfactory for the health and well-being of France. Barrès made use of all opportunities and people to stress this necessity for unity. In his call to all parts of the nation to be inspired by eternal France, Barrès saw, as in a similar fashion he was to see the Union Sacrée of 1914, the fete of Joan of Arc as one where Frenchmen of all parties could unite in a great fraternal gathering around the heroine of the country.

For Barrès a leader was necessary both for personal and national reasons. "Perenially in opposition, disheartened both emotionally and rationally from the task of governing," it was personally attractive to him to be a member of a mass movement dominated by a leader because he could "taste profoundly the instinctive pleasure of being in a flock."[9] Politi-cally, he would link himself with the patriots of the school of Déroulède, the regionalists, and with those, whether Catho-lic or positivist, who wanted a national and social discipline.

For the sake of France, it was necessary to find the strong man who would open the windows to throw out gossip and allow in fresh air, a man who would be capable of acting. In Boulanger, he found the figure around whom to rally. Instead of belonging to political parties, the people uniting in the

[9] *Mes Cahiers*, i:39; viii:96.

Boulangist movement wanted to find the party of France, a party that would renounce oratorical chicanery in order to concern itself with general interests, a party, without factions, that would be concerned only with work and peace, and that would put national honor on its banner. Parties must become national ones, and collaboration must take place between all those serving the national interest. Barrès himself, unattached to any one party electorally or in the Chamber, said, "I do not want to fight for a party, I do not want to fight for parties."[10] Boulangism was for him a movement of very diverse people representing very varied, even opposite, social conceptions, but united in their belief in the *élan*, the psychological unity of Boulangism and in Boulanger himself, a real man.

Maurras similarly continuously stressed national unity, opposing the democratic system which meant division, struggles of class and religion inside France, and foreign intrusion into the national consciousness.

To Maurras, unity was more important than tolerance. Liberalism in politics meant civil war, in religion it meant schism. A democratic system meant both that government was divided, disunited, and bitterly opposed by other parties and groups, and that it was a factor in dividing, since it perpetuated the opposition. A government was 10 ministers, each with his own faction and party.[11] The Place Beauvau (Ministry of the Interior), warred on the Quai d'Orsay (Foreign Ministry), while the Rue Oudinot (Ministry of the Colonies), was not always in agreement with the other two. In 1899, during the Dreyfus Affair, a struggle had taken place between the important Information Service, organ of French national defense, and the Sûreté Générale, which was concerned with the defense of the Republic only. The democratic Republican regime, which excited and fed a hundred internal quarrels, had ruined the moral unity of the country. Maurras deplored the absence of a power strong enough to make the varied interests unite. It was because of this desire to main-

[10] *Mes Cahiers*, vɪ:143; ɪx:252.   [11] *Kiel et Tanger*, p. 232.

tain unity that he at first refused to mention the Dreyfus Affair, and even when he did, in an article in *Soleil* on October 23, 1897, it was only to say that it was necessary to forget Dreyfus for the welfare of the country.

Maurras was opposed, as was Barrès, to the idea of class conflict, since it was a divisive factor in the country. He argued that it was in the name of the unfortunate myth of class struggle that some dreamt of dismembering the vertical organization of nations for the profit of a horizontal and international alliance of classes. To the dialectical myth of Hegel and Marx, comments Mr. Roudiez, Maurras preferred his own, based on certain conceptions of Aquinas, that conciliation and harmony were possible between classes.[12] For Maurras, national and professional communities were more important than classes; on the one hand he denied the validity of class struggle, and on the other he asserted the possibility of industrial and social concord. It was not true that there was a venerable quarrel of the farm and the bourgeois house with the castle; the peasant and the castle owner, the castle owner and the petty bourgeois had more common than opposed interests.[13] It was unfortunate that too many people had an interest, an electoral interest, in upsetting the relations of capital and labor.

Maurras would substitute for class struggle, not the fusion of classes, but the reclassification of producers to include employers as well as workers, in the interest of production and in their own interest. Workers and employers together would regulate their common interests, with the King protecting workers against possible abuses of capital. He accepted the ideas of Le Play, de Mun, and La Tour du Pin with very few modifications, and was interested in the maintenance of social peace and the reconciliation of all workers. He complimented de Mun for his campaign in favor of the establishment of mixed syndicats to which employers and employees would be admitted, and approved the desire of the Socialists to found arbitration tribunals composed of

---

12 Leon S. Roudiez, *Maurras jusqu'à l'action française*, p. 266.
13 *Les Princes des nuées*, p. 74.

representatives of both sides.[14] Believing in the desirability of class collaboration, Maurras advocated the aspiration of the workers to a kind of *embourgeoisement* and the ownership of some property.

To this analysis Sorel was totally opposed. "The decisive word in Sorel's vocabulary is 'scission,'" argues Mr. Meisel.[15] Certainly, one of his principal preoccupations was the undesirable unity in the democratic system. As in ancient times, the great question was still that of scission, but it did not seem to him that socialism had as many resources as primitive Christianity to remain inviolate. Therefore, any individual or factor encouraging scission was desirable. Those teachers who wrote of the revolutionary tendencies of the proletariat and the evils of social peace were to be applauded as Corneillian heroes.[16]

In this connection a democratic system was undesirable because it always sought unity, and had perfected unitary theory. Social economists worked hard to give the workers the illusion of solidarity existing between the different social classes. This attempt to create unity was shown in the Dreyfus Affair, the chief result of which was not the separation of Church and State, or the smashing of military control over the government, but the strengthening of the philosophy of *Solidarité*, the political and economic expression of which was the theory of social peace,[17] and which was really a philosophy of wicked hypocrisy. The bourgeoisie had taken over the devices of a bureaucratic centralization from the *ancien régime*, and had developed the unitary concept even further in several ways. By the system of popular universal education, the children of workers became *embourgeoisé*, and therefore the proletariat was deprived of future leaders. In trade unions this meant that the leadership was bought off by concessions and bribes, and the labor councils were becoming amiable cigar-smoking clubs. In politics, bureaucracy

[14] Charles Maurras, "L'Evolution des idées sociales."
[15] J. H. Meisel, *The Genesis of Georges Sorel*, p. 275.
[16] *Matériaux*, p. 413.
[17] *La Révolution Dreyfusienne*, p. 21.

was in control of organizations, and legislation was largely inspired by ideas of pacifism and state socialism. The Socialist press itself was affected by this desire for conciliation, and sought to move bourgeois opinion by appealing to sentiments of goodness, humanity, solidarity, and bourgeois ethics; socialism was soliciting the protection of the class which was the irreconcilable enemy of the proletariat.[18]

This allegation of democracy that it was above class conflicts and its concern with the mixing of classes Sorel regarded as disastrous. Social peace was not a Socialist conception, but merely the order established by the governing classes and accepted by docile workers. The great social question was still that of scission. It was necessary that society be divided into two camps, and into two only, as on a battlefield.[19] Bourgeoisie and proletariat must face each other with all the rigor of which they were capable. The best way in which this could be done was by the myth of the General Strike and the use of violence—violence, not force, for as in war, everything was carried on without hatred or a spirit of vengeance. Violent strikes would take the place of the ancient religious persecutions in fostering the necessary and desirable warlike state. This state was necessary because it was the best means by which the *élan* of the people could be stimulated, decadence averted, the taste for moderation and the desire for social peace overcome, and a new juridical system created. Asked about Bourget's play, *La Barricade*, which was based on the ideas of his *Reflections on Violence*, Sorel answered that he would be happy if it would help force the bourgeoisie to defend itself and to abandon its guilty and inglorious resignation in the face of the courageous ardor of its adversary. And in reality, the influence of Sorel did lead middle-class writers to urge the bourgeoisie to resist violently in order to safeguard its own privileges.

Sorel was right in seeing political issues as clashes of power, but there was inherent in his argument a plea for purposeless

[18] Georges Sorel, "Le Syndicalisme révolutionnaire," *Le Mouvement socialiste* (November 1, 1905), 17:278.
[19] *Reflections on Violence*, p. 144.

activity. As a moralist, he urged the reanimation of the spirit of the people, as a technician he urged the increase of industrial production, but the two concepts are not connected, and may even be opposed. The analogy he made in *Reflections on Violence* between the worker and the soldier was considerably overdrawn, while his idea of conflict inevitably producing the heroic individual was based on a curious view of human nature. It is unlikely that heroism can be a continuous manifestation of man's character. Conflict, moreover, must be a disruptive influence, and the continuity Sorel praised elsewhere was forgotten in his plea for violence.

THE DEMAND FOR DECENTRALIZATION

If the three writers differed on the need for unity or scission to overcome the existing malaise, they were agreed on the need for decentralization. Michels has said, "We owe to Sorel the rediscovery of the relationships between democracy in general and absolutism, and their point of intersection in centralization,"[20] but this is as true of Maurras and Barrès as of Sorel. The regionalist movement in France had many objectives, as Gooch has shown.[21] It wanted to make secure liberty and vitality in the regions, to revitalize patriotism, to provide a guarantee against despotism and a barrier against revolution, to restore individual initiative, to safeguard the variety of customs and habits. Although the aims might be laudable, there was not, with Sorel, Barrès, or Maurras, any clear conception of what regionalism or decentralization or federalism might mean from the political, administrative, industrial, or intellectual point of view. Decentralization provided an effective rallying cry, it did not supply a basis for political reform. In fact, it may have produced exactly the opposite result, with the opposition of Radical-Socialists to examining the problem at least partly due to the support of regionalism by Catholics and Royalists.

[20] Robert Michels, *Political Parties*, London, 1915, p. 234.
[21] R. K. Gooch, *Regionalism in France*, New York, 1931, passim.

Sorel saw the whole democratic movement as one which strengthened state power. The state was the expression of the domination of a group of men who had succeeded in taking over concentrated and organized force.[22] All French political crises consisted in the replacement of intellectuals by other intellectuals to maintain the state or to strengthen it, since the preservation of the state was necessary for intellectuals. Sorel regarded all the revolutionary disturbances of the 19th century as having ended by strengthening the power of the state. In the contemporary regime, all politicians, Socialists as well as bourgeois, upheld the exercise of violence by the state and propagated the superstitution of authority. This led to unwarranted and inevitably unsuccessful state activity. The consequence was that industry became submerged under the increasing expansions of authority mixing in affairs formerly regarded as essentially private.

This expansion of the economic powers of the state meant not only error, waste, and embezzlement, but also the deflection of the working-class movement from its true objective. Sorel indicated the danger of the revival of the Saint-Simonian spirit among socialist intellectuals,[23] and criticized the parliamentary Socialists who continued to speak of revolution while they were really concerned with social reforms, and who pretended to lead France to libertarian communism while in fact transforming all producers into officials. Excellent examples of these parliamentary figures were Millerand and Waldeck-Rousseau, whom Sorel regarded as typical representatives of that kind of state socialism which was really based on a monarchical tradition. All this meant that the working class became ardently interested in questions unrelated to its class interest, and uninterested in securing its own emancipation by itself. During the Dreyfus Affair, it needed only two years of democratic agitation for the fruits of 20 years of Socialist propaganda to be lost.

[22] *Introduction à l'économie moderne*, p. 230.
[23] Sorel, "Quelques mots sur Proudhon," *Cahiers de la quinzaine* (June 1901) 2nd Series, No. 13, p. 25.

History had shown that the search by philosophers and founders of religious orders for the happiness of man was futile. When the state had to any large extent attempted to promote the happiness of man it had failed, and it hardly seemed likely that the contemporary state Socialists were any more capable in this respect than was Plato.[24] The ideal of the Socratics had been the transformation of the state into a church, and though contemporary socialism did not really resemble religion, it too possessed that belief in the total power of the state that antiquity had had to an extraordinary degree. Sorel revolted from socialism because, in origin a philosophic doctrine, it had become a sect, then a political party, combining with other allied or antagonistic forces to administer business, ameliorate legislation, and direct the state. In fact, the spirit of the state had crept back into Marxism because Socialists, wanting to capture power, had organized workers into a political party.

Sorel would support all ideas diminishing the role of the state. If capitalist society had been characterized by the march toward unity in the state, the working-class movement would stress local division.[25] The essence of syndicalism, he wrote in an article reviewing a book by Péguy, in the *Action française* on April 14, 1910, was to free itself from its Jacobin tutelage. He supported the antipatriotic doctrine of the syndicalists; it was not a question of loving or not loving one's country, but simply of the most tangible manifestation of the struggle against the state. To deny one's country would be a demonstration of a refusal to compromise with the bourgeois order. To decrease the power of the state, Sorel advocated administrative decentralization and the resurrection of communal and provincial life. But it is possible that what Sorel called "federative government" was another of his myths, for the reality of federalism, he argued, was not absolutely necessary for the realization of federalist tendencies.[26] More-

[24] Sorel, "Le Socialisme en 1907," *Le Mouvement socialiste* (May 1907), 21:481.
[25] Sorel, "Les Dissensions de la social démocratie en Allemagne," *Revue politique et parlementaire* (July 1900), 25:63.
[26] *Introduction à l'économie moderne*, p. 161.

over, he acknowledged that the federalist ideas of Proudhon would not be realized in his time. These ideas seemed to be popular only in the small manufacturing towns; they were not easily understood by the workers of large towns.

Barrès was as opposed as Sorel to the increasing power of the state, and to the overcentralization he saw in all fields. In the realm of politics, all power was concentrated in the Chamber of Deputies. In the field of administration, officials received their orders from Paris. The intellectual world was dominated by the universities, humanistic, Kantian, teaching in terms of abstractions, and creating *déracinés* who became Parisian men of letters. This meant domination by the state and centralization of authority. There was, Barrès claimed, too much state intervention (he apparently forgot he was at the same time pleading for protectionism in economic affairs) and too little liberty of association. He agreed with Taine that the domination by the state paralyzed the spontaneity of all associations, of local groups and moral groups, leading to two great evils, the lack of local life and the incapacity for spontaneous cooperation.[27] The local group ought to have been a gathering of neighbors, an involuntary company, a natural and limited society.

The provinces suffered from not being allowed any activity worthy of them. The transfer of their powers, as in the case of Lorraine, to the bureaus of Paris had ruined their autonomous development. The provinces had degenerated from directors of their own affairs into clients of Paris. The situation was even more aggravated by the fact that in 1888 it was the deputies who controlled everything and made the decisions, whereas 20 years previously, when a prefect made his decisions he at least resided in the department. The intrigue in Paris meant it was there that one had to influence people in order to succeed. This in itself was more difficult, for it was necessary to convince not one or two people, but a great many deputies. Moreover, the centralist system was dominated by cosmopolitan businessmen, important Jews, and foreigners—men like Reinach and Herz, bands of vagrants.[28]

[27] *Scènes*, p. 490.
[28] Maurice Barrès, *Assainissement et fédéralisme*, Paris, 1895, p. 7.

If Paris continued to develop in the direction of a casino, consistently preferring foreigners to Frenchmen and following ends more and more irreconcilable with the destinies of the provinces, the latter would have to be concerned with supplying the brain power that the capital would have ceased to provide.

Only decentralization could save France; it would take the form of communal and regional autonomy under national unity. The dilemma for Barrès was the unit to choose for decentralization. Since the department was an arbitrary administrative unit, and the optimum region for each economic activity varied, he returned to the old provinces. French nationality was created out of provincial nationalities; the force of the word *Frenchman* was doubled when to it was added *Breton, Lorrainer,* or *Alsatian.* Decentralization could restore the effective life of the provinces politically and culturally, could liberate France from the influence of foreigners, could restore Alsace and Lorraine, the provinces that had been lost by a centralist regime. It could also become a means of social transformation because the communes and the regions were sociological laboratories, and their political and economic experiments would be of benefit to all.

Thibaudet has suggested that "Barrès more than anyone created a spirit of decentralization."[29] In his youth, Barrès had worked on the journal, *Les Chroniques,* which, if not a regionalist review, at least did not neglect the problem.[30] Although he abstained when his fellow workers on *La Cocarde* voted to found the Ligue Républicaine de Décentralisation, in October 1895, he did call a federalist and internationalist congress in Paris. Barrès had indicated that all types of people, Catholics, moderates, liberals, and conservatives were in favor of decentralization, and even Bonapartists were not necessarily in favor of centralization. He pointed out Déroulède as an example of a Bonapartist who, formerly opposed to decentralization, had shifted to its support. Yet the contradic-

[29] Albert Thibaudet, *La Vie de Maurice Barrès,* p. 276.
[30] Leon Dubreuil, (ed.), "Lettres de Maurice Barrès à Charles le Goffic," *Annales de Bretagne* (1951), 58:19-88.

tion remained between the apologist of federalism and the admirer of the professor of energy, the archcentralizer, Napoleon. His idea "to put an authority at the head of the state and develop local and corporative autonomies,"[31] was more illusionary than any concept that existed in the contemporary system. Moreover, while Barrès was pleading for the recognition of a distinct culture in each province, it is difficult to see what there was in common between his seven *déracinés* from Lorraine, except that they all had left their native land.

For Maurras the problem was simple—the Republic was overcentralized, and both the Republic and the overcentralization must be ended. To centralize was the fate of the Republic, to decentralize was in the interests of France. One or the other had to be destroyed.[32] The Republic was in a continual dilemma. It could not decentralize for several reasons. Being weak, it had to take military precautions, and that needed the concentration of power. It needed electoral links between the elector, official, and elected, for it was by centralization that the ruling parties were chosen and rechosen; their election would be unlikely in a decentralized system, and therefore Parliament would not be likely to commit suicide by decentralizing. A republic, once established, could not become decentralized; the natural trend of an elective government was democratic state socialism. It reserved in its own hands the administration of public services, and there was no power to make the transfer to a decentralized state. State intervention had gone too far in the Republic; every day it invented some new occasion to molest the initiative of citizens.

This overcentralization produced certain difficulties. The Republic encouraged those migrations from the provinces which destroyed the professional families and enfeebled everything. The general interest was left unrepresented. Centralization encouraged idleness; the administration and bureaucracy played in relation to the people the same role that the intendants had played in relation to the dissipated youth before the Revolution.[33]

[31] *Mes Cahiers*, iii:37.
[32] *L'Action française*, April 22, 1908.
[33] Maurras, *L'Anglais qui a connu la France*, Paris, 1928, p. 37.

Maurras traced the source of the urge to centralize back to 1789 when the National Assembly abolished the old provinces of France and divided the country arbitrarily into 81 departments. Jacobinism would not admit the free existence of a variety of provinces in a unified nation, and preferred to absorb them and dismember them, but it was acting on a theory of profiting a France that was unreal.[34] Local areas were being emptied of their people, their activity, their vitality, their industry, their agriculture, and their commercial importance. There was no local life—all the Girondins had been beaten; there were no small centers—communes had become impoverished; the state had become the engineer and the chaplain of the communes.

How different everything was before the Revolution! French royalty had never permitted that outrage against the soul of France, as Taine called it, which was perpetrated by the division into departments.[35] In 1783 there was an infinite number of small and large autonomous organizations federated by the King of France without being enslaved by him, capable of putting at his disposal free contributions taken on collective capital rather than on an individual basis. From 1780 to 1787 all the men interested in the public good had wanted to establish provincial assemblies on the model of the bodies of Languedoc and of Provence, whose excellent administration was the admiration of France. From the year VIII, Frenchmen were not citizens, but *administrés*; on August 4, 1789, the franchises of towns and national provinces died.

It is interesting, but not surprising, that Tocqueville drew quite different conclusions from the good administration in some of the *pays d'états*, and that he should have entitled one of his chapters, "How the administrative centralization was an institution of the old regime and not, as is often thought, a creation of the Revolution or the Napoleonic period." The Maurrasian version of pre-Revolutionary history was an incredible travesty of the truth with its refusal to acknowledge that provincial independence had been abolished by the mon-

[34] *L'Action française*, February 10, 1924.
[35] Maurras, *L'Ordre et le désordre*, p. 54.

archy, which had sent its nominees to govern most of the country.

But to Maurras the idea of decentralization was of sentimental as well as of political interest. It was on the second floor of the town hall of Martigues, in leafing through the old registers of the municipal archives that he learned "to render justice to our past . . . and felt myself what I have always been, municipal Republican, provincial federalist, and passionate Royalist."[36] In 1888 he met Mistral for the first time, and became aware of the interest in Provençal, and of the fact that Félibrige was not simply an intellectual amusement. But his appreciation of the true extent of Provençal culture was a totally unrealistic one. Reviewing a book by Mistral, Maurras wrote that while the peasants, shepherds, and poets of Provence thanked Mistral for having rescued the speech of their ancestors, there would be everywhere readers of the *Tresor* who would derive perpetual enlightenment on the mystery of races, languages, and blood from it. This, as Richard Aldington has aptly commented, about a book that cost 120 francs in 1900.[37]

Maurras was in favor of restoring the power of the provinces, of making the universities autonomous, strengthening the family by suppressing the law of equal inheritance, encouraging the tenure of land and industry, making the *syndicats* autonomous, and restoring the authority of the religious congregations. To secure these ends, he wanted economic and territorial decentralization in which all orders and degrees of the political, administrative, juridical, and civil hierarchy would participate. He had argued that a federalist system was not possible, since neither of the two factors normally responsible for its formation was present; there were no organized bodies like Swiss cantons or American states already in existence, nor was there a common enemy creating unity. Yet in 1892, he paid his first visit to La Tour du Pin to talk of federalism. With his friend Amouretti, Maurras decided that the Félibrige of Paris ought to be more than simply a

---

[36] *L'Etang de Berre*, p. 44.
[37] Richard Aldington, *Introduction to Mistral*, London, 1956, p. 142.

meeting place for dinner, and with two others, René de Saint-Pons and Joseph Mange, signed a *Declaration des Félibres Fédéralistes* on February 22, 1892, urging immediate autonomy for the provinces and a greater independence of the communes. It is typical of the whole career of Maurras that the movement should have expelled him for this excess of enthusiasm.

The concrete suggestions he made were not strikingly dissimilar to that division of power, coordinate and separate, which is the chief feature of a federal system. The central government would retain the power of diplomacy, control of the armies of land and sea, and, to a lesser degree, general finance. Other organizations—the clergy, university, communes, *arrondissements*, provinces, public assistance, and judicial bodies—would be autonomous, the center reserving for itself only the supervisory, police, arbitration, and judicial powers. Caution must be exercised, however, about the professional group, for they might be without deep roots in French tradition, and thus a menace to it because of infiltration of ideas of international revolution and cosmopolitan anarchy.

Maurras' idea of territorial decentralization was equally vague. To the communes must be left the management of all affairs that were specially their own; to the provinces the questions that concerned the provinces. Thus, the supreme national organization might be relieved of all the functions that sapped its strength and might bring a greater continuity and energy of purpose to the direction of the national destinies of the country. In addition to economic and geographic decentralization, there ought also to be a decentralization of customs, so that as the number and importance of officials were diminished, citizens would lose the habit of turning incessantly to the state for aid. The role of the state would be reduced to, at most, that of a protector, a watchman.[38] It would be confined to acting as guarantor of individual existence, of the independence of the country, of the free usage of

[38] Maurras, "Une Monarchie fédérale," *Le Soleil*, March 9, 1898.

the native idiom, and the maintenance of customs and national traditions. In this way, organization and life would be substituted for mechanical administration. But only a king of France could bring this about. Only he could decentralize without risk, ensure the defeat of the cosmopolitans, and restore political authority. Being neither a creature nor a courtesan of his people, he would not reduce them to servitude nor deprive them of the free exercise of their power as citizens.[39]

But the paradox remained of Maurras, on one hand the Félibre and Provençal, on the other the creator of unity through monarchy. The paradox was that decentralization needed a strong power and that it would be effected only through nationalism and a central hereditary power. Maurras' compromise, "Never say, 'Long live the Republic,' but at the right time, 'Long live the republics, under the King of France,' " is more difficult to understand than the simple slogan of Déroulède, "A bas les Parlementaires; vive la République!"

The tragedy of this overstatement of the position by the three writers is that there was a genuine case to be made out against overcentralization in France. The gibe that government consisted of holding France at the end of a telegraph wire starting from Paris was shown to be not too far from the truth when in 1896 President Faure visited the Alpes Maritimes. Everyone who intended to call on the President was obliged to submit his name to the mayor of the town, who redirected it to the prefect, who telegraphed it to the Minister of the Interior. The control by the prefect over actions of the mayor and municipal council, and by the Minister of the Interior over the mayor meant that in every field of government, simple decisions had to be referred to the central authority. Bureaus in Paris decided whether a certain warden ought to be appointed in a particular gaol, whether a doctor in an asylum could prolong his leave, whether the name of a street could be changed, whether the

39 Maurras, *La République de Martigues*, Paris, 1929, p. 77.

nomination of a captain of a fire brigade ought to be authorized.

These practical difficulties helped produce French political pluralism. In this era, when the monistic theory of the state was being attacked, and the value and importance of groups in society emphasized, pluralists like Duguit and good Republicans like Charles Brun and Paul Boncour were impressed by the necessity to decentralize. It is a commentary on the extremist, uncompromising position of Maurras, Barrès, and Sorel that they took little account of the useful work being done by other critics and that their own criticisms were limited to confusing abstractions. Nowhere in any of the three writers can a clear outline of what is entailed in decentralization be found. Sorel's syndicalist ideas, for example, would seem to imply little if any control by central governmental agencies and a general absence of political power. But paradoxically enough, the syndicalist movement, which for him was the prototype of a decentralized organization, was itself strengthening its central body as opposition by government and employers became stronger. The formation of the Comité des Forges by leading employers meant greater resistance to union activity. The government, by arresting syndicalists in 1908 and 1913, by using troops to smash several strikes between 1910 and 1912, and by threatening the C.G.T. with dissolution in 1913, attempted to stem the tide of syndicalism. The response of the C.G.T. was to create larger and more centralized bodies. The Marseilles conference of the C.G.T. in 1908 invited all craft federations to become industrial, and in general, the local Bourses du Travail were losing power to larger bodies. Part of Sorel's myth was disappearing without his awareness.

THE CRISIS IN EDUCATION

The attack on centralization was carried over from political and social matters to the educational system, the writers attacking the uniformity or unity of the system. Maurras attacked the system because it provided the wrong kind of uniformity, egalitarian teaching that molded young brains

165

according to the necessities and desires of the state. Sorel was concerned because he felt that the system increased the power of the State because, although modern liberalism professed to be diametrically opposed to the absolutist theory of the Church, in fact it held the same view that education ought to be as complete and as uniform as possible.[40] Popular education led to absolutism and to lack of freedom because of uniform instruction. Barrès objected to the centralized system because this meant that in the provinces, university teaching was by Parisian professors, without any roots in the provinces, who taught an abstract philosophy having no relation to the necessities of national life.

The particular criticisms the three writers made about the harmful effects of the system differed widely. Barrès opposed the abstract philosophy being taught because it corrupted the young, led to the acceptance of unreal and fallacious ideas, and produced a pedagogical product who was deaf to the needs of France. Barrès' continuing hatred toward his teachers, M. Burdeau, portrayed in his books as M. Bouteiller, and M. Lagneau, "ce nigaud," as he once called him, was caused by their false teachings. They corrupted the young, inspired in them contempt for their parents, introduced new gods, inspired in their best pupils dreams of domination. This official teaching of the state, inspired by Kant, transported human beings into a world apart, a world that was poetic and heroic, but a world completely unreal. Barrès stated, "One of my favourite theses is to demand that education not be given to children without regard for their individuality."[41] In Les Déracinés, he denounced the puerile functioning of intelligence, abstract and devoid of all reality, on which the foundations for the work of an individual could be laid. The Sorbonne, like the 18th century philosophes, was intoxicated by the belief that science could provide a complete explanation of the world, and that university had destroyed all the old moral supports. To the mediocrity of the salons

[40] Le Procès de Socrate, p. 188.
[41] Barrès, "A Propos de la réimpression de 'l'Homme Libre,'" Révue politique et littéraire (September 10, 1904), 41:322.

and the demiculture of the graduates, Barrès preferred the creative, disinterested, spontaneous masses.[42] Besides the abtract teaching of the university, its chief fault was that it preached the love of humanity before that of the national collectivity. This resulted in a rationalism foreign to French habits and local and family traditions. Barrès objected that young Frenchmen were being taught as if one day they would have to do without their country.[43] The university despised or ignored tangible reality, with the result that its students hardly understood that the race of their country existed, that the earth of their country was a reality, and that, more real than earth or race, the spirit of each country was the instrument of education and of life for its sons.

Barrès made similar criticisms of the system of primary education and asked that it provide the opportunity for individuals to enjoy the heritage of the past. The hymns and the sacred songs on which a child ought to be nourished would encourage in him family, regional, historical, and corporative influences.

Barrès' own personal experience and criticism was largely an illustration of Taine's criticism of the *lycées* as huge stone boxes isolated in each large town and having as their rule strict confinement in their communal life.[44] This led to deficiency in social graces, unfortunate attitudes toward women, and these, combined with a desire to throw off the excessive discipline, meant that the student was tempted by low life in hygiene, money, or sex. Barrès followed Taine's conclusion that some young men at twenty-four, through their education in idealism, were not ready for life, that there was a growing disparity between education and life and that there was a need for regional universities.

On the question of the humanities, Barrès and Sorel took opposite points of view from Maurras. It was in character for Sorel to complain of the fatal influence exercised over

[42] *Le Jardin de Bérénice*, p. 124; *Mes Cahiers*, ix:19-20.
[43] *Les Déracinés*, i:35-39.
[44] Hippolyte Taine, *The Modern Regime*, 2 vols., New York, 1890-94, i:231-264.

the French mind by classicism,[45] an influence which developed
the defects of one's nature and which led to a state of ideological dissociation in which the country had lost the sense
of the reality of things. He criticized the professional schools
for devoting too much time to pure culture. The great schools
neglected technology for pure science; the Ecole Polytechnique hardly merited its title. The state was as incapable
of taking care of education as it was of industry. Education,
instead of developing a monstrous egoism which subordinated
everything to the desires of the individual appetite, and which
instilled a distaste for manual work, must be directed toward
a practical end. This end must be achieved through a double
process. Apprenticeship must be taken seriously and not
treated as a game or as an intellectual exercise. At the same
time, young men must be taught to love their work and to
consider everything they made as carefully created works
of art. It was the function of the educational process to make
individuals conscientious, artists and scholars in everything
relating to production.[46] The anarchistic and aristocratic idea
of the complete man was not suitable for a society in which
education had to be oriented to scientific division of work,
enlightened by a socialist philosophy and social ethics.

Barrès, differing from Sorel in his belief that there was a
need to give to children an inner faculty of expansion, "a
continual enchantment," agreed that the system of humanities did not render man more apt for agriculture, for commerce, or for industry, but, on the contrary, turned him from
them. The administration had prepared students only to become officials or Parisian men of letters. The university gave
birth to a proletariat of *bacheliers et filles*, to unemployed
intellectuals. The conclusion reached by Barrès was amply
borne out by the fact that the French publishing crisis last-
ing from 1890 until 1910 or 1911 did in fact leave a generation

[45] *La Ruine du monde antique*, p. 84; *Les Illusions du progrès*, pp. 256-
267; *Le Procès de Socrate*, p. 192. Sorel did admit, however, that the
decline of classicism would be undesirable if education could not be
founded on industrial practice.
[46] Sorel, "La Science dans l'éducation," *Le Devenir social* (May 1896),
2:461.

of frustrated aesthetes.[47] Both in France and in other countries where similar situations existed, an important impact on extremist political movements was to be the result.

Barrès' criticism, however, was a contradictory one. He reproached the system for its Kantism, its cold moralism, and its rigorous discipline, but he also accused it of leaving everything in a turmoil, and of anarchy in lacking a doctrine or discipline. The suicide of two schoolboys had led him to condemn the whole school system in a speech on June 21, 1909. In his desire for a discipline he said in a speech in the Chamber, "I accept . . . a school against the Church if that school has a positive value, fecund and living."[48]

Maurras agreed with Barrès that the schools taught the religion of the state, Kantism, and the defense of the Rights of Man, with the result that ethics were based on conscience rather than on will and reason. This created bewilderment in the minds of students, and was both antinational and antiscientific. But Maurras also criticized the system for having reduced the study of humanities and thus prevented the development of judgment and the formation of a critical sense. In this way the teaching of the state produced in young people either a complete lack of interest in public affairs or pure revolutionary ideas, so that French faculties of letters became seminaries of anarchism or of dilettantism. Maurras, like Barrès, objected to the lack of tradition in the teaching system. There was no indoctrination of the greatness of the past. The state, said Maurras, made use of the teacher in the village as an electoral agent; the teachers, with the ardor of proselytes, were sectarians in the fight against tradition and religion. Barrès complained that a large majority of the body of teachers was impregnated with pacifism.[49] Both he and Maurras thought that education should be run by local authorities rather than by the central government, and that each region should maintain and develop its own university.

[47] R. F. Byrnes, "The French Publishing Industry and Its Crisis in the 1890's," *Journal of Modern History* (September 1951), 23:232-242.
[48] *Journal Officiel*, January 18, 1910, p. 156.
[49] Barrès, preface to Paul Pilant, *Le Patriotisme en France et à l'étranger*, Paris, 1912, p. xii.

Sorel was aware that the system had a deleterious moral effect, and that it might further the degeneration in the social system because the educational system affected family relationships. Parents struggled to get an education for their children, who then despised them, but families were forced to send their children to schools to receive school doctrine. Under the existing system, Sorel dreaded mass education, and hoped the state would not succeed in suppressing consciences. He cited Proudhon's opinion that the teaching of the young, with the exception of the privileged, was a philanthropic dream. Education created an oligarchy of the erudite who, hallucinated by the idea of despotism over a poor clientele, flattered the popular masses in order best to succeed in dominating the state, and who would always be ready to sacrifice the future of the country to their vanity, their hates, and their corporate interests.[50] A classical education did not help pupils make much money, but it did give them prestige over the masses. The bourgeois control of the school meant both that the proletariat was placed under the direction of an ideology foreign to it and that an attempt was made to impose unity through teaching.

Sorel feared the effect on the proletariat. Through the system of universal education, the bourgeoisie deprived the proletariat of potential leaders on the principle that it was wiser to subsidize the barbarians than to fight them. Education would not be useful to the proletariat; the primary school was empoisoned with many old ideas, and its lay and bourgeois catechism rendered the masses more easily accessible to all the nonsense uttered by politicians.[51] If the popular university movement had succeeded in leading the most intelligent workers in the direction hoped for by the bourgeoisie, socialism would have fallen into the democratic rut. Sorel accepted Proudhon's idea that a good system of education must be founded on working-class associations in which apprenticeship would be based on the value of work rather than the culture of the mind.

[50] *Le Procès de Socrate*, pp. 8-9, 180, 192.
[51] *Les Illusions du progrès*, p. 196.

Once habit and tradition have lost their hold on a people, the problems of obtaining agreement on fundamental basic principles and of reconciling the majority principle with minority rights will always exist in a democratic community. In a country with serious internal and external problems, and with the presence of competing ideologies, the failure to find easy solutions to these problems provokes abundant criticism.

The attack of Barrès and Maurras was typical of the Right in its condemnation of the absence of unity and of discipline, in its demand that unity be dedicated to the power of the state rather than to a Rousseauist conception of general well-being, and in its appeal to a higher entity than the individual. The basic fault in the plea for unity by the two nationalists was the unstated premise that there is a fixed hierarchy for individuals and groups in a rigid, stratified society. Their argument that above all else it was best not to have a pretext for civil war implied that any attempt at change would pose a threat to the well-being, traditions, and institutions of society. Sorel's attack was typical of a disciple of Proudhon, opposing unity imposed from above and advocating multiplicity, change, and conflict as a moral concept, in the belief that the production of an attitude of tension in the community was in itself desirable. The initial fault in Sorel's position was his assumption of the cowardice of government and of the middle class, with the implication that both were condemned to death. But both in fact were lively corpses, and their resistance to working class activity indicated this. Since Sorel, in another connection, himself admitted that *amour propre* was a force in social history that had often been more important than material interests and religious passions, it should have come as no surprise that the middle class would look after its own interests. His plea for an artificial creation of tension became as unnecessary as it was illusory. Moreover, Sorel was wrong in stating, as he did in an early work, that while the worker or peasant was interested in revolutionary traditions, the miracles of Lourdes, the devotion of the Sacré Coeur, the beatification of Joan of Arc interested the bourgeoisie. The crowd at the Gare de Lyon surrounding

171

General Boulanger, animated, as Barrès argued, by national subconscious and obscure ancestral sentiments, could have shown Sorel that tension could be produced by the heritage of the past as well as by the promise of the future.

Their criticisms of the educational system were another manifestation of the illiberalism of the three writers. A liberal education, especially in its classical formulation by Newman, seeks to develop such attributes as freedom, equitableness, calmness, moderation, and wisdom. Implicit are the premises that the acquisition of knowledge is a desirable end in itself, and that education is basically concerned with individual growth. Maurras, Barrès, and Sorel would not approve a liberal education defined in this way, for they believed that education should be motivated as a preparation for a certain task to be undertaken in adult life. In the case of the Nationalists, the purpose of education was to produce a passionate and devoted love of country, and in the case of Sorel, to produce a worker devoted to his work. Pertinent though the criticisms of the educational system by the three writers may have been, the Republic could hardly agree. For both Republicans and their enemies, the school was the symbol of the regime. If, as Ernest Barker said, the educational policy of the Third Republic was the work of M. Lebureau, the official would be most concerned with its lay character. To Ferry, Catholic schools were "schools of counter-revolution where one learns to detest and hate all ideas which are the honor and *raison d'être* of modern France." To end this clerical threat he began the series of educational changes that were the administrative implementation of Gambetta's famous slogan. The proposal of Pochon in the Chamber that no Frenchman be eligible for state employment unless educated in a lay school might have been an extreme measure, but it was an indication that Republicans looked to the lay school for loyalty and that this would normally be forthcoming.

CHAPTER IX

ATTACK ON THE POLITICS
OF THE REPUBLIC

THE political institutions of the Third Republic were subject to sharp attack for numerous reasons, many of which were justifiable. Among the most substantial criticisms were the ineffectiveness of the institutions and the vulgarity of the Republic, the parliamentary disorganization and continual crises, the lack of strong political leaders and the weakness of the office of the President of the Republic, the power of the legislature over the executive, the short-lived administrations, the lack of governmental policy and the power of groups, the absence of a general interest and the presence of pressing private interests, the dishonesty of politicians, the camaraderie of the self-interested politicians, the management of elections and the power of the committees outside Parliament, the continuous pressure of constituents on deputies and the scandals, the unfavorable financial and budgetary situation, and the failure to introduce social reforms.

Maurras, Barrès, and Sorel joined in this onslaught against the regime. They attacked the institutions of the parliamentary system, the party system through which they operated, the personalities of the deputies who were elected and their inefficiency and corrupt natures, the demagoguery of which they made use, and the plutocrats who were the real rulers of the country.

Maurras saw the Republic as nothing but a long list of evils, and he conducted against it what Cormier has called "a 60-year Trojan War."[1] The Republican doctrine was absurd and puerile; the Republican institutions were the last degree of French decadence, the cause and effect of French humiliation. The Republic was an idea and only an idea, corresponding to nothing real, profound, useful, solid, or good.[2]

[1] Aristide Cormier, *La Vie intérieure de Charles Maurras*, Paris, 1955, p. 14.
[2] *Les Princes des nuées*, p. 184.

Because its view on the essential nature of man was so wrong, the Republic was a permanent conspiracy against the public welfare. This conspiracy was even more dangerous because there were no controls on the Republic as there were controls in a monarchical system over the will of the monarch. The Republic was bureaucratic, envious, possessed of little initiative, and responsible for social evils like the fall in the birthrate, deforestation, the growth of alcoholism, and the desiccation of local life.

Maurras regarded the Republic as a regime of discussion for the sake of discussion, and of criticism for the sake of criticism.[3] The regime had no method, no continuity, no stability. The continuous flux of opinions, the routine of the bureaus, the agitations and official parades, the colonial adventures, the operations of parliamentary and financial interests—these sporadic impulses did not make a policy. Parliamentarianism, said Maurras, was not the palladium of liberty. Even corrected by a prince, parliamentarianism would always be the regime of the competition of parties, if not of civil war. It was garrulous, indiscreet, prodigious, halting, and thoughtless. It meant the oppression of minorities. The leaders of parliamentarianism would never represent anything but parties, coteries, personal rivalries, conflicting passions.

Barrès joined in this criticism. The Nationalists were divided on some matters, said Barrès, but they were united in complete disgust for the Republic and for the parliamentary regime in which the Chamber was an ideal place for deceit[4] and for a minority to terrorize the majority. The ignorance, falsehood, and insolence of the parliamentary illiterates were a perpetual insult to French intellectual inheritance.

The Nationalists looked on the Republic as a sickness, and consistently used medical metaphors of decomposition and poison in discussing it. Barrès thought that Boulanger had understood that parliamentarism was a poison of the brain

3 *L'Action française*, November 22, 1912.
4 *L'Appel au soldat*, 1:131.

like alcohol, saturnism, syphilis, and that every Frenchman was intoxicated by the exuberance and vacuity of his verbosity. It was because Boulanger represented the opposition to the parliamentarian regime that Barrès had rallied to him,[5] and Barrès never ceased regretting that machinations with parliamentarianism had led Boulanger to duplicity, alliances, and secret procedures.

It was necessary to put an end to the present institutions, although this was regrettable. Barrès found it pitiable that men who, like himself, were partisans of the need for preserving French ways of life, and who wanted to live in accord with the spirit of eternal France were so often reduced to wishing for revolutionary changes against which their intelligence protested. Nevertheless, reform of the Constitution was the indispensable condition without which those with the best wills would be powerless to serve the individual and society. However, Barrès' program for constitutional reform hardly suggests clarity of thought behind the necessary corrective measures he proposed: referendum, separation of powers, abolition of the Senate, abolition of the office of President of the Republic, or the possibility for the electors to dismiss the head of the executive.

Sorel was opposed not merely to the political institutions of the Republic but to the power of the state in general. All the efforts made by philosophers to moralize the state were in vain. Whenever the power of the state was very great it provoked conspiracies, and parties violently opposed each other in order to steal, massacre, or oppress once they captured the state power. Statism tended to transform the worker into a machine, to stupefy officials, and to look on scientific methods with abhorrence. Sorel explained the prosperity of the United States as due, in spite of the vices of its politicians, to the fact that the state played only a small part in life, while industrial production offered opportunity to men of adventurous spirit.[6] Unlike Barrès, he was opposed to protection

[5] Maurice Barrès, "M. le général Boulanger et la nouvelle génération," *La Revue indépendante* (April 1888), 7:59.

[6] Daniel Halévy, "Un Entretien sur la démocratie," *"Pages libres"* (January 25, 1908), 15:98-100.

of industry or agriculture, so that his economic views were almost pure liberalism. For Sorel, the Republic was simply another of the manifestations of the power of the state that had to be destroyed. He rejected all political institutions, partly because they represented the state power and partly because the economic foundation of society was always more important and ought to be examined before the political. He rejected outright the slogan Maurras used, "Politique d'abord." When man had ascended to a higher culture, the religion of political magic would disappear.

But this rejection by Sorel of the validity of political action was totally misguided if we define "political action" in the realistic fashion that Bertrand de Jouvenel has done, as "action which inclines to his (individual) will the wills of others,"[7] and accept the view that the political process is something much wider and more general than what is commonly denoted by the word *political*. Sorel's attitude to the state was similar to that of Proudhon and Engels. They pleaded for and anticipated the disappearance of political authority. In this way, all discussion of the institutions necessary for fostering the new society became unnecessary and irrelevant. Sorel always saw the state as parasitical, and as unfavorable to production. Admittedly the state had not yet become an instrument in the smooth functioning of the economic system, and Sorel can hardly be criticized for not being at least a precursor of Keynes. But the state was concerning itself increasingly with social legislation, and to this intervention Sorel was not simply benevolently neutral, but overtly hostile. It is for this lack of interest in real social progress that damaging criticism can be made of Sorel.

The criticism that Ascoli made of Sorel is one which can be applied to all the three writers.[8] Looking at modern society as they did, one wonders not why it went so badly, but how, if it had so many buffoons and rascals, it could continue to function at all.

[7] Bertrand de Jouvenel, *Sovereignty*, Chicago, 1957, p. 16.
[8] Max Ascoli, *Georges Sorel*, Paris, 1921.

THE GAME OF POLITICS

Politics are the preoccupation of politicians, and all three writers were contemptuous of politicians. The three attacked the self-interest, the limited capacity, the inefficiency, the demagoguery, the pretence of infallibility, and the harmful consequences that resulted from the activity of politicians. They all assailed bitterly the political and literary figures who supported the regime. For Sorel, Jaurès was "a Sibyllin obscure oracle," a man whose peasant duplicity could be compared to a cattle-dealer, a man who in the Chamber was like a fish in water, Zola "un petit esprit," de Pressensé, "a mediocre scribbler of dull chronicles," Briand "a Boulanger with artistic hairdo, moustache still a little sticky from *apératifs*." There were few old politicians who were not elderly tricksters. For Barrès, Clemenceau was "the little bull with the large breast and the square snout," Ribot "the large hawk on the icy pool," Waldeck-Rousseau was "congealed in his silence like a pike in its jelly," and Zola "a *déraciné* Venetian." Barrès referred to contemporary politicians as frogs, sparrow hawks, bellowing beasts who had escaped from the judicial slaughterhouses, beasts who knew where to find their hay.[9] Caillaux, Briand, and Barthou were three young dogs, vigorous beasts of the same litter, who had formed alliances while playing together in the parliamentary dog kennel. "Look, my child, at these men," said Barrès' character, Mme Thuringe, "and learn to despise them; they are all *canaille*." Barrès proposed that deputies be dipped in the Seine, like dogs being cleaned from fleas.[10] Similarly, the columns of the *Action française* were full of the acrid venom which Maurras unloosed on politicians, and which led at least twice to physical attacks on prominent politicians.

For Sorel, politicians were self-interested, had lost all ideals, and had lowered the moral tone of life. He regarded politicians as people whose interests were singularly sharpened by their voracious appetites, and referred to them as people in whom

[9] *Mes Cahiers*, i:185; viii:61; *Leurs Figures*, p. 6.

[10] Barrès, *Dans le Cloaque*, Paris, 1914, p. 55; *Une Journée parlementaire*, Paris, 1894, p. 83; *L'Appel au soldat*, i:209.

the pursuit of fat jobs had developed the cunning of Apaches. Since they acted only in favor of a group that would support them, they caused a lowering of ethical standards.[11] They entered a deliberative assembly only in the hope of obtaining concessions from their adversaries. Political democracy in fact meant the creation of a special class of politicians who would thrive on the capitalists. Politicians distorted history because, being interested only in the ways of increasing the chances for success of their party, they recognized in history only those aspects that could be utilized in their behalf. They opposed the contemporary social organization only to the extent that it created obstacles to their ambition. They used the word *country* when they needed to develop in the people the tendency to submit to power.

Sorel's most bitter contempt was reserved for the parliamentary Socialists. He wrote to Croce that he "wanted to show how the leaders of socialism work to corrupt the moral tendencies without which socialism can do nothing."[12] Political socialism meant an era of frightful servitude; it could only dishearten men having some sentiment of honor. It is curious to find such a fierce hater as Sorel arguing that "parliamentary Socialists have a doctrine of hate, and that is not true nobility."[13] Sorel enthusiastically quoted Reinach's observation that the parliamentary Socialists tried to deceive the people "by throwing to them every morning monks and priests, just as the Caesars had formerly thrown them bread and circuses."[14] Sorel prophesied that the leaders of the Socialist party would end by becoming a sort of political clergy as harmful to socialism as clericalism was to religion. These leaders had forgotten or abused the idea of revolution. The Socialists, instead of conquering power by a single coup, contented themselves with gaining individual positions which allowed them to play a part in administrative details. They created an electoral clientele, and in the Chamber they

[11] *Reflections on Violence*, pp. 168, 247.
[12] Letter to Croce, October 30, 1903, *La Critica* (1928), 26:34.
[13] *Reflections on Violence*, p. 109.
[14] *La Révolution Dreyfusienne*, p. 42.

solicited favors for their friends and proposed laws likely to please the workers.

In 1902 Sorel was writing that the Socialist sects hoped to reach power and to use the state to make life easier for their friends—every question was reduced to a problem of compromises among the different factions in order that a majority be obtained. He regarded the parliamentary Socialists as inferior thinkers, who spoke of solidarity, but in fact made the compromises that were necessary in parliamentary life. The result was that modern socialism was becoming a more or less confused concept, varying from simple demagoguery to a socialism of professors, the end of which would be the purification of the capitalist regime.[15] But it was noticeable that the degeneration of the movement increased as its members took part in the life of the political institutions of the bourgeoisie. Parliamentary Socialists utilized the strike movement for their own political ends and subordinated proletarian movements to demagogic politics. Strikes became less and less the result of economic questions, and became manipulated by politicians. In 1908 Sorel confessed that he had abandoned his interest in the *Mouvement socialiste*, with which he had been closely associated for three years, because he believed that politicians were using the journal and the syndicalist movement for their own ends.[16]

But it was time to end the revolutions of politicians. Nothing great could come of a working-class movement led by politicians—the working class had to oppose democracy, at least to the extent that it favored the progress of political socialism. One of the results of the Dreyfus Affair had been to direct the Socialist movement in France towards electoral politics, but it had also demonstrated that it was necessary for the working class to turn to syndicalism. The proletariat must refuse to allow itself to be organized into new hierarchies. In carrying out the general strike, it would get rid of all the

[15] Georges Sorel, preface to F. Pelloutier, *Histoire des bourses du travail*, Paris, 1902, p. 16.
[16] Letter to Delesalle, November 2, 1908, in *Lettres à Paul Delesalle: 1914-24*, Paris, 1947.

matters with which the old liberals had been concerned—the eloquence of orators, the handling of public opinion, the combinations of political parties.[17] For the workers, the revolution must be something more than the victory of a party, it must be the emancipation of the producers from political tutelage. Sorel, who always maintained his admiration for the young syndicalist, Pelloutier, praised the men at the head of the syndicalist movement in France, who were not great philosophers, but were men of sense and experience with a distrust of political organizations.

Barrès would not follow Sorel in his denunciation of all politicians and political activity, but he made out an equally strong case against the self-interestedness of politicians. "Parliamentarians have no notion of morality or of personal dignity . . . but are certain that the flock will be well guarded if each guards his own interests."[18] The mind of the deputy was concerned with his re-election, his popularity, his desire to become a minister. Before becoming ministers, deputies remained inactive in order to become ministers; after becoming ministers, they continued to do nothing in order to remain ministers. In the Palais-Bourbon, there was a multitude of sharpers and deceivers . . . a considerable number of *canaille*; an honest man seemed like an imbecile. The dominant law in the Chamber was never to vote according to one's own beliefs or on the questions presented, but always for or against the ministry, and to follow the machinations of the corridors. Candidates entered the Chamber attached to a party and with the resolution to overturn all cabinets without caring about country or the public tranquillity. No deputy except those affiliated to Boulangism was independent enough to displease Parliament.[19]

Yet Barrès himself always had mixed feelings about the Chamber. It was the meeting place of scoundrels, but it was also a forum of excitement, of civil war, that could provide

[17] Sorel, "Le Syndicalisme Révolutionnaire," *Le Mouvement socialiste* (November 1, 1905), 17-167:267.

[18] *Les Déracinés*, II:11.

[19] *Leurs Figures*, pp. 7, 102; *L'Appel au soldat*, I:193.

an appropriate setting for the development of his ego. Talking of Chateaubriand, Lamartine, and Hugo, but thinking of himself, he defended their aloofness in the parliamentary body. As great artists, they had decorated parties; they did not have to mix in the daily intrigues, but were correct in reserving themselves for great occasions.[20]

All the writers agreed that politicians were both inefficient and ineffectual. "Even good people like de Mun, Pelletan, Ribot, Simon," said Barrès, "once in the parliamentary swim, are powerless to utilize the gifts that Providence has given them, and are consumed by the vain agitation of mediocrity."[21] Politics, he told himself, was a very costly pleasure, in money, in time, and in grudges.

In the same way, Sorel could not see the democratic system as anything but inefficient. Led by instincts of destruction, it did not want administrations to function with the regularity that was dear to good employers. A parliamentary regime passed unreasonable laws, distributed money to many parasites, and maintained great economic confusion.

Maurras claimed it was the Dreyfus Affair which made him understand clearly why the Republic was powerless to resolve an affair of state. A great country needed an infinity of decisions and choices to be made, rapid and continuous initiatives to be taken, that were impossible in a republic, a purely critical type of government. The rhythm of democracy necessitated the periodic change of public employees, and this meant absence of continuity. A democratic regime venerated anarchy as its free expression and logical form. The state, the slave of the Chambers, of political parties, of electoral coteries, was also the slave of unforeseen events and of changes of opinion. The government was overburdened by petty functions that would normally be performed by a ceremonial leader. Diplomacy and military affairs, national life and welfare must not depend upon the incompetent. But in the Republic, the chief offices were occupied by lawyers, men

20 Barrès, "Se Prêter, non se donner," *Le Journal,* August 10, 1894.
21 Barrès, "M. le général Boulanger," p. 63.

of the "Bible and the Code," as Barrès had described them.[22]

All three writers felt that demagoguery was one of the main characteristics of the parliamentary system. Maurras commented on the parliamentary humbuggery, the obscurity, uncertainty, and malaise of good minds.[23] Barrès called the parliamentary regime "Blagomachie," a strange system which sought the truth through eloquence and often through barbarian ballets of attitude, gesture, physiognomy, and facial expression. All that the deputies had in common was pugnacity and virtuosity. Sorel complained of demagoguery because it was a sign of mediocrity and because it had a pernicious effect on the proletariat. Demagoguery had ruined all countries it had governed; it generally began to triumph when the first signs of decadence were manifested in a nation, and it increased economic decadence.[24] Democracy was in reality a government of demagogues who talked of utopias rather than showing people the true nature of their activity, and created illusions favorable to their tyranny. Orators would always adopt the politics capable of procuring the most applause in a large assembly. Social democracy was in the last analysis an organization of workers under the direction of vehement orators. It was an oligarchy of demagogues who governed the working class. As the professional haranguers of crowds used words more abundantly, more audaciously and more noisily, the emptier their brains became. The conflicts taking place after the Dreyfus Affair increased the amount of demagoguery in the system. At first in his *L'Avenir socialist des syndicats*, Sorel had hardly distinguished between political and proletarian socialism, but in *Matériaux d'une théorie du prolétariat*, he asserted that proletarian or syndicalist socialism would fully realize itself only if it were a working-class movement directed against demagogues.[25] If the workers remained under the control of demagogues they

[22] *Enquête sur la monarchie*, pp. 126, 213.
[23] *L'Ordre et le désordre*, p. 28.
[24] Sorel, "Socialismes nationaux," p. 55.
[25] *Matériaux*, p. 268.

would never be able to realize their existence as a class. At the same time, France would be lost if demagoguery, supported by philanthropy and the brainless bourgeoisie, became paramount.

THE PARTY SYSTEM

For the two Nationalists, Barrès and Maurras, the party system was the expression and perpetuation of the lack of unity in the state. For Sorel, it was another means by which the intellectuals and the bourgeoisie could maintain their leadership.

Sorel was contemptuous of parties. They were coalitions formed to obtain the advantages which the authority of the State could give, whether their promoters were motivated by hate, sought material profit, or above all, were anxious to impose their will. The party had as its object, in all countries and at all times, the conquest of the State and its utilization in the best interests of the party and its allies.[26] When an individual belonged to a party, he could not see anything beyond what the party was interested in having its members see. The development of associations did not appear capable of limiting the abuse of parties in democracies, because it was difficult for associations to live without political parties. Rousseau would find the existing groups too organized, too servile, the opposite of the democracy of which he dreamed.

Sorel was most caustic at the expense of intellectuals who were the leaders of parties, especially of Socialist parties, and its wealthy women revolutionaries. A party, even a revolutionary one, was nothing but a syndicate of the discontented, a coalition of the poor, at the head of which was a staff composed of lawyers without briefs, doctors without patients, and students of billiards. The development of the Socialist party meant in reality that the proletariat was working to give itself new masters who had no other aim but to imitate ancient royalty. The official leaders of the Socialist party too often resembled sailors who, having never before seen the sea,

[26] *La Décomposition du Marxisme*, pp. 24, 48.

once launched upon it, navigated without knowing how to find their way on a map.[27]

Though Barrès had declared himself unable to belong to any party, and always attacked the dissociation of France, the isolation of individuals and groups struggling in different directions without coordination of efforts, he did make one speech, in April 1914, attacking interest groupings rather than parties. The members of these interest groups, who were connected with financial groups, gave their support momentarily to leaders in order to obtain decorations and favors. It was necessary to put national interest before the camaraderie and the struggle of the groups where *petit papiers* replaced programs. Barrès regarded as undesirable Boulanger's entry into the Chamber and his parliamentary program. He believed that these actions would lead to Boulanger's becoming merely an addition to the existing political parties and would force him to play the same parliamentary game, dissatisfaction with which had brought the nation to him.

For Maurras, the basis of parliamentarianism did not exist in France. There were no parties in the English sense, and parties, in the French sense, were only plunderers who lived on the State. Maurras' masters—de Maistre, Bonald, Comte, Le Play, Fustel, Renan, and Taine—had all enumerated the general characteristics of party government: feebleness and tyranny, continued abuse of force, eternal subjection to fear of falling.[28] The electoral battles were instruments of French division. France was split because those who governed it were not statesmen, but party men. If they were honest, they believed only in the good of the party; if dishonest, in filling their pockets. The political parties were pillaging the State.

The system made for self-interest and for weakness. The so-called Republican elections had been only coalitions of interests, organized by uneasy petty officials. Radicals believed in statism in order to dominate, in anticlericalism in order to pervert, in opportunism in order to avoid being swept away.

27 Sorel, "Le Prétendu socialisme juridique," *Le Mouvement socialiste* (April 1907), 21:336.
28 Charles Maurras, "Les Idées royalistes," *La Revue hebdomadaire* (March 1910), 3:42.

Party government was placed above national government. "Parti" had been substituted for "Patrie." What should be repressed by the law was placed above the law and given the power to administer the law. Party government was the natural enemy of the history of France . . . the party had a school, a press, a public opinion, an opinion which was a lie destined to destroy not only itself but also the country's pride and the nation's will to live.[29] The national interest was being neglected by all parties. Preference was given to internal struggles of parties over external fights against the enemy; the entente with the foreigner was the essential and classical ingredient of the party system. It was necessary to have a government independent of parties and free to operate, politically autonomous and capable of forcing action on others instead of being always forcibly activated by them.

CORRUPTION

All the writers saw corruption as an essential part of a republican political system; indeed, it was from the criticism of the Panama scandal that much of the impetus of the right-wing Nationalist movement developed.

Barrès devoted two whole books and a play to the subject. He argued that the operation of the political system produced a certain parliamentary type, prudent and cunning, the antithesis of the heroic figure, and ever ready to seek his own advantage. At the Palais-Bourbon, theft, so long as there was no scandal, was only a fault against good taste, something that lowered a person in estimation but did not mean party ostracism. No party made any difficulty about admitting a thief if he had sufficient nerve and stomach. In spite of the fact that there was no law in France against guilty ministers, deputies were unwilling to discuss Panama, each fearing to throw light on the shadowy band of criminals.[30]

In a country where, on the one hand, everyone dreamed of becoming an official, and on the other, money was sub-

[29] *Réflexions sur la révolution*, p. 170.
[30] *Leurs Figures*, pp. 8, 17; *L'Appel au soldat*, 1:71.

stituted for moral discipline as the regulator of morals, rich entrepreneurs provided a means of support for the government which they corrupted. In a liberal political system, where barter and blackmail were the rule, the barterers knew the exact price for which a person could be bought, and had a large stock of receipts to prove how successful they were at it. In this way Herz, the evil genius of the Panama scandal, had obtained concessions from the municipal council, from the government, from individuals.

Sorel saw moral and physical corruption in the political system, as he had complained of corruption in the small towns where he had resided as an engineer. Not only was it true that administrations were corrupted to the degree that politics became more democratic,[31] but the corruption was on a broader basis—another example of the decadence in the system. Bourgeois democracy corrupted the people by its vile appetites, its deplorable manners, its frequent imbecility and also bv attempting to obtain the allegiance of the proletariat, which was the only class that could preserve itself from contamination. Thus, a democratic republic corrupted the creative power of the industrial bourgeoisie while at the same time it attempted to deny and to remove desirable conflict among classes. After the Dreyfus Affair, the period 1899 to 1906 was one of corruption and compromise, in which the parliamentary Socialists played a sordid role. "There was a mad scramble for melons, and in the rush the Socialists were not the least cynical." The anticlerical policy that was stressed in those years was a return to the political manners of the 18th century, with a government directed by coteries of courtesans, male and female.[32]

PLUTOCRACY

All three writers took a neo-Marxian view of the real rulers of society, the financial elements.

Sorel was concerned with the undesirable moral effects of financial domination. Democracy was the paradise of which

[31] *Matériaux*, p. 88. [32] *La Révolution Dreyfusienne*, p. 62.

unscrupulous financiers dreamed. In a plutocratic system, economic ideas not only obscured the moral law but also corrupted political principles; of all governments, the worst was that where the rich and the able divided power. The present orientation of the wealthy classes was terrifying to those who believed in the importance of juridical sentiments. The consequence of this domination by the plutocracy meant that their undesirable moral attitude penetrated throughout the system. Shopkeepers had often been reproached for lacking patriotism when they spoke of their horror of war and applauded universal fraternity and humanitarian progress; but it was necessary to understand that they were defending their material interests which were being menaced.[33]

Barrès began his political career by attacking the financial interests supporting the parliamentarians. In 1889 he said, "The opportunists . . . are a financial society organized for the exploitation of France under the Third Republic."[34] To play a political role, Barrès argued, one had to attach oneself to the world of finance; it was the center of influence and of government.[35] France was not really a democracy but a plutocracy, and the crime of the government was that it provided no counterweight to the power of money.

Maurras held that intelligence and opinion were the organs of industry, commerce, and finance, whose help was needed for all work of publicity, library, or the press. Worse than that of a government of the multitude and of numbers, the government of money created derision and crime. Instead of hierarchies and order, instead of the authority of princes of French blood, France had passed under the control of money merchants who were of another skin, that is to say, of another language and of another thought. Only a leader would be able to restrain the power of money; the last obstacle to the imperialism of money, the last fortress of free thought was

[33] *Le Système historique de Renan*, p. 133.
[34] *Courier de l'Est*, January 22, 1889, as cited in J. Rey, "Une Campaigne electorale en 1889," *Candide*, April 30, 1936, p. 5.
[35] *Les Déracinés*, II:4.

justly represented by the Church, the last autonomous organ of pure spirit.[36]

In his political history of France, Bodley argued that the root of the evil lay not in the Republican form of the regime, but in its parliamentary system. Certainly the criticisms that Maurras, Barrès, and Sorel made of this system were often justified. Corruption played too large a part, for the Wilson and Panama scandals were only the two most important of a whole series. In the first scandal, it was disturbing to see that President Grévy was forced to resign for the misdemeanors of his son-in-law. It was even more disturbing that while MacMahon, embodiment of the old regime in the Elysée, came out of power poorer than when he had entered, Grévy had emerged richer.[37] In the Panama scandal, the whole parliamentary world, as Barrès said, was devoured by a cancer of rage and fear. Yet, apart from Clemenceau, Proust, and de la Fauconnerie, all the deputies compromised in the Panama scandal were re-elected, while those who had been most opposed—Déroulède, Millevoye, and Delahaye—were defeated. To the extreme Right, Parliament was a "great Begging Order of the nineteenth century," ruling over clients, not citizens.

Lack of strongly held convictions meant that the typical politician was the compromiser, the man who was to be found in the corridors during the crises, and not the strong man. Gambetta who, "coming into a room could raise its temperature by ten degrees," was turned out of office in 1882 and Ferry in 1885. To keep Ferry out of the Elysée, combinations were formed and the dark horse, Sadi-Carnot, by no means deserving Clemenceau's unkind gibe, "the most stupid," was chosen. With poetic justice, Clemenceau himself, the destroyer of ministries, was to be kept out of office for many years, and was never to gain the presidency. Instead, Paul Deschanel, of whom it was said that if he ever formed a cabinet, it would be a cabinet de toilette, was chosen.

[36] *L'Avenir de l'intelligence,* pp. 13, 44, 77; *Mes Idées politiques,* p. 136.

[37] Daniel Halévy, *La République des comités,* p. 43.

188

The great difficulty, as Clemenceau said, was that most of the parliamentarians wanted to be ministers, and sacrifices, especially of principle, would be made to this end. The career of Briand was a series of betrayals, from revolutionary sydicalist and leading exponent of the general strike to a follower of Jaurès and a member of the Socialist party to a Radical ministerial position from which he was in contact with the Catholics. More than one minister, like Goblet defending the maintenance of the Concordat which he had attacked, quickly changed their views. In the Parliament of 1900 there were more than 200 ex-ministers. Politicians of all parties retained their seats for considerable periods, Mackau for fifty years, Brisson from 1871 until his death, Ribot from 1878 until he entered the Senate, and Deschanel from 1885 until he was elected President. Sarrien, known in Parliament as "la vieille bête," was a deputy from 1876 to 1908, and a senator from 1908 until his death.

But the insuperable problem was the weakness of executive authority. The continuous series of cabinet crises was due to the multiplicity of groups, to the lack since the 16th of May of executive discretion to dissolve the Chamber, to the power of the Senate being greater and more crippling than had originally been intended, to the power of the parliamentary commissions, to the feebleness of the presidential office, the extent of local influence especially through the *cumul de mandats*, and to the extra-parliamentary action of the political parties.

Ineffectiveness or lack of policy was largely the result of the controlling power of the deputies. Omnipotent, affecting administration, annihilating ministries, imposing its wishes on its agents, members of the Chamber could appear as "Banquo terrifying the ministers of the Republic."[38] Intervention by individual members over acts of the administration, and the indiscriminate use of interpellations wasted time and gave rise to intrigues and combinations. From 1902 to 1906 there were 262 requests for interpellations, of which as

[38] Henry Leyret, *La Tyrannie des politiciens*, p. 65.

many as 140 were actually discussed. From June 1910 until November 1911, of 232 requests, 108 were discussed. In the slow legislative procedure, the committees became all-important, often heirs apparent of ministers, or like the finance committee, "wreckers of ministers." In the great permanent committees of the Chamber, Poincaré saw the origin of enfeebled government.

The result of the political maneuvering and the lack of principle was the short negative ministries. From October 1885 to May 1914, there were 42 ministries, many of them upset on trivial issues in which no matter of policy was involved. In 1892, Loubet fell because of an autopsy refused on someone involved in the Panama scandal, in 1894 Casimir-Périer fell because of the refusal to allow some employees of state railroads to attend a labor union congress. There never was a homogeneous ministry based on a homogeneous majority. The difficulty that Bourgeois had in finding a Foreign Minister when he was attempting to obtain a homogeneous Radical administration was a disillusioning experience.[39]

Every Prime Minister had to give up measures he wanted and support those he did not want. Clemenceau had been appalled when Gambetta entered into negotiations with the new Pope, Leo XIII, and with German representatives, but he in his turn was to carry out a policy of "facility." A Prime Minister looked to his colleagues, not for competence, but for ability to make combinations. Brisson and his "cabinet of concentration" of Radicals and Moderates made the Chamber adopt the very motions proposed by Jules Ferry to which it had just refused its vote. A Cabinet was a political, not an efficient administrative, body; the Prime Minister a person of oratorical skill, not a man of action.

But the disturbing nature of the system was ameliorated to some extent by the continuity of individual ministers, the same ministers being actors who came before the public after having changed costume in the wings. Yet even this can be overemphasized. From 1875 to 1913 there were only seven

39 J. D. Hargreaves, "Entente Manquée: Anglo-French Relations 1895-96," *Cambridge Historical Journal* (1953), 11:73.

cabinets not containing members of a preceding ministry. Often over half were retained; in three, eight out of ten remained. But the fact that there were, between 1871 and 1929, 82 cabinets and 349 ministers would seem to indicate, taking 12 as the average number in a ministry, that each served on an average about two and a half to three times. However, 132 ministers served only one term, 79 two terms, and 54 three terms.[40]

Political difficulties were also overcome by the rally to the Republic in vital moments, the organization of effective political machinery, and by stability in other institutions. The German Ambassador at the time of Panama remarked that the Loubet-Ribot Ministry which fell in the Panama Canal had been revived in the form of the Ribot-Loubet Ministry. Between 1899 and 1910, there were only six ministries, three of which lasted over two years, and one of which resigned without being defeated.

From 1899 to 1905, the Bloc des Gauches kept the Republic together after the Affair. Its steering committee, the Délégation des Gauches, composed of delegates from the four groups forming the ministerial majorities in which Jaurès was the leading influence, stopped internal disputes, maintained a common policy, ensured the easy transfer of power from Waldeck-Rousseau to Combes, and claimed the Presidency of the Chamber and two Vice-Presidents.[41] Until its dissolution in 1905 it offered a salutary example of coherent democratic politics. But it took on itself the role of initiative and of direction which must belong to the ministry. It even laid the groundwork for the 1906 Clemenceau Government, promising to govern with "l'esprit socialiste," setting up a Ministry of Labor, appealing to Viviani and Briand, and generally oriented to the Left.

Continuity was also assured in other ways. The prefects were a fixed part of the political landscape—the behavior of

[40] John G. Heinberg, "The Personnel of French Cabinets 1871-1930," *American Political Science Review* (May 1931), 25:389-396.

[41] R. A. Winnacker, "The Délégation des gauches," *Journal of Modern History* (December 1937), 9:449-470.

Anatole France's M. Worms-Clavelin, who survived all ministries, and would even remain under a monarchy—may not be typical, but it is indicative. Philippe Berthelot remained a power at the Quai d'Orsay under many ministers. Jusserand served in Washington for almost twenty years. Eugène Etienne, Under-Secretary for the Colonies, had a great influence on most measures for Morocco and the Empire in general. In twenty years, there was hardly a change in the three Directors of Public Instruction who held among them the three offices of primary, secondary, and superior education. The whole administrative framework endured—the Conseil d'Etat, the Corps des Ponts-et-Chaussées, the Mines, inspection of finance, universities, diplomatic corps.

When all just criticism has been allowed, the criticism of Maurras, Barrès, and Sorel is seen to be unfair. They complained both that the Republic could not exert authority and also that it was a regime of intolerable authoritarianism. They complained that the Republic could do nothing, but attacked it when it began acquiring a large colonial empire. They attacked Delcassé fiercely although his anti-German orientation was as strong as their own. Although it was the heavy military expenditure that caused budgetary difficulties, the three were unwilling to admit that this was the price that had to be paid for a strong France. A regime liberal, with well-made laws, but deficient in dealing with social matters, the Republic was after all the first regime in France since Louis XV that had lasted over 30 years.

CHAPTER X

THE WEAKNESS OF THE REPUBLIC

THE THREE WRITERS directed much criticism at the weaknesses of France. According to them it was weak internally because of the division of opinion in the country. Externally, it was weak in relation to the growing strength of other countries.

The Nationalists, Barrès and Maurras, were keenly aware of the reduction in glory in relation to France's past, and were afraid that she had become a second-class power. For Barrès, this was inevitable in a parliamentary system which not only lacked leadership but also kept France weak. In this it was self-interested; it dreaded a victory in Alsace-Lorraine more than anything, since the system could not last in the face of a victorious army.[1] Because the country lacked leadership and was "divided and headless," it had mistaken its direction, and there were anarchy and disorganization in the country as a whole as well as in the Palais-Bourbon.[2] The tragedy of France lay in the fact that it lacked a great man. Barrès urged that it was necessary to have a man who was above parties, one who was the expression of the needs of the country and able to lead it out of its demoralized condition. Opposed to monarchy, but calling himself an adherent of dictatorship, he looked to the man "who will represent, who will unite in himself, the different groups, who will be the national man, the general delegate, the leader."[3]

His first book, *Sous l'oeil des barbares*, had ended with an appeal to the supreme figure: "Thou alone, O master, if you exist somewhere, axiom, religion, or prince of man." Even if the leader had feet of clay, as General Boulanger did, the need remained, and other Boulangisms would follow. The force of Boulangism rested on ancestral concepts, hereditary sentiments, on the national conscience. It was part of the effort made by the nation, whose nature had been transformed by the intrigues of foreigners, to recover its true direction. And

[1] *Scènes*, p. 299.   [2] *Mes Cahiers*, ix:211.   [3] *Les Déracinés*, p. 258.

193

it was also a moral discipline through which national energy would be recreated. But above all, "What one asks of General Boulanger is first to serve as a soldier, and to see to the recapture of Metz and Strasbourg."[4] In this way, one would know that there had not been a definitive acceptance of the humiliating Treaty of Frankfurt.

Maurras agreed with Barrès that the division of the country was disastrous and that a leader was sorely needed. Both the writers had regarded the Dreyfus Affair as an important cause of the division of the country. Barrès argued that the Affair had been invented and manipulated in order to make use of antimilitary and internationalist doctrines, with the result that the higher officers had been discredited and the army enfeebled.[5] For Maurras, the price paid to establish the innocence of Dreyfus was too high. The capitulation of April 1905 was the result of the disorder into which the authors of the Dreyfus Affair had thrown the military, naval, political, and moral forces of the *pays légal*.[6] He went even further and argued that "we can imagine greater horrors than the life imprisonment of a presumably innocent man—an army vanquished, corpses lying by the thousands, a four-year war and 1,700,000 deaths."[7]

Internal quarrels, Maurras said, led to inertia. The Constitution of the Third Republic divided and enfeebled the state militarily at the same time that it centralized the state and stretched its diminished powers to the limit. This was demonstrated by the fact that Marchand had been beaten not at Fashoda, where victory was possible, but in Paris, where it was not. The lack of the stabilizing influence of a powerful supreme leader, coupled with the fact of a divided government, meant that no Frenchman could act as Bismarck had done at Ems, or was capable of working without consultation.

Moreover, in these internal struggles, politicians played with the greatest secrets of foreign affairs in the country. A discussion on foreign affairs was still regarded in the Palais-Bourbon as a tournament of academicians, who, with heads

4 *L'Appel au soldat*, ii:61, 148.   5 *Scènes*, p. 66.
6 *Kiel et Tanger*, p. 10.   7 *Au Signe de Flore*, pp. 69-70.

in the clouds, had no relation to the business in hand. This lack of realism had unhappy results. Regimes since the Revolution had lost French territory and humiliated the country. They had cost the country Flanders, Artois, and Alsace, a hundred years of European supremacy, the empire on sea and land. The Revolution itself had led to Trafalgar, Waterloo, Sedan, Fashoda, Tangier, and Agadir.[8]

The history of the Republic and of the Empire since the Revolution had been one of invasion and abasement, civil, religious, and moral agitation. By 1914, the follies of the Republic had led to six invasions in 125 years, and of these, it was noticeable that none had occurred under the regimes of Louis XVIII, Charles X, and Louis-Philippe. Under the Bourbons, the farthest a foreign invasion had reached was Corbie, in 1636, and from then until the Revolution there had been no great invasions. What was Pavia, what was Rosbach, in comparison with Sedan or Waterloo? Since the Revolution, the state had been bankrupted, Paris entered three times, and two civil wars had taken place—and all this during a period which had seen Italian and German unity and the inordinate increase of the Anglo-Saxon empire.

The regime created weakness on all sides—lack of discipline and demoralization among the people, and neglect of building a navy, army, and police force. From 1900 to 1912 the army, navy, and diplomacy were organs of state condemned to obsolescence and already out of date. Before the Revolution, France had been an equal of Britain on the sea, but the present regime, without either a great minister or a great hereditary king, could not provide a strong navy. The Minister of War methodically disorganized the armies and Parliament gave its fullest approval to the ministerial general who reduced all military expenditure. The Dreyfus Affair had disorganized the general staff and destroyed the French Information Service.

The historic role of France was to forge ahead as leader or as guide, but under the Republic, this was forbidden. How

[8] *L'Action française*, September 27, 1912.

could one compare the politics of the French Republic since Sedan to the politics of the Prussian monarchy since Jena?[9] Russia could have a policy, but France could not, and was condemned to fill the worthless office of satellite to the Czar during those times when she was not a satellite to a system of superior powers. Never had political France been so small.

Maurras attacked every policy undertaken by the Republic, the alliance with Russia as well as the acquisition of a colonial empire. Once he had thought that "the Crown of Russia, after the most unfortunate of wars (1905) still proved by the vigor and the seriousness of its defense what resource there was in its principle."[10] Hindsight told him that Russia was an uncertain, expensive ally, open to the enemy because of its courtesans, its intellectuals, its revolutionaries, and its Jews. His argument in *Kiel et Tanger* that it was possible to defeat Germany without the aid of the British, Russians, or Italians was correctly described by Jules Cambon as utter idiocy.

Maurras held that the colonies raised problems of their own. France did not have enough ships to defend or even to visit them, and these overseas territories did nothing but become objects of passionate envy. Properly speaking, there was no negligence in colonial policy because there was nothing that one could even call a plan. This very weakness of France in diplomatic planning created dangers of its own. Since foreign policy was forbidden to the Republic, the regime was condemned to irritating maneuvers, dangerous for the integrity of the country and the independence of the inhabitants.[11] Great issues were neglected and excessive attention paid to small questions. All true ideas of patriotism were being lost.

Perhaps the greatest danger of all under the Republic was that of war. Democracy was both incapable of making war and incapable of avoiding it. In fact the greater the influence of the people on politics, the greater the danger of war. Maurras thought that peace depended, not on the rulers of France, but on the foreigner, and would last as long as it pleased

9 *Enquête sur la monarchie*, pp. 2, 301, 496; *Kiel et Tanger*, p. 14.
10 *La Démocratie religieuse*, p. 85.
11 *Kiel et Tanger*, pp. 11, 29.

the rivals of France to prolong the state of peace. But at the same time, he held that the *mystique* of 1789 and of 1793 had led to wars contrary to the general interest of the country. Léon Bourgeois, "un sot calibré," was the person most responsible both for spilling French blood and for so many deaths during the 1914-1918 war, because he had prevented France from arming.[12] Perhaps 100,000, perhaps 500,000 young Frenchmen would have been alive if Bourgeois had not existed. The Third Republic, applying itself more and more to maintaining peace at any price, even that of disarmament, had led to four years of a great war. Without conscious or unconscious irony, Maurras argued that France for a hundred years had been living, or rather, dying of democracy.

The only way for the country to survive was to adopt the laws, customs, procedures of those opposing the regime. The sentiment of *la revanche* had kept France united for a long time and maintained respect for a rended, humiliated flag above all the French party divisions. The choice for France now was between disappearance as a great power and re-establishment of a true monarchy, with the King of France as the arbiter of the peace of the world.

In some respects the Nationalist attack was justified, for the Radicals had sadly neglected foreign affairs. There were few debates on the subject; between 1898 and 1902 when the Dreyfus Affair was at its height, there was not one important debate.[13] In the sixteen years before 1914, only two members of the Radical-Socialist party, Bourgeois for a few weeks and Doumergue just before the war, occupied the Quai d'Orsay. In this political vacuum, the colonial pressure group exerted a large influence, and since many of the group were masons—the Café Petite Vache was the main rendezvous of colonialists and masons—there was a double reason for the attacks of Maurras.

The Right in fact merged its internal and external enemies. Colonial politics suffered because of the personal quarrel with

[12] *Les Princes des nuées*, p. 384.

[13] B. Leaman, "The Influence of Domestic Policy on Foreign Affairs in France 1898-1905," *Journal of Modern History* (December 1942), 14:449-479.

Ferry, who was both Minister, and the author of Article 7 restricting religious schools. When Ferry was overthrown in March 1885, revenge was taken on the anticlerical through the Colonial Minister. For Maurras and Barrès it became an act of impiety to substitute Tonkin or Madagascar for Alsace and Lorraine. For them, all issues of foreign and colonial policy were considered almost exclusively as they bore on the dominant factor of the German menace.

THE ENEMY WITHOUT

A marked characteristic of the philosophy of the Right is xenophobia. It was therefore in character that Maurras and Barrès concentrated their powers of vehement denunciation against foreigners. Even on a personal level, relations with the foreigner were undesirable. Barrès' heroine, Colette Baudoche, perceived that "between her and [the German soldier] M. Asmus, it was not a personal question, but a French one." Barrès' advice, in a prize-giving speech on June 24, 1904, to the girls in a Lorraine orphanage, was "to turn your friendship toward the boys who live in the country of your parents.[14]

The premise behind this hatred of the foreigner was that France was the apex of the civilization of the world, which was now being threatened. Maurras saw civilization as Mediterranean. In a famous contrast between Maurras and Péguy, Halévy said of the former that he was "a man of the Mediterranean, whose mind conceived clear-cut forms to which death would put an end.[15] Maurras himself admitted that the sun of Provence was in his veins.[16] His demand for simplicity and purity and his scale of hierarchical values extended to nations and cultures as to other phenomena. These values, of which classicism was the expression, were threatened by cosmopolitanism, which Maurras regarded as a confused mixture of nationalities, threatening to lead not to an intelligent and reasonable federation of modern peoples, but to vague

[14] *Colette Baudoche*, pp. 252, 266.
[15] Daniel Halévy, *Péguy et les cahiers de la quinzaine*, New York, 1947, pp. 132-136.
[16] Aristide Cormier, *La Vie intérieure de Charles Maurras*, p. 63.

THE WEAKNESS OF THE REPUBLIC

disorders. He argued that the realistic, as opposed to the idealistic view of change led not to peace but to war, not to cosmopolitanism but to national retrenchment, not to universal democracy but to rival aristocracies.

Whatever was foreign to classical literature, both to the common Hellenic-Latin treasure and to great French writing, Maurras called barbarian.[17] This was reinforced by personal experience. During his voyage to Greece, he had felt that barbarian languages such as German and English, particularly in the American version, accorded badly with a setting as delightful as Athens, the source of civilization. A few individuals were exempt from this severe castigation. There were some "romanized barbarians" who had a feeling for the art of writing and who, like Liebniz, Goethe, Heine, Schopenhauer, and Nietzsche, knew how to direct and to develop their thoughts.[18]

That Maurras was so virulent does not disguise the fact that many of his own associates were keenly interested in German culture. Pujo and Daudet, fluent in German, were ardent Wagnerians. Bainville was the author of a biography of Louis II of Bavaria. Vaugeois was a Kantian, and Lasserre wrote a preface to extracts from Goethe. "We have all played with German philosophy on coming out of school or college," confessed Maurras, "but Barrès is truly one of the first to free himself."[19] Barrès, in fact, in spite of an early flirtation with Wagner, and in spite of his frequent allusions to Goethe, rejected German culture, as Blum said,[20] because of his Latin taste, Western taste, meridional taste, and his detestation of the man of the north.

The two Nationalists believed that France was in danger, partly because Frenchmen had opened the gates to foreigners or supported their actions, and partly because foreigners were continuously conspiring against France.

[17] *Prologue d'un Essai sur la critique*, p. 85.

[18] Maurras, "L'Annexion intellectuelle," *Gazette de France*, July 29, 1895, as cited in Roudiez, "Charles Maurras: The Formative Years," p. 214.

[19] *L'Action française*, December 10, 1923.

[20] Léon Blum, *Oeuvres I*, p. 81.

Maurras criticized all his political opponents for ignoring the national problem. The national problem was the key to all others, the strategic position commanding all other French problems. Socialists, liberals, Radicals—all were condemned for having turned their back on the national problem. All of them, moreover, had been of assistance to Germany. The clemency of the two Napoleons toward Germany was one of the most potent explanations of Prussian success and German fortune. The liberal parties at all times were the friends of Germany, and even of Prussia; all the liberal literature of the 19th century from Thiers to Michelet was infected with Prussianism. Democracy, whether under the Girondins, Napoleon, or the 19th century liberals, was the greatest external builder of German unity.[21] Democracy and Germany together proclaimed their insolent rights to empire. The Socialists also were at fault. The most vulnerable point of Jaurès was not his Republican democratic ideas, but rather the foolish foreign policy undertaken because of his incurable friendship with Germany. The campaign of Jaurès against the commemoration of the 75th anniversary of Fustel de Coulanges showed that it was the spirit of Germany, the true country of his heart, that animated and stirred him.[22]

German influence was being manifested everywhere: in Monod teaching history, in Croiset in letters, in Lachelier in philosophy, in Jaurès in the political world. The international Socialist council, dominated by Germans and Belgians, had established its authority over the French proletariat. The defense of the revolutionary point of view in France was bound to a defense of the whole German system. Barrès and Maurras both agreed that Kantism was the religion of the Third Republic.

Both clericalism and anticlericalism were active on behalf of Germany. The condemnation of his works to the Index in 1914, Maurras insisted, was due to falsification by the German Secretary of the Congregation of the Index. Even Sicilian politics were imposed by Rome on the French, for

21 *Le Procès Maurras*, Paris, 1946, p. 59.
22 *Pour un jeune Français*, p. 127; *Les Princes des nuées*, p. 344.

it was to the Sicilian Cardinal Rampolla that the initiative for the politics of the *Ralliement* must be attributed. The anticlericalism of Gambettism, encouraged and paid for by Bismarck, separated France from Vienna and the Vatican. William II was supporting the anticlerical movement in order to stop the efforts of the French diplomats and soldiers in North West Africa.[23]

Barrès, the Lorrainer who never forgot the 1870 invasion—the Alsatians living in terror, the hostages, the burned houses, the war taxes,[24] the Uhlans, revolvers in hand, entering his town—and who remembered that his father and grandfather had been taken hostages to prevent the French from firing on German troop trains, was always the eight-year old on the road from Mirecourt. Wagner, Nietzsche, the excellent administrative system of the Germans counted little compared with the humiliation of the invasion. Barrès' unswerving and dominating political idea was the recapture of Metz and Strasbourg. As early as 1884 he was writing of "our special task, to recover the stolen territory," and he always believed that French resistance to Germanization was a matter of organic necessity.[25] Not without reason Léon Daudet once called him "the watchman of the frontier." It was galling to Barrès that the German edition of Zola's *La Débâcle* had sold heavily, and that it showed a German soldier standing on the French flag. But it was also a question of understanding the Germans in order to be shielded from their attractiveness, in the same way France was warned against the dangers of opium and morphine. To this end, therefore, Barrès warned of the legends of Germany, which were violent and horrible, marked, like the story of Tristan and Isolde, by an enthusiasm for suicide.

Both Barrès and Maurras were ambivalent in their appreciation of the relative dangers of Germany and Britain. Maurras attacked Hanotaux for being pro-German and Delcassé for being pro-British. Germany, England, international socialism,

23 *Quand les français,* p. 79; *Enquête sur la monarchie,* pp. LV, 194.
24 *Mes Cahiers,* x:209.
25 *L'Appel au soldat,* ii:75; *Les Amitiés françaises,* p. 24.

all were conspiring against France; Maurras never decided which was the greatest danger and most serious threat to French national interests. An example of this threat was the Dreyfus Affair. Sorel had been disappointed by the results of the Affair, and had wondered whether it had not been the result of a German plot, in which the prestige of the French high command was to be destroyed. Certainly, he felt Germany had organized a great agitation around Dreyfus.[26] In the same way, Maurras alternatively chose England and Germany as prime mover in the Affair. English guineas had operated for Dreyfus against the Méline-Hanotaux cabinet.[27] The advisers of Queen Victoria had plotted during the Affair in order to stop Marchand in East Africa.

If the French universally submitted themselves to German influences, Maurras wrote, their Anglomania also contradicted the course of French development. The Republic was abased before England and was being manipulated by her. The parliamentary committees had easily become playthings of Edward VII, with his cigars and dinners.[28] The very blood in the regime was British, for parliamentarianism—government by the Chambers, or rather, by one Chamber—was an institution that was born English and had remained so despite transplantation.

England had fomented the Revolution by gaining command of the seas during the reign of Louis XVI, had provoked the 1830 and 1848 uprisings, had instigated the Second Republic, and had subsidized the series of intrigues and conflicts leading to the Third Republic. Perfidious Albion indeed. England was the nation that had profited most from the disasters of the French Revolution and the continental divisions that followed it. It is paradoxical that Maurras' only mention of Burke was as "an enemy of France."

In spite of his enthusiasm for monarchy, and although he spoke of England as being as antidemocratic as it was possible to be—aristocratic, traditional, adapted to government—

26 *La Révolution Dreyfusienne*, pp. 5-6.
27 *La Démocratie religieuse*, pp. 338-339.
28 *Kiel et Tanger*, p. 161; *L'Action française*, September 16, 1909.

Maurras refused to learn the British art of adapting monarchy to contemporary conditions. The reason was partly that England was not only the foreigner but also the northerner, and therefore the non-Mediterranean.

THE ENEMY WITHIN

Barrès, Maurras, and Sorel felt that the strangers within France were as dangerous as those without. All three writers had attacked the plutocrats, the real rulers of a democracy, and all continued by attacking the foreign element in the economy, the international financiers, and the oligarchy of money. The specter of international finance was haunting France. The Rothschilds, favorite symbol in 1890 as in 1930, were the true masters of modern society. All three writers agreed with the sentiment of Barrès: "If the state is not the powerful master, it is the slave of the bank; no middle ground is possible."

But the attack was not limited to financiers. As early as his first electoral program in Nancy in 1889, Barrès was aware of the problem of foreigners, foreign goods and workers, and part of his program was directed toward this problem. Politically, the opportunist system which discriminated against Frenchmen in favor of Jews, foreigners, and cosmopolitans was to be ended. Economically, there was to be protection against both foreign competition and foreign workers, passage from the old liberalism to general protectionism. Stringent restrictions were to be put on the employment of foreigners— a tax on all foreign labor in France, a tax on all French employers using foreign labor, the deportation of all indigent foreign laborers, a refusal to allow foreign capitalists to own land, property, or businesses in France, a refusal to allow French laborers to work abroad. Terror ought to be used against speculators; Jews ought to be deprived of political rights.[29]

Barrès was equally harsh to the newcomers in French life. He said, "A nation is a group of men united by common

[29] *Scènes,* II:157-167.

legends, traditions, habits in the same milieu during a more or less long time."[30] Therefore, naturalization was only a legal fiction which allowed a person to obtain the advantages of a nation without giving him its character. The naturalized, influential Alfred Edwards, with whom he disputed so fiercely, Barrès refused to regard as a citizen. "He remains a foreigner although we facilitate his stay among us." Barrès saw the Dreyfus Affair as an example of the danger of allowing political influence to those too recently naturalized, who did not have French secular interests at heart.

Exceptions would of course be made for friendship or for political reasons. Stanislas de Guita, the school friend with whom Barrès had recited the poetry of Baudelaire, whose grandfather had served in the wars of the First Empire and had acquired French nationality, was a satisfactory candidate for admission to the French nation. Even more important, the fact that the mother of Boulanger was a Scotswoman from Aberdeen was conveniently forgotten. Barrès even greatly admired one *déracinée*, Marie Bashkirtseff, "the cosmopolitan who belonged neither to heaven nor earth nor society," and whom he called "Notre-Dame du Sleeping Car."[31]

Included among the newcomers were the Jews and Protestants, and Barrès decried the fact that the parliamentarians were giving to the Jewish and Protestant minorities a favored place in the system. The Reinach family, of German descent, was allowed to insult a French general, born a Breton.[32] In spite of all the advantages they had obtained, Reinach and Herz, these foreigners raised by parliamentarianism from the lowest depths to the heights, refused to be satisfied by the benefits and honors, monstrous and contrary to public welfare and to laws, that they had received. Commenting on "the millionaire traitor Dreyfus," Barrès agreed with his mentor, Jules Soury, director of studies at the Ecole des Hautes-Etudes, on the danger of foreigners who, "once installed in

[30] *La Cocarde*, October 1894, as cited in A. Zévaès, *Notes et souvenirs d'un militant*, Paris, 1913, pp. 225-226.
[31] *Trois stations de psychothérapie*, p. 47.
[32] *L'Appel au soldat*, II:84.

France, work to transform the national conscience according to their own sentiments . . . Déroulède is put in jail, while Dreyfus has a gay villa at Vaucluse."[33]

Barrès regarded the Dreyfus Affair as a battlefield where a Frenchman, inheritor of the tradition of his earth and dead, had to accept the challenge of the naturalized and of foreigners. The Dreyfus syndicate was attempting to sacrifice a French general to the coalition of financiers and spies. "We are with the flag" against the band of politicians, the governmental world enslaved to Judaism and composed for the most part of notorious traitors who would not let Dreyfus be condemned. Barrès confessed himself struck by the fact that the Protestant friends of Dreyfus came from Alsace.[34] The disorder in the country was created by imported truths— useful truths were drawn only from French foundations. The danger was equally acute in daily life. France was being cosmopolitanized. There were Neapolitan gypsy songs in the restaurants and the cafes. A true government would banish them and would substitute French songs. It would purge the language of the foreign words that had crept into it.

With this analysis, Maurras completely agreed. The declaration of the Ligue d'Action Française of 1905, for which he was partly responsible, categorically stated, "The Republic in France is the reign of the foreigner. . . . It is necessary to give France a regime that is French." Maurras believed foreigners were using social institutions, moral ones like the school and the press, material ones like the soil and money, to get rid of French values. A bad government, too favorable toward foreigners, left the task of defending common interests to the individual. A good government, one taking the national interest as its political guide, would make it unnecessary for its nationals to be unsociable toward foreigners. It would protect national industry and act not only against the industry and work of the foreigners, but also against the cosmopolitan speculators established in France.

[33] Jules Soury, *Une Campagne nationaliste*, Paris, 1902, p. 79.
[34] *Mes Cahiers*, ii:157; iii:228.

The foreign elements within France made up "an international cluster of public powers,"[35] from the real rulers—the forces of oligarchy and money—to the leaders of the Socialist movement. This meant that the French Republic was in fact much more Republican than French. Writing in 1903, Maurras stated that the French parties had been defeated by the political forces of the foreigner in 1877, 1881, 1885, 1889, 1893, 1898, 1902, to speak only of legislative battles.[36] Every increase in the powers of central authority would be put to the profit and service of the foreigner. On reading of the vast number of defeats suffered, one wonders how the "French parties" of Maurras were able to survive and how they were capable of emerging ready for the next, seemingly inevitable, defeat.

But who were these foreigners, this disciplined and organized international elite in the Republic, this powerful army in the confused multitude that was France? They were the four *Etats Confédérés*, the masons, cosmopolitan and servile; the Protestants, Swiss, English, and Germans who influenced through their thought; the Jews, who were powerful through their money; and the *métèques*, who connived, and of whom the Monod family was a good, or a bad, example.

In December 1894, in an article in Barrès' journal, *La Cocarde*, Maurras introduced the word "métèque" into the French language (it was officially admitted by the Academy in 1927), meaning by it a recently domiciled or naturalized guest or his children—someone like the father of Gambetta, Steeg, Spuller, Waddington. An opponent like the philosopher Parodi was "un métèque crétois." The Monod family was attacked most viciously because it was a large, successful, and influential one.[37] When in 1905 Gabriel Monod, lecturer at the Ecole Normale and Professor of the College of France, attempted to prevent the official commemoration of the 75th anniversary of Fustel de Coulanges, Maurras and the Action Française opposed and defeated him. To fight the *métèques*,

[35] *"Les Idées royalistes,"* p. 47.
[36] *La Démocratie religieuse,* p. 61.
[37] *Pour un jeune français,* p. 29; *Au Signe de Flore,* pp. 155-240.

Maurras supported a bill to exclude all those not having three generations of French ancestors from holding public office.

But, as Barrès had made an exception for his friend de Guita, so Maurras similarly excused Jean Moréas, because he was a guest, respectful of French language and taste, not one of those who had opened the gates to the aesthetics of Wagner, the ethics of Ibsen, the politics of Tolstoy. In general, with young doctors losing their practices and young workers losing their jobs because of the competition of these newcomers, Maurras was firmly convinced that charity began at home.

Masonry, a secret society with its tentacles all over the country, exploited the country to its profit. The lodge was in control of Parliament, and to be antimasonic was to be antiparliamentary. In 1899 Maurras had called masonry the only constituted oligarchy, but later, due to the large number of masons in political life, he came to the conclusion that it was the only one of the four *Etats Confédérés* whose domination was possible.[38] Cosmopolitan by its nature, masonry was successfully infiltrating revolutionary ideas into France.

Maurras and all the Right attributed a pernicious influence to the masonic movement. "We shall lack the key to many matters as long as the proceedings of the masonic bodies remain unpublished," wrote the publicist of *L'Action française*, Jacques Bainville.[39] A considerable number of politicians were masons. In the 1880's practically every Cabinet included some masons and after the early 1890's sometimes over half of the members.[40] The Bourgeois Government of 1896 contained eight in its ten members. At least thirteen Prime Ministers were masons. In 1903 Combes, then Prime Minister, sent a message of good wishes to the meeting of the masonic general assembly.

The masonic leaders were figures of political importance. Almost all the Presidents of the Council of the Order of the Grand Orient held political posts, as did some of the Grand

[38] *Enquête sur la monarchie*, p. 255.
[39] Jacques Bainville, *La Troisième République*, Paris, 1935, p. 11.
[40] Mildred J. Headings, *French Freemasonry under the Third Republic*, Baltimore, 1949, p. 79.

Masters of the Grand Lodge. The Grand Orient, moreover, was supposed to have an official delegate to the Prime Minister, Lelarge under Combes. Masons played a large part in the proposal of legislation, in the fall of governments, in the influence of administration. It was said that in a critical vote on November 8, 1900, Brisson, hands raised above his head, had given the masonic sign of distress. There was a close correlation between the subjects discussed in the masonic assemblies, and in the Radical and Radical-Socialist party congresses. All over the country, argued Anatole France's character, the Abbé Lantaigne, the prefect "had been able to turn the masonic lodges of the departments into boards vested with the preliminary choice of candidates for public offices, for electoral functions, and for party favors."

Masonry was both keenly Republican and anticlerical, many of its members from the Moderate Republicans to the extreme Leftists belonging to the League of the Rights of Man founded in 1898 to defend the Republic. The speaker at the general assembly of the Grand Orient in 1902 who declared, "The Republic is Freemasonry emerged from its temples," was only dramatizing an obvious truth. When André Gide invented a joint conspiracy of the Monarchists and Freemasons against the Pope in 1893 in his *Les Caves du Vatican* he was allowing himself considerable poetic licence.

Masonic influence was not as great as Maurras claimed. The total number of Freemasons in 1889 was 20,000, and in 1908 32,000. Brisson who had been either President of the Chamber or Prime Minister from 1877 to 1885, was not chosen as President of the Chamber in 1893, nor was he chosen President of the Republic in 1894 when Casimir-Périer was elected by a large majority. But undoubtedly masons played a formidable role in colonial affairs and in the educational process. It was noticeable that the Ministry of Public Education was almost a permanent possession of the masons and that the masonic movement included many teachers, the Grand Orient making special provision for them by reducing the initiation fee by half. If the Second Empire had been defeated in 1870 by the German schoolmaster, the Third

Republic was determined not to be defeated by the French curé.

Maurras attacked the third enemy, Protestantism, by quoting approvingly Comte's view of the Reformation as "the systematic sedition of the individual against the species."[41] Never had the intellectual, aesthetic, political, and moral capital stored up for 30 centuries run greater risks than in the frightful period of the Reformation. Neither the Revolution nor French romanticism could be explained without the previous division of conscience that the Reformation had imposed on France, and which exposed the intellectual frontiers to the north and the east. The fathers of the Revolution were in Geneva, in Wittenberg, and, further still, in Jerusalem.

Protestantism meant the supremacy of the individual and of personal freedom of interpretation. It substituted private judgment for reason that judged by fixed principles and by eternal laws, and so allowed judgment to be made under the influence of the imagination, the emotions, the caprices, the passions, the temperament of each individual. The Protestant spirit menaced the French spirit, and was the principal cause of its decadence. Originating from individual anarchy, Protestantism ended in the insurrection of citizens, convulsions of society, and in anarchy. Protestants were Frenchmen who, for three centuries, submitting to a cause more political than religious, tended to "de-Franchise" themselves in order to accept the ideas of Switzerland, Germany, or England.[42] Born of the French race, language, and customs, Protestants nevertheless were infiltrated by foreign ideas. As a body, the Protestant community made itself the accomplice of the foreigner in order to tyrannize the country.

To see Protestantism both as a past and contemporary revolutionary force was another of Maurras' obsessions. In 1789 only two per cent of the French population was Protestant, and this small minority, then, as a century later, lived largely in the South. Perhaps it was this concentration in Gard, the department adjacent to Maurras' own Bouches-du-

[41] *Réflexions sur la révolution*, p. 64.
[42] *La Démocratie religieuse*, pp. 90, 225.

Rhône, that was particularly distressing to Maurras, for apart from the Lutherans on the Eastern frontier, Protestants were almost nonexistent in the rest of the country, let alone a threat to the state. Maurras was equally prepared to forget the loss sustained by France by the emigration of the Huguenots, and the contributions in his own time that a Renouvier, a Curie, a Monod, a Gide were making to French civilization.

The Jewish Problem

But the most consistent and heaviest attack on foreigners was on the Jewish problem. All three writers had anti-Semitic tendencies, though the degree and virulence varied widely, and each cast his anti-Semitism in the pattern of the rest of his ideas. For Sorel, the Jew was the nonproductive plutocrat or the materialist, a rationalist intellectual, cosmopolitan and without tradition. For Barrès, the Jew was the powerful foreign element in the French body and soul. For Maurras, the Jew was the source of harmful ideas, a member of the real ruling body in France, and an essential element causing weakness of the country.

Sorel was ambivalent in his attitude toward Jews and was aware of the political and material value of the anti-Semitic movement. He saw contemporary anti-Semitism as born of superficiality, in the same way that Fourier's in a previous age had been, created by journalists without economic or philosophic culture. Sorel was remarkably prophetic in his estimation of the anti-Semitic movement. Anti-Semitism was not an unnatural phenomenon. "I believe it will last so long as socialism has not completely vanquished demagoguery, so that it (the anti-Semitic movement) will not devote itself to following practical ends, reforms capable of interesting the classes furnishing the chief contingent of anti-Semitism."[43] It had not been studied as closely as it deserved to be; Sorel prophesied that its future would be more significant than one might imagine. In reality, an anti-Semitic movement was a union of the masses which was held together by pure nega-

[43] *De l'Eglise et de l'état*, p. 54.

tions, and that made it formidable. It was an example of ochlocracy, a regime in which ignorant, credulous masses were played upon by agitators using state power in tyrannic fashion.[44]

In an early work, Sorel had held that the Jewish Bible had a great social value, since it was the book of a peasant democracy, of the workers in the fields claiming justice against the people of the towns, the magistrates, and the priests who oppressed them. The Jews, more than any other people, admired work, and they were, even in his own day, excellent workers in southern countries.

Yet he attacked both the "big Jew bankers,"[45] and the rich Jews sympathetic toward utopias and socialism. Judaism bequeathed to a modern world the materialism and corruption of commercial capital. At different times Sorel saw Jews as intellectuals, consumers, and nontraditionalists. They lived on the margin of production: they were concerned with literature, music, and financial speculation. As Mr. Schlesinger has pointed out, it is a short step from hatred of international bankers to hatred of Jews.[46] In fact, Sorel began to argue, "The French should defend their state, their customs, and their ideas against the Jewish invaders." In 1907, although he had been favorably disposed to revisionism during the Dreyfus Affair, he remarked scornfully that Le Mouvement socialiste had displeased the Jews because there had been an article there against the illegal rehabilitation of Dreyfus.[47]

Sorel became more hostile in his attitude during the period he was associated with the Right and the monarchists. His article in L'Indépendance, June 15, 1911, on the ritual murders in Russia, found them all more or less proved. The Jewish question helped to separate Sorel from Péguy and to end his association with the Cahiers de la quinzaine. Sorel remarked to Berth. "Péguy has a clientele of 300 Jews whom he cannot

---

[44] Sorel, "Les Aspects juridiques du socialisme," p. 396.
[45] Reflections on Violence, p. 58; Les Illusions du progrès, p. 213.
[46] Arthur Schlesinger, Jr., The Vital Center, p. 38.
[47] L'Indépendance, January 1, 1912; Letter to Croce, La Critica (1928), 26:99.

offend too much."[48] In an appendix to the *Reflections on Violence*, written after the Russian Revolution, Sorel even argued that the "so-called excesses of the Bolsheviks were due to the Jewish elements that had penetrated the movement."[49]

The anti-Semitism of Barrès was not always of an extreme kind. He thought that Drumont, the cofounder in 1889 of the "Anti-Semitic National League of France," the author of *La France juive*, and editor of the violently anti-Semitic paper, *La Libre parole*, had rendered France a notable service, and dedicated his own book, *Leurs Figures*, to him. But Barrès reacted sharply to Drumont's proposals of exile or confiscation for Jews in France. "We repudiate, detest these savage words . . . the Jew is what you Christians have made him; what astonishes me is that he does not hate you more."

However, Barrès saw the Jews as a powerful foreign element, deficient in the desirable qualities, and subversive of French tradition. The Jews had no tradition in the Barresian sense. Country meant the soil and ancestors, the "earth of our dead," but for the Jews it was the spot where they found their greatest interest. In the homes of the Jews, the wives had salons, a respectable façade; at the same time, "the husbands intrigue to destroy our traditional ideal and our country, our ideas and our institutions."[50] All the injuries of Dreyfus counted nothing as against the attacks of the Dreyfusard party on military honor and French thought. De Morès, "magnificent example of humanity, precious son of France," was for Barrès a hero of anti-Semitism.

Everyone agreed that there was a Jewish question. Was it possible to assimilate them? The Jew was a different being. Anatole France's Abbé Guitrel had argued that since the Jew had never received baptism nor been instructed in the truth, he could not rightly be called a heretic. In the same way, Barrès suggested that for some people the Jew could never be a traitor because he could never be a citizen; he belonged only where he found his greatest profit.

[48] Pierre Andreu, *Notre Maître Sorel*, p. 282.
[49] *Reflections on Violence* (1950 Edition), p. 309.
[50] *Mes Cahiers*, 1:232.

With much imprecision, Barrès talked of races. One could speak of an Indo-European race and of a Semitic one. "This is not to talk about races among us, but these are provincial varieties."[51] The Jews were an inferior race having only negative characteristics, no mythology, no epic poetry, no philosophy, no science, no plastic arts, and no civil life. This inferiority was shown by their behavior. Apparently Jews worked by intellect, not by instinct. With Jews, said Barrès, there was nothing noble by reflex. It was by reasoning that they could reach, could understand something. The Jew was an incomparable logician. His reasoning was as clean and impersonal as a bank account. The Jewish state of mind was one used to dealing in values. The Jew did not become more attached to any philosophical outlook; he only became more skillful in classifying everything.[52]

In his Nancy electoral program in 1889, Barrès tied the Jewish question to the national question. The Jews had kept their distinctive character and had become dominators. They violated the principles of the Revolution by their isolated action, by their manner of monopolizing, by speculation, and by cosmopolitanism. In the army, the magistrature, the ministries, and all French administrations they infinitely exceeded the normal proportion to which their number could give them a right. They had been named prefects, judges, treasurers, officers because they had enough money to corrupt the country. This dangerous disproportion had to be corrected and more respect obtained for true French nationals. Obstacles ought to be put in the way of easy naturalization. By 1890, Barrès had anticipated the National Socialist position. Fundamentally, the word *Jew* was only an adjective designating monopolist, usurer, player of the Bourse. Anti-Semitism was a natural ally of socialism. *La France juive* was an excellent preparation for *La Revue socialiste*.[53] In view of his opinions on this question, it was ironical that Barrès should be defeated in the 1898 election by an anti-Semitic candidate more extreme than himself.

[51] *Mes Cahiers*, ii:117, 141.   [52] *Scènes*, p. 433.
[53] Barrès, "La Formule antijuive," *Le Figaro*, February 22, 1890.

Jews were powerful both in France and abroad, as the evidence of the Panama scandal had shown. The naturalized German, Baron Reinach, thought of using his money to influence government personally, enlightening parliamentarians and even ministers on public business. After an incident between Barrès and Joseph Reinach in the Chamber, Barrès refused to acknowledge the right of non-Catholics to discuss the affairs of Catholics. "Each to his own—M. Reinach to Frankfurt."[54] Barrès accused the Jewish Naquet of being the cause of transformation of Boulanger from an enemy of parliamentarianism to one who played in parliamentary politics, and so of having reduced Boulangism simply to parliamentary verbalism.

Maurras was wary of the idea of race. Politics was one thing, medicine another. They had points of contact, but were not identical. "Race" in biology was far from corresponding to "race" in history or politics, and there were laws of human society different from those of biology.[55] Race, however, was a general factor it was necessary to consider. It was too badly known to serve for the founding of any law, but it furnished the basis for physical and moral observations that politics could utilize. It was not surprising to find Maurras denouncing Gobineau, who had placed the Aryan race so high in his hierarchy, as "inept, false, lying."

Anti-Semitism, argued Maurras, was not a clerical movement. It was not a religious quarrel, not even a question of race, but simply one of national defense. The Jews were united, powerful in finance, education, and journalism, and therefore anti-Semitism existed because the French were reduced to wondering if they remained masters in their own home. Anyone attacked by the Jews became automatically an ally. "The hatred with which Jewry always pursued Méline will make us honor him."[56]

The Jews were a foreign element in the French body politic. They formed a very distinct state in the French State, allied

54 *Mes Cahiers*, vi:360.
55 *De Démos à César*, p. 135; *Enquête sur la monarchie*, p. xcvi.
56 *Kiel et Tanger*, p. 62.

with their fellow Jews in north and south Europe. More even than the Protestants, the Jewish world was a natural group. Agreement among themselves on the great issues which interested the Jewish community was reached spontaneously. The too-numerous marital alliances with Jews and Americans had contributed to the uprooting of a part of the French aristocracy.[57]

The Jews were permitted to carry on their activities in complete security, sheltered by a state without head or name. If Jewish pride, the Jewish spirit of domination and of anarchy did indeed exist, it was assisted very effectively by Republican doctrine. All the nerve centers of the central administration were affected and infected by the Jewish microbe. Jews were able to establish their power through centralization, therefore an added advantage of decentralization would be that France would get rid of the Jews.

The Jewish element, the real core of the Republican party, through its fixity of purpose, its wealth, its hereditary and religious organization, was able, working with its three allies— masonry, Protestantism, *métèques*—to control and to direct the entire political life of France. The influence of the Jews both on parliamentary activity and on the life of the country in general was wholly disproportionate to their numbers. Jews had held all parliamentary and governmental positions, and all presidencies in the system, except that of the President of the Republic. The danger for France was that Dreyfus, Jerusalem, and the cosmopolitan elements were associated together against the French army.

The Dreyfus Affair, the cause of the birth of the Action Française movement, was never to be forgotten by Maurras. The Dreyfus Affair remained the allegory, the symbol of a regime founded on the dream of vague moral progress. "He kept the Affair going for five acts," commented Thibaudet, "and indeed, never let it die." For years the *Action française* kept a daily calendar of events of the Affair on its front page, just above the racing news. The Affair was the supreme in-

[57] *La Contre-révolution spontanée*, p. 15.

stance of Jewish dominance and treachery, and Republican incompetence, resulting in army leaders being removed, the Information Service being suppressed, and regiments being demoralized. This obsession of Maurras with the Affair remained until the end of his life. On receiving his sentence from the court on January 27, 1945, of "réclusion perpétuelle, dégradation nationale," it was not surprising that he should shout, "It is the revenge of Dreyfus!"

Maurras always found an individual Jewish whipping boy to be thrashed—Baron Reinach, Joseph Reinach, Dreyfus, Albert Milhaud, Bergson. The ex-Jewish Henri Michel was for him the "Mimi Pinson Professor of Philosophy." More than once, his reply to Jewish criticism was:

> "Juif insolent, tais-toi
> Voici venir le Roi."

Maurras kept alive the memory of the battle of the Affair by guarding in a drawer "the precious nose of the Jew Bernard Lazare, to whom the Dreyfusards had erected a statue at the entrance of the Jardin de la Fontaine at Nimes."[58]

Joseph Reinach, antipatriot, comedian of French patriotism, covered with French blood and benefiting from the ruins of France, a kind of perpetual minister without portfolio, was more than a minister, as Warwick had been more than a king. Benda, Basch, and Durkheim were Jews, and as such, automatically powerful in state and society.[59] The Jewish salons —Maurras himself had been an habitué of that of Mme de Caillavet—were influential in Paris; Jews controlled the newspapers, an important part of the university and of the judiciary, and to a lesser but still appreciable degree, of the higher ranks of the army. Even on the General Staff the Jews had their man, Picquart.[60]

Jews contributed to the weakness of France. Israel had put its garrisons in Paris, and French forces belonged to France

[58] ibid., p. 93.   [59] Quand les français, p. 129.
[60] Charles Maurras, "Souvenirs politiques," La Revue universelle (May 15, 1930), 41:387. In reality, Picquart, who had played such an important part in the cause of revisionism in the Affair, was himself anti-Semitic.

no longer, but to Jewry. Maurras attributed the carnage of World War I to the moral feebleness of the years 1897 to 1899. The various difficulties—the decline in the army, the incompetent officers, the refusal to vote military credits unanimously as previously, the two-year law, the break with the Vatican, the dissolution of the Congregations—all were due to Jewish influence. International Jewry marched as one man for Kaiser William, for the Reich, for Bolshevism. They aggravated the defection from tradition and immobility because they became small traders and never peasants.

Not only were Jews in themselves harmful to the regime. They were also the source of many of the current false ideas. They were revolutionary agents. The invention of supernatural justice came from Judea, as did the idea of equality among men.[61] It was from the Jew that the Protestant had received his monotheism, his belief in prophets, his anarchical thought.

Maurras' attack on Jews was of a personal as well as an impersonal nature. On January 25, 1912, before the Second Chambre Correctionnelle du Tribunal at Versailles, he refused to answer a question put to him by the President of the court, M. Worms. "I am French, you are of Jewish nationality. It is impossible for me to reply to a Jewish judge."

What was to be done with these strangers in the midst of France? "It remains for us to cry 'Down with the Jews,'" Anatole France's nationalist character, the Duc de Brecé, had argued. "The Jews will bring misfortune on France. Why don't we get rid of them? Nothing would be easier."[62] Maurras thought in the same way. True Frenchmen had the absolute right to make the conditions for the nomads under their roofs. Maurras had been opposed to the outright persecutions of Protestants; all that was owed the Jews was protection and justice, and a care that they not be offended as human beings. But Jews must not be admitted to any official position.[63] They must be put in their place. Maurras never made clear whether this meant a physical or occupational or economic isolation.

[61] *Anthinéa*, p. 236.
[62] Anatole France, *The Amethyst Ring*, New York, 1919, p. 20.
[63] Maurras, "Intermède philosophique," *Gazette de France* (January 7, 1899), as cited in Roudiez, "Charles Maurras: The Formative Years," p. 215.

The way for Maurras' fierce diatribes had been prepared by La Tour du Pin in his attacks on the economic strength of Jews, the position of masons and Protestants, as well as his contempt for the Revolution. But both were only symptomatic of the virus of anti-Semitism that began in the 1880's with the resentment of the greater part played by Jews in the world of politics and finance, the increasing immigration from Eastern Europe, and later, of the role of Baron Reinach and Herz in the Panama scandal. The disease was not limited to any particular political or social group. On one level of life, the Princess of Guermantes would never have been home to Mme Alphonse de Rothschild, nor would the Prince allow Swann in the house. On another level, Déroulède had accused French Jews of wishing to "de-Christianise" France, and Francis Laur had demanded the expulsion of the Rothschild family. At the wedding of the daughter of Gustave de Rothschild, de Morès had gathered a band of ruffians to throw rubbish at her as she emerged from the synagogue.

The publisher Albert Savine, Anglophobe and promoter of the Félibre, encouraged his authors to attack Jews, and from 1886 to 1893, his house produced over fifty anti-Semitic books and pamphlets.[64] La France juive, the book of the most devoted and influential anti-Semite, Drumont, was the best seller in 1886, and within a year of publication, 100,000 copies were sold. The technique of the big lie was familiar before the days of Hitler. In 1900 the Jewish population in France was about 80,000, but Drumont insisted it was 500,000. When Caserio assassinated President Carnot, Drumont's paper, La Libre parole, argued that he must be a Jew. The incredible nonsense of Leo Taxil, his account of the visits of the devil to the lodges of Freemasons, and announcement of the birth of the Anti-Christ's grandmother, a Jewess, in an Egyptian hotel, were eagerly awaited and accepted. His fictitious heroine, Diana Vaughan, was even blessed by Leo XIII himself.

Anti-Semitism began to be significant in political movements in socialist as well as right-wing and Catholic groups.

[64] Robert F. Byrnes, "The French Publishing Industry and its Crisis in the 1890's," op.cit., pp. 232-242.

In 1889-1890, Drumont joined with Jacques de Biez, Morès, and Millot to found the "national anti-Semitic league of France," but its work of "national awakening, protection of the conscience of each individual, mutual and fraternal assistance," lasted only a few months. In 1892, Drumont started his *Libre parole*, with its masthead, "France for the French." The Boulangist movement had not been anti-Semitic at first, and it was not until the secession of Eugène Mayer of the *Lanterne*, attacks by Joseph Reinach, and a refusal of Rothschild to recommend the Boulangist candidates in Algeria, that the movement, temporarily at least, linked hands with Drumont. It was not surprising that the Union Nationale formed in 1892 "to return the masses to religion," became an anti-Semitic electoral league three years later. Nor was it unusual to find Drumont as president of the Christian Democratic Congress at Lyons in 1896, nor to see him as one of the nineteen members of the anti-Semitic right-wing group in the Chamber. But anti-Semitism penetrated the Left as well as the extreme Right. Malon's *La Revue socialiste* applauded Drumont, and Auguste Chirac gave the subtitle, "History of Jewishness" to his two volumes on *Kings of the Republic*. Séverine, the clever journalist, who was to become a Dreyfusard, began her career as a collaborator of Drumont.

Yet it was still true that anti-Semitism found its greatest strength in the petty bourgeoisie rather than the worker, and it was not without significance that in 1909 Drumont was beaten by Marcel Prevost in his attempt to enter the Academy.

The dislike of foreigners, both internally and externally, is not limited to reactionary groups, for it is a disease from which radical movements in all countries have not been totally immune. But in reactionary groups it tends to become more than an incidental in their political behavior. It becomes one of the main bonds holding the group together and often its most appealing slogan. Diderot's argument in the *Encyclopédie* against those who would rather spread darkness over the foreigner or even plunge all the rest of the world in barbarism than enlighten him, is even more valid now than when written. The ultimate error in those who suffer from xenophobia is to mistake the present for eternity, and accept a given power relationship as an inevitable and sanctified value. To regard foreigners and minority internal groups both as hostile and inferior as did Maurras, Barrès, and, to some extent, Sorel, was to pity the plumage and forget the growing bird. Goethe once told Eckermann that national hatred was always strongest and most violent in those possessing the lowest culture. The emergence of the modern nationalists was sadly to belie him.

CHAPTER XI

TRADITIONAL INSTITUTIONS AND A POLITICAL SCIENCE

ALL THREE WRITERS had spoken of the necessity of upholding traditions, but what traditions were to be upheld? Sorel denied being a traditionalist of the kind that the Action Française was producing if, as he wrote in a letter to Edouard Dolléans on October 13, 1912, "one means by traditionalist the supporters of monarchical and Catholic institutions."[1] He agreed he was a traditionalist in the sense that he attached major importance to historical evidence in cultural matters, but not in the sense of being an ally of Maurras. Sorel criticized the choice of intellectual parentage the Nationalists had made. They had passed over Chateaubriand because he was a romantic and had overpraised Fustel de Coulanges. The Nationalists refused to recognize that modern ideas of tradition came from Savigny, a German, while Bonald, even if he had given the idea of the general will to God, had borrowed the concept from Rousseau.[2]

Sorel was not even sure that tradition was of primary importance. He had stated that a time had arrived when the complaints of the oppressed individual seemed more sacred than traditions, the necessities of order, and the principles on which society rested. But he was sufficiently a traditionalist to argue, in an article in *L'Indépendance* in November, 1912, that, "A people belonging to the category of great races must make continual efforts to create the novel by depending on the legacy of the past."[3]

All the writers dealt with the Church, the army, the importance of rural values, and a series of accepted values, which in the case of Maurras, amounted to a political science.

[1] Edouard Dolléans, "Le Visage de Georges Sorel," *Revue d'histoire économique et sociale* (1940-1947), 26:107.

[2] Book review of Louis Dimier, *Les Maîtres de la Contre-révolution au XIX siècle, Le Mouvement socialiste* (January 1907), 182:102-104.

[3] As cited in Pierre Andreu, "Bergson et Sorel," *Les Etudes Bergsoniennes* (1952), 3:58.

221

THE CHURCH AND THE ARMY

The three writers were basically nonreligious. Though some have claimed Barrès as a spiritual Catholic, the substance of his work does not bear this out. Maurras was put on the Index specifically for the nonreligious nature of his work. Sorel, both by temperament and by training, was agnostic. But all were interested in the political and social role that the Church played, though Sorel was somewhat contradictory on the matter.

Sometimes Sorel stressed the heroic morality of the persecuted Christians in ancient times; at other times he praised the legal system of the Romans and denounced Christians as destroyers of society. In one book, *La Ruine du monde antique*, he argued that Christianity had accelerated the fall of Rome, while in others he denied its responsibility. For Sorel, there was no true social morality in Christianity, for it could not teach what it was necessary to do in modern civil society.[4] The Church attached itself to the military class partly because it sought to find support for a course of external politics conforming to Catholic interests.[5] When he was still an ardent Dreyfusard, Sorel believed that the Church had committed no greater fault in modern times than having taken part against the revision of the Dreyfus trial. Indeed, the Church was a greater danger than the army, for while the priest was in daily contact with the citizen, the military oligarchy exercised only an intermittent tyranny. But Sorel praised Christianity both for the value of its myths and for the heroic energy which had been exercised in its behalf in previous generations.

Barrès was not a defender of the Catholic Church and religion because of any spiritual or theological impulse. "We reject revealed religions because of what they include, in which we cannot believe."[6] In a letter of April, 1902, he stated that although he did not want Catholicism to be degraded, at the same time he did not intend to go to confession, or to associate

---

4 *La Ruine du monde antique*, p. 311.
5 *De l'Eglise et de l'état*, p. 55.
6 *Mes Cahiers*, 1:129.

himself with the campaigns of the vestries against free thinkers. Barrès did occasionally talk of "the mystery at the bottom
of all reality," the great states of religious emotion, and the
need for the divine. But in his political trilogy, *Les Déracinés,
L'Appel au soldat,* and *Leurs Figures,* there was little place
for religion. Of his seven young men from Lorraine, only
Saint-Phlin was religious in any meaningful way.

Catholicism, however, was valuable in a double sense. Barrès
ranged himself among its defenders, "not as a faithful believer, but because I am patriotic, in the name of the national
interest."[7] He believed that French nationality was tied
strictly to Catholicism, that it was formed and developed in
a Catholic atmosphere, and that, in trying to destroy and tear
Catholicism away from the nation, no one could foresee what
would be demolished. Politically it was valuable because it
was a force, a treasure to protect. Between Catholicism and
French civilization no distinction could be made. In a pic-
turesque metaphor, Barrès said, "The Church planted in the
village square makes the soil healthy. Around it the human
plant develops in an atmosphere of civilization."[8] The Church
was still what men had found strongest and most valuable
in maintaining order. Even when he confessed that "nationalism lacks the infinite," and that he felt himself "sliding from
nationalism to Catholicism,"[9] Barrès still found it necessary
"for Maurras as for me, that the gods of France become the
gods of civilization."

But Catholicism was useful also for personal reasons.
Catholicism, like individualism, tradition, and nationalism,
was valuable in heightening his own sensibility, and at times
his sensuality, to the point of voluptuousness. The Catholic
religion "is the poem that most satisfies me"; it was in the
churches that "my intelligence and my heart find the formulas
of the highest poetry." Catholicism had made him what he
was; it was the milieu which offended him least, which would
best accept his divine manifestations, and which was most

[7] *Journal Officiel,* December 21, 1906, p. 3400.
[8] *Journal Officiel,* January 16, 1911, p. 88.
[9] *Mes Cahiers,* viii:80-81.

favorable to his natural activity. The wiping out of the Protestant bands by the Duke Antoine was a happy victory which allowed the preservation of the truths from which Barrès benefited. The truths were not to be judged but only to be seen in correspondence with the developments of his soul. Religion, in fact, was more than a simple means of maintaining public order. The virtues that Catholicism had bequeathed to the nation were both social health and the exaltation of the highest powers of the soul. Catholicism not only provided laws in accordance with the laws of health for the individual and for peoples but it also was the most favorable atmosphere for the existence of magnanimous sentiments. "It is not enough to say Catholicism is a guide, it is necessary to add that it is an immense reservoir of the pleasures of the soul." For Barrès, Catholicism did not find its proof in history, but in his soul. The Church, moreover, taught how to honor the dead, and "The dead are my sacred things. I honor them in common with the dignified among the living."[10]

For Maurras, Catholicism conserved and perfected all his favorite ideas: order, tradition, discipline, hierarchy, authority, continuity, unity, work, family, corporation, decentralization, autonomy, working-class organization. Religious life had become a matter of tradition more than of faith. Religion itself was not necessary for the people, religion and education were necessary only for the leaders of the people. A realistic view of politics would place less emphasis on the importance of celestial justice than on the terrestrial necessity of public welfare.

A patriot could very well not believe in Catholicism. However, it was necessary to be concerned with it as a political element of the country. Catholicism, to which were owed the organization and the conservation of the country, had not ceased to be the center of the firmest resistance to the effects of anarchy and revolution which had been disturbing France for a century.[11] "Maurras accepts the Church and not the evangelist. He wants the Pope, not Christ," wrote Barrès.[12]

10 *Mes Cahiers*, vi:25,60.
11 *La Démocratie religieuse*, pp. 33, 464.
12 *Mes Cahiers*, xi:232.

Maurras, "a cerebral Christian," as Bernanos called him, had little sympathy for religious dogma or feeling. For him the Christianity of the Evangelists was odious, a philosophy of pure and barbarous sensibility. His story, "Les Serviteurs," in his early book, *Le Chemin de paradis,* is, in effect, a symbolic attack on the morality of Christianity, similar in content to that of Nietzsche. The virtue of the Church was that it had organized the idea of God. In a famous passage in *La Démocratie religieuse,*[13] explaining why he was "a son of Rome," nowhere did Maurras mention any spiritual reasons. It is significant that none of the leaders of the Action Française were religious, and that the political intimates of Maurras— Vaugeois, Pujo, Moreau, Bainville—were all agnostics. In an epoch when the Church was making many converts among intellectuals, Maurras remained agnostic. It is perhaps revealing that in 1926 the Church accepted Cocteau and rejected Maurras.

In a re-edition of *Le Chemin de paradis,* Maurras said, "I wanted to avoid offending Catholics. My intention has never been adverse to them . . . the alliance with Catholics seems desirable to me."[14] In re-editing his writings, he had cut out what might offend "the Church that I saluted as the oldest, the most venerable, or the most fecund of visible things and the noblest and most holy ideas of the Universe . . . the Church of Order."[15] He omitted, among other things, the autobiographical story, "Le Conte de la bonne mort," which had described his loss of faith. This covering of his intellectual tracks, in fact, makes it difficult to discover passages like the famous one, "The Gospel written by four obscure Jews," so often quoted against him, but it did not prevent him from being made an outcast by the Church, and having his work put on the Index.

Maurras was always conscious of his debt to Comte; there were, he held, sympathies and affinities between positivism and Catholicism on questions of the family, the origin of

13 *La Démocratie religieuse,* p. 26.
14 *Le Chemin de paradis,* p. xxxvi.
15 *La Démocratie religieuse,* p. 528.

political authorities, tradition, order, and civilization, and they had common enemies. There was no French positivist who did not believe that, if it was the Capetians who had made France, it was the bishops and the clergy who had been the first to cooperate. The Catholic Church, for 20 centuries, had been the vessel of civilized order containing most of the seeds of progress for the human species. Maurras dedicated *Le Dilemme de Marc Sangnier* to the Roman Church, "the Church of Order," and to Catholicism, "the most general notion of order." Inheritor of the work of the Latins and of Hellenism, the Church had stood firm against revolution and anarchy. It had been able both to formulate laws of conscience for the relations between men and society and also, as a living authority, to interpret cases arising out of these relations.

All other religions were the product of the foreigner and were anti-French in idea and action. Antipatriotism was linked to anti-Catholicism, intellectual and moral dissent to the Huguenots. For Maurras, the Church and the monarchy were mutually beneficial. If on the one hand God became the first gendarme of the monarchy, on the other, there was no possible security for the Catholic Church outside of monarchy. But, as Catholic critics were quick to point out, in the political alliance that Maurras envisaged, the Church occupied a secondary position, and was always an obedient auxiliary force. The very slogan of Maurras, "Politique d'abord," meant that primacy must be given to political organization over all others. When Maurras combined his political preoccupation with an intense nationalism, the Church became even more wary. To Catholics, the formula of the national interest was one under which all the Gallican and Josephite enterprises had been supported against Catholicism.[16] The attitude of the Catholic to the Maurrasian version of Catholicism might well echo the old Norman proverb: "Lord, preserve me from my friends; I will preserve myself from mine enemies."

Next to the Church, the second traditional body was the army. The Nationalists were convinced that it was important

[16] Etienne Lamy, "Quelques précisions," *Le Correspondant* (June 10, 1908), 231:986-987.

to uphold the army, symbol of order and defense. This dictated their attitude in the Dreyfus Affair, which meant more than the fate of an individual. For them, besides the conscious treason of Dreyfus, the serious consequences of the Affair were the destruction of the country's faith in the army, the abolition of military jurisdiction, and the ruin of the army itself. The worst crime of Dreyfus was not that he had stolen the documents enumerated in the *bordereau*, but that for five years he had disturbed the army and the whole nation.

Barrès was a supporter of the army for both material and ideological reasons. An army was necessary for France to remain independent and strong. He regarded General Mercier, who, during the Dreyfus Affair, had proved so deficient in character and in honesty, as "my fellow Lorrainer and my friend. He is incapable of failing in honor."[17]

But Barrès also admired soldiers as possessors of the virtue of energy and the means of overcoming the feebleness and emptiness of life. The army, moreover, was a school of character. Through it, young people could use and develop their various aptitudes for the good of the country and their own development. The army was the image of the nation, and that image could justifiably be upheld by the noble lie. Barrès confided that old Boulangists like himself had learned to support deceptions and to nourish themselves on chimeras.

The army, for Maurras, was necessary for both internal and external reasons: internally, in order to prevent an anarchist or socialist revolution, and externally, in order to restore France to its former glory. The army was the only permanent group escaping the fluctuations and the mutual hostilities of the parties. In the absence of the king, it was the only way to get unity. The army disliked political control, it was hostile to the parliamentary system, it detested humanitarianism, left-wing or pacific ideas. Maurras never talked in the way that de Maistre or Veuillot did of the divinity of war, for he always regarded war as harmful. But the army must be at the service of a just idea, the principle of order itself.

[17] *Journal Officiel*, July 13, 1906, p. 2363.

The proper use of the army was denied both by democratic ideology and by the Republic. Democracy was harmful to the military idea, while the Republic had led to antimilitarism, to the sabotaging of the Information Service, and the appointment of incompetent military leaders. The Republic and the party system were in contradiction to the normal life and safety of France. The Republic dishonored the old royal army, venerable institution of French unity, heroic element in the formation of France. Throughout the Dreyfus Affair, a democratic rottenness penetrated the army with the increase of civilian influence. Since then, "The liberty of insulting the 'galonnards' has been virtually inscribed in the Charter of our liberties."[18]

Sorel, too, upheld the integrity of the army for his own particular reasons. Contemporary experience, especially in France, taught that there was no profession which was more antipathetic to intellectuals and less intelligible for them than the profession of arms.[19] The army embodied the idea of heroic action, and would always provide the model for a true movement of the workers.

"Life is a swallow and theory a snail," R. H. Tawney once wrote. While the nationalists were propounding what was essentially an aristocratic conception of the army, technology was altering the very institution about which they were talking. Easier communication and methods of transport and more capable administration meant that in the future mass armies would be based on conscription, and that from now on the political role that military leaders would like to see the army play could not be assured. The syndicalists, attempting to get the conscripts to desert their barracks, were laying the foundations for the political revolts of soldiers and workers in other countries in 1917 and 1918. Moreover the growing interconnection between economic and military problems and the enormous increase in armaments meant that planning of a considerable part of the national economy was necessary in order to produce the required equipment. The independent

18 *L'Action française*, November 30, 1912.
19 *Le Système de Renan*, p. 134.

power of army leaders was therefore likely to be reduced because of the greater control exercised by politicians. But the military leaders were still a power with which the Republic had to reckon. If Clemenceau was right to gibe at the military competence of the army leaders during the World War, the prewar politicians were even more correct in their constant fear of political intervention by those leaders.

THE RURAL MYTH

"A true and complete philosophy of tradition is always agrarian," argued Thibaudet.[20] With its more homogeneous population, its smaller number of outsiders, its relative immobility and little contact with foreigners, the rural area has a more developed nationalist and traditionalist attitude in the sense of love of country than the urban area.[21] All the theorists developed this contrast between the urban and rural areas, attacked the city, symbol of decadence, responsible for the decline of tradition.

The great observation of Barrès, one critic has said, was that one thought in a truer and more fruitful manner in the countryside, for him the Lorraine countryside, than in a city library.[22] One of the main reasons for so violently attacking Bouteiller, the teacher in Les Déracinés, was that he had implanted the idea of city ambition in his young students. Barrès waxed lyrical about the countryside, its ruins, the glory of its stones. "What I see in Lorraine, what I hear, is the peasant, the word of the peasant." When Lucien Herr dismissed him as "a typical product of small French towns," Barrès took this as a compliment, and added, "I have the happiness to be that."[23] Barrès was fond of talking of the song of the small town, which was an eternal repetition of the ideas of religion, authority, marriage, saving, heritage. Small town people lived

20 Albert Thibaudet, Les Idées politiques de la France, p. 79.
21 Carl J. Friedrich, "The Agricultural Basis of Emotional Nationalism," Public Opinion Quarterly (April 1937), 1:50-61.
22 Robert Kanters, "Barrès invisible et présent," La Nef (August 1947), 4:66.
23 Mes Cahiers, 11:236.

at a slower rate, and their aims were limited, but there was something to be revered in that monotony, that insignificance, that smallness. This concern for the small town was coupled with Barrès' regard for other traditional values. It is noticeable that several of his more important speeches were on the necessity for the care and preservation of the small parish churches of the country.

Similarly Maurras, "ce fils de la mer," as René Benjamin called him, equated the true and national traditions with the countryside. When he spoke of "the people," he had the peasants and fishermen of Martigues in mind.[24]

In this respect as in so many others a firm disciple of Proudhon, Sorel contrasted the undesirable qualities to be found in the cities with the favorable ones to be found in the rural areas. On one side, there were skepticism and vice; on the other, faith and morality. The city was flippant and cynical; the rural area was serious and dignified. The city with its heterogeneous population, its cosmopolitan ideas, was based on trade, finance, international banking and mercantile activities, attracted strangers, and weakened traditional morality and religion. The rural area provided the opportunity for the peasant to become an artist, for work in the fields to have an aesthetic character, and for a common concern in the administration of collective things.

Again he drew parallels from history to justify his case. The trial of Socrates was, in essence, the result of the underlying conflict between the agriculturalists who respected the laws and did not want change, and the Sophists, the urban element, who mocked traditional ideas. Athenian democracy, like contemporary democracy, was an oligarchy of shopkeepers and small artisans, and the city, the home of their activity, was a marketplace ruled by self-interest.

Sorel found as features or characteristics of the town all the institutions or ideas he detested—the system of exchange, the merchant and the market, the fair, the apparatus of the state, governmental, parliamentary, and judicial institutions,

[24] Roudiez, "Charles Maurras: The Formative Years," p. 182.

politicians, intellectuals, abstract ideas, and democratic ideas. For him, modern democracies were characterized by individuals who felt no attachment to the past, had no deep love for their home, and were concerned only mildly for future generations. The true place for these individuals was the large town, where men passed like shadows and where political committees had taken the place of the old social authorities overthrown by revolutions.

Essentially an urban phenomenon, democracy had a false sense of values. It took as its ideal citizen the man of letters, the orator, the journalist. In this way the domination of the cities was established in France under the fallacious pretext that the citizens of towns, by reading newspapers and journals, were more enlightened than countrymen. This was amply illustrated by the doctrine of the bourgeois Socialists that city workers had a kind of historic-economic mission. This doctrine was in fact a reflection of the dictatorship of the cities.[25] The Socialist leader, Jaurès himself, had indeed only discovered the peasants in 1900, and then only for electoral purposes.

Sorel contrasted to this unfortunate urban influence the virtues of the countryside, moral and national. The rural population, stable and homogeneous, holding its property in the form of land, had a feeling of national sentiment. Whereas the immigrant or foreigner could engage in the activities of the city, he could not infiltrate the countryside and obtain land, since the supply was limited. From the theoretical point of view, starting from the rural element was valuable. In *Le Procès de Socrate*, Sorel had praised Oeconomicus for his stress on rural, domestic economy, and in the *Introduction à l'économie moderne*, he criticized the starting point of Marxism, which believed that urban phenomena ought to be the base for economic research. To find the theory of all societies it was necessary to study the life of agricultural societies.[26] In this way a rural socialism, bound to moral forces and to an

[25] *Le Procès de Socrate*, p. 179; *Matériaux*, pp. 386-390; *Introduction*, pp. 42, 203.
[26] Georges Sorel, "Socialismes nationaux," p. 59.

organization of work where progress was easy to measure, would be practical. While industry depended above all on mechanics and was an abstract science, agriculture, on the contrary, was "a biological industry," much more complex, much more concrete than industrial production, and therefore capable of providing a more realistic clue to the complexity of reality. From the moral point of view, the countryside was equally valuable. The worker in a trade, the urban worker in general, the man in one of the liberal professions, was not sufficiently absorbed in his work; it remained external and unintelligible to him. But the peasant, on the other hand, was absorbed by the earth that he cultivated. An agricultural enterprise had at its head a man loving the earth, and love of profession was the first element of success. It was ridiculous to talk as Marx had done in the *Communist Manifesto* of the idiocy of the life of the countryside. The agriculturist became the servant of the earth, preoccupied with it and its future.

In so stressing the desirability of rural values, Sorel left unresolved contradictory features of his theory. On the one hand, he argued that tension must be maintained in order for heroism to be manifested, that industrial technique must be advanced, and that the peaceful life was undesirable. On the other hand, he made a claim for rural values and for peasants, although these will normally be the most conservative elements in a political system. It is paradoxical that the group he castigated most severely, the men of liberal professions, are in fact the group most likely to carry out the cardinal necessity Sorel stressed, that of being sufficiently absorbed in their work.

A POLITICAL SCIENCE AND THE TRADITIONAL VALUES

The Right always claims the inevitability of certain characteristics, if a society is to exist, and chief among these are order, stability, and authority. If the Right is opposed to abstractions like justice or liberty, it is also, under the guise

232

of realism and a concern for the concrete, just as much attached to its own abstractions. It was the aim of Maurras to erect these concepts into a system which became a political science of tradition.

Sorel thought that a science of politics could not be formulated. Since each individual was a separate person, all serious study of man had to be based on the impossibility of interpreting emotional states. Human activities could be studied only by analyzing objective processes. Since it was impossible to formulate a science of human acts, all one could hope to do was to gather "systematic data," which would be revised from time to time.[27] Sorel wrote to Croce, "The philosopher must be a modest man, not proposing universal panaceas." The creator of a system worked like an artist, interpreting with extreme liberty what he observed around him. In modern economy and in a large number of social phenomena, movements were blind, unconscious, or quasi-material.[28] History was more of an art than a science, and no general formula could be established as a guide in historical research. Legislative acts could never resemble mathematical formulae.

Maurras agreed with Sorel that there was no general law of history which could provide the key to historical understanding. He criticized Comte for having believed that he had discovered such a "law of history"; there were, Maurras argued, laws of history, but no Law of History.[29] But to the rest of Sorel's analysis he was totally opposed. Maurras believed that there was a chronological primacy about politics, and that a good political state was the necessary foundation for satisfactory conditions in every other sphere. He made a religion of politics. The intellectual problem, the ethical problem, the social problem, all led back to the political problem.

The ambition of Maurras was to build a political science, a science that was based on a combination of experience and

27 *D'Aristote à Marx*, pp. 177-188.
28 Georges Sorel, Preface to E. R. A. Seligman, *L'interprétation économique de l'histoire*, Paris, 1911, pp. xxxviii-xxxix.
29 *Le Chemin de paradis*, p. xlix; *L'Action française*, January 7, 1927.

history. His political doctrine was "not deduced, but induced from the facts, from the interconnection of facts that are called laws."[30] He agreed with Montesquieu that civil and political laws were related to the nature of things, to places, times, and states. These laws were not imperative laws in the sense of order and command, but laws of constancy and sequence, induced from the field of history and the general behavior of mankind. Politics was not morals; the art and the science of the conduct of the state were not the art and science of the conduct of man. There was no direct relationship between moral perfection and the perfection of political forms, the latter being bound to factors like geographical or social conditions foreign to the morality of man. He said, "I do not believe in moralism or in idealism."[31]

The first principle of his political science therefore was that law was not arbitrary but the result of an appreciation of a given situation. Law was not the expression of the general will but of necessity, of the general well-being of the public interest. A parallel could be drawn from science. There was no liberty of conscience in astronomy, physiology, chemistry, or physics in the sense that principles established in these sciences by competent men would be declared absurd.[32] Similarly, all societies existed according to natural necessities; it was a question of knowing exactly the essence of these necessities, not of affirming what was just or well-founded. Society had the choice only between obedience to the necessary political laws or death, and many former societies, such as the Republic of Poland or Athenian democracy, had in fact chosen death, dissolution, and ruin. This would be the fate of the democratic Republic, for it had as its base revolutionary illuminism, which was in manifest and complete disagreement with the views of positive politics or what Maurras called organicist empiricism.

This empiricist approach to a political science was based on certain premises. The first of these premises was that

30 *L'Action française*, January 7, 1927.
31 Letter to Barrès, October 26, 1912, as cited in *Mes Cahiers*, ix:372.
32 *L'Avenir de l'intelligence*, p. 111.

societies were facts of nature, of necessity, not born of contracts or wills. Society was a natural whole, not a voluntary association. It was not wished for, it was not elected by its members, for individuals did not choose their blood, their country, their language, or their tradition. The community was the first condition not only of progress but of the existence of the individual. A society could no more be broken up into the individuals that composed it than a geometric surface could be broken up into straight lines or a straight line into points. Society was the condition and the generator of justice, not the reverse. One had seen societies without justice, but no one had ever seen justice without society. Parliamentary democracy pretended to provide a government of principles. But all governments before being governments of "principles," must first be governments, and must therefore exist. The task of political science was first to defend, then to conserve societies and states.[33]

Together with the first premise was another that society was wiser than the individual and its preservation more important. In this way, Maurras believed that in the Dreyfus Affair, a King of France would have done what the King of Italy or the Emperor of Germany would have done: before allowing the story of the judicial error to be propagated, he would have called those interested in the propagation proven agitators. Nothing ought to stand in the way of the existing social institutions. If by chance Dreyfus were innocent, he ought to be named Marshal of France, but a dozen of his chief defenders should be shot for the harm they did to France, peace, and reason, a list which Maurras later extended to include the army, justice, order, state, country, civilization.[34]

A third premise was that of an unchanging human nature, viewed realistically. One could take the nature of man, alternatively with the face of a god and that of a wolf, as constant. Man needed his fellow man, but was also afraid of him. Man was an animal with reason, and it was this

---

[33] *La Démocratie religieuse*, p. 97; *Au Signe de Flore*, p. 61.
[34] *Au Signe de Flore*, p. 55; *La Contre-révolution spontanée*, p. 49.

reason which distinguished him, without separating him from the rest of nature. But he was also limited by the laws of life. By instinct he was an accumulator, conservative, traditionalist. He had been formed by 50 centuries of civilization; if he trembled in the desert, it was from solitude.[35]

Another essential premise was that Maurras' view of politics and political behavior was a realistic one, while that of a democratic republic was illogical and unsound. He regarded democrats as "princes des nuées," because they believed that the edifice of civilization rested on ideas, without wondering if they were true or false, or on wills, without considering the realities behind these wills.[36] They refused to face the fact that force was a natural phenomenon. But there was no place for sentimentality or for humanitarianism in politics. The existence of reasoning without force behind it could not be conceived. Power was not an idea but a fact. There would always be conquest and a conqueror, just as there would always be assassinations in the course of the game of interests.

From his political science Maurras outlined certain values, of which the most important were stability and order, authority and leadership, inequality and the hereditary principle as the basis of rule.

Stability and order.—Maurras argued that a political liberal regime was one of instability and therefore of disorder, discontinuity, and revolution. Its companion, romanticism, meant disorder, exaggeration, self-abandonment, talk of the infinity of human things. Nothing was more variable than feeling, and for about a century, sensibility had been making disquieting progress. Romantics attacked the laws and the state, public and private discipline, the fatherland, family, and property.[37]

But politics was a matter of continuous work, of coherence because of its invariable laws, and of science and order. Nothing was easier than revolutions . . . the beautiful, the diffi-

[35] *Prologue d'un essai,* p. 50; *Mes Idées politiques,* p. 23.
[36] *Les Princes des nuées,* p. 426.
[37] *L'Avenir de l'intelligence,* p. 51.

cult thing was to avoid clashes, to guard against subversion, to aid nature in its fight against the enemy of life. In language that would no doubt be approved by Professor Oakeshott himself, Maurras said that to navigate and to steer to port, to endure and to make endure, these were the political miracles. Those who held the contrary idea only served the interests of the forces of death.

Order was inscribed in the nature of things. For Maurras this was both an aesthetic delight and political wisdom. Order in man, thought, and the state meant discipline, composition, and conformity, the absence of anarchy, the avoidance of chaos and of formless mass. For the Greek, beauty was fused with the idea of order itself because it was composition, hierarchy, gradation.[38] There was no beauty of detail, all detail changing its value as soon as its place was changed. Just as order meant beauty in the arts, it would mean happiness in the city.

Disorder and destruction were the same thing, and the disorder of the French State would result in the destruction of France itself. Liberal thought was disorganized, leading to skepticism and corruption. But human life was great and good as it resisted death; to maintain was not only to be able to create, but also to conserve for the future. All organizations, whether spiritual or temporal, had the same interest in not allowing the living accumulation of sentiments and the more humble impulses to decompose, and thus assured to the universe the immense benefits of order.[39]

Anything that disturbed the public order was an injustice, so that true justice meant respect for public order. Nobody could take upon himself a right of upsetting everything in order to redress a judicial error, even where the error was proved in a way that the one involved in the Dreyfus Affair was not. Laws were sacred, but the most sacred law of all was that of public safety. If Colonel Henry was wrong to resort to forgery, his error was not a crime, for he was seeking to maintain this safety. It was Maurras' two articles in *Ga-*

[38] *Quand les français*, p. 187.
[39] *Le Chemin de paradis*, pp. LVI-LVII; *La Démocratie religieuse*, p. 108.

zette de France, September 6th and 7th, 1898, justifying this forgery, that established him as the spokesman of the right.

Maurras agreed with La Tour du Pin that order was not born spontaneously in society.[40] Authority preceded and engendered it. Greece, Rome, and the Catholic Church had all contributed to the order of the world. France needed a strong army, respect for property, the sound establishment of public peace, the friendship of Catholicism, and enmity towards the revolutionary dogmas. From the point of view of peace, the worst government was still worth more than the best absence of government. The minimum of order in national and international relations was more favorable to the maintenance of peace than the savage struggle which was born everywhere because of the lack of a leader.

But the Maurrasian conception of order meant absence of tolerance and of diversity of opinion. "Under the pretext of organizing life," commented Guy-Grand,[41] "he removed the taste of living and substituted suffocation." In his desire to perpetuate the political forms he favored, he chose, as Blum said,[42] "purely arbitrary ones and pretended they were eternal." Spinoza once urged that the task of the political thinker was to show how men, even when full of passion, could still have fixed and stable laws. Maurras' solution was not to permit the passion. But to believe as he did in a rigid, stable society is both to misjudge the temper of politics and to put a high price on the conformity it necessarily entails. This kind of belief misjudges politics because instability is and has been the inevitable norm of a vital society. And the price paid for not believing this is to deny dissent and doubt, the means by which society progresses and through which freedom can survive.

Authority and leadership.—The Maurrasian concept of authority was Aristotelian. What humanity venerated most was authority, and what counted most was obedience. Political

---

[40] *Enquête sur la monarchie*, p. 204.

[41] Georges Guy-Grand, *Le Conflit des idées dans la France d'aujourd'hui*, Paris, 1921, p. 86.

[42] Léon Blum, *Oeuvres* I, p. 227.

science established that authority was a necessary means of social life, and the instinct of obedience of the greatest interest to the crowds which wanted to be governed, and well governed, by firmness. "For Maurras in politics it is not a matter of knowing what pleases us, but what is good for us,"[43] commented Barrès.

Authority was an absolute value like virtue or genius or beauty. It was authority not liberty, which was general, necessary, and human. If a strong superior authority was not present to impose order, the human race would be decomposed and thrown into chaos. Authority was a natural phenomenon; it was not made either from below or from above, but was born. It was a characteristic possessed by some and denied to others. The true man of authority imposed himself naturally on others. But care was still necessary, for obedience was fallible and people could be deceived in taking a Boulanger for Julius Caesar or a Bonaparte for Louis XIV.

A state without a head would lead only to disaster. A people needed a leader as man needed bread. When threatened by an enemy, people must be commanded, when disorder reigned, they must be led back to order. To maintain order and stability, organization was essential in society. This meant differentiation of organs and division of functions, because inequality was a basic characteristic of all political and social activity. Society and civilization were born of inequality, and neither society nor civilization could arise where individuals were equal.

Dictatorship was in the order of necessity of things—the single leader alone could successfully blend his interests with those of the general interest. Moreover, he alone would be clearly responsible for his actions, unlike elected representatives who escaped responsibility. The good dictator and the national dictator were necessary for a decentralized system, based on classicism and rationally oriented. But the country did not want the dictatorship of money or of electoral opinion, it did not want dictatorship against France. Maurras had nothing but contempt for the false leader. The English Monk

[43] *Mes Cahiers*, x:27.

was able to be victorious without spilling blood. But if Boulanger captured power, he would install fountains of wine, and, if he were obliged to put a dozen republicans in jail, he would send them champagne.[44]

Heredity.—A national authority was a necessity, but an electoral authority was an absurdity, irrational and contradictory, because it was based on competition and party division. The effect of election was to enfeeble or destroy authority, while the effect of heredity was to establish tranquillity, order, and duration. The only true authority, the only one to create unity, would be a hereditary one. All that was happy, durable, and truly strong would acquire its happiness, its duration, and its force from the power and the natural laws of blood, from the French nation and its earth.[45] The aptitudes of a nation were fixed to some degree by blood, but even more by oral tradition and education. Although Maurras argued that an aristocracy was transmitted by blood, and that an aristocracy of birth was the foundation of aristocracies of intelligence, probity, and fortune, the social attributes were more important than the physical. It had been professional heredity, not the heredity of the nobility, that selected the families from which the *ancien régime* was able to produce such a remarkable group of officers, judges, diplomats, and artisans.

All societies were governed on such a hereditary base. Even in contemporary France, it was such a group, the four *Etats Confédérés*, who brought to France whatever it possessed of stability and continuity. What was universal and eternal was not monarchy, but the hereditary government of families. In fact, the only rational form of authority of one person was that which rested in a family. The family was the means of continuing heritage and tradition. The two existing facts of hierarchy and tradition were politically united only when there was heredity. Where Bonaparte had failed, Capet had succeeded because Bonaparte had not had behind him what had supported Capet, three generations of dukes of France.[46]

44 *Enquête sur la monarchie*, p. 488; *Mes Idées politiques*, pp. 40, 48-49.
45 *L'Action française*, September 16, 1911; March 21, 1912.
46 *De Démos à César*, ii:197.

Napoleon had ignored the value of traditions, and so could not establish a dynasty; he was only a dictator, an employer, a leader of a band, not a king.

In his presentation of the laws of politics, Maurras provided an analysis that was coherent and at the same time based on a totally unrealistic view of French political life and history. He oscillated, as Parodi said, between an empirical conception of social laws and a completely romantic conception of the national interest.[47] He suggested he was stating a certain number of given empirical facts, but really was presenting a picture of society as he would have liked to have seen it.

[47] D. Parodi, "L'Action française," "*Pages libres*" (June 6, 1908), 15:630.

CHAPTER XII

THE PROPOSED SOLUTIONS

To the deficiencies of the regime the three writers gave their answers: monarchy, nationalism, syndicalism, or heroic moral action.

MAURRAS' MONARCHY

There were significant differences in the political approaches of Barrès and Maurras, and one of them was on the question of monarchy. Barrès admitted it was true that the Capetian family had been associated for many centuries with the destinies of France, but regarded it as of secondary importance. "What do we owe to the Royal Family?" he asked. "Nothing, but we owe everything to France and its culture." He even looked on monarchy as a German idea.[1]

For Maurras, monarchy was the pole around which he spun his theories, and which he defended in the name of science and history. He had carved the initials *V.H.V.* (*Vive Henri V*) on his school desk, but it was not until his visit to Greece that he became converted politically to monarchism. Maurras refused to admit that the restoration of the monarchy was a forlorn hope. Monarchy was an institution, a regime, not a man or woman, and such an institution and regime was not a corpse. There had been, he said, a hundred examples of restorations in republican countries.[2]

He linked his ideas on monarchy to those on heredity. What was eternal, he had argued, was the principle of heredity. Monarchy was not the only good form of government; there were many countries and times where a republic with a hereditary aristocracy and in certain determined conditions could flourish. But a government of families was less frequent in history than one of monarchy, which had succeeded more often, being more simple. Stability was thus doubly insured, on the one hand by the system of hereditary succession, and on the other by the person of the prince.

[1] *Mes Cahiers*, ii:160, 194, 251.   [2] *Kiel et Tanger*, p. 350.

Royalty was not a personal preference. The popularity of monarchs resulted from their position, not the reverse. There was no particular divine right in royalty; the proper rights of royalty were historic ones. Because the basis for monarchy was a historic one, Maurras again rejected the electoral principle. The electoral principle enfeebled the state without giving the necessary guarantees; possession of power was always being questioned, and therefore enfeebled. It was because the Empire of Napoleon III had been founded on the plebiscite that it had had to find at all costs a means of manipulating public opinion by continual displays of exaltation or diversions. The Empire, a government of opinion, elective, democratic, and plebiscitary, had therefore been dependent and not independent. Also, the Capetians had made the kingdom of France, but the Bonapartes had unmade it. Brumaire and Marengo were more than canceled out by Leipzig and Waterloo, as was December by Sedan.

A true monarchy was essential if the decline of France was to be stopped. Without monarchy, France would perish, and the contemporary generation of Frenchmen be the last. In politics it was necessary to consider not the morality of kings, nor even their glory, but the result of their reign. French kings had increased the national capital and had improved things. The worst mistresses of the worst of princes had always been less fatal than the caprices of the parliamentary or dictatorial exercises of national sovereignty. Moreover, kings were more easily controlled than were assemblies. The worst monarchy could be terminated eventually by regicide.[3]

The advantages of a return to monarchy were many—it provided a known ruler, it would strengthen France, it would create unity and expel the foreigners.

It was necessary to have a known ruler and to destroy the anonymous Caesarism of the present administration. It was necessary to get a group to put its powers at the service of a person of flesh and blood, the result and synthesis of ten centuries of history, a person who was already alive and did

[3] *Enquête sur la monarchie*, pp. 124-128; *Kiel et Tanger*, p. 351.

not need to be created artificially. The presence of such an individual would be the method by which unity would be created and a government of parties overcome. A King of France was the only point around which different forces had grouped closely, and without him, they would disperse. He could reconcile, conciliate, reunite the interests of the ephemeral citizens with the interests of the development of the state because it was in him that French heritage was deposited and personified. The initial step in the formation of French unity had been taken on the day when the Duke of France had become the King of France. From that dated French advances in religion, civilization, the life of provinces, the towns, material and moral progress.[4] Without a king, Frenchmen had nothing in common; he was the brain, the central nervous system of the whole nation.

His presence meant not only unity but continuity. France was a work of art, a work of political art, born of the collaboration of favorable circumstances and of the activities of French kings. French patriotism needed a permanent expression which could be found only in a king, or a series of kings. What was called France was born of Capetian organization; every loss France had suffered under Capetian regimes had been followed by exemplary reparations. The dynasty had provided harmony in the nation. Whenever the hereditary principle was interrupted, the results were less happy. The restoration of the royal family, therefore, would be the symbol of the restoration of families in general.

A monarchy providing unity and continuity would enormously strengthen France and revive it nationally. Hereditary power was the only political institution that could not only take account of national difficulties but also provide the maximum power to end these difficulties and lead to peace and security. Maurras was willing to admit that monarchy of itself did not avert the misfortunes by which civil or foreign wars, physical epidemics, or moral pests could menace nations. But what he urged was that in countries like France, heredi-

---

[4] *De Démos à César*, ii:130.

tary monarchy provided not merely the best but the only basis for defense against these misfortunes.[5]

It was this work of defense and organization that had been a characteristic feature of the Capetian house. At all times the hereditary monarchy had strengthened France. Louis XIV had won great victories and placed on the Spanish throne a prince of French blood, a natural friend of France. Louis XV had annexed Lorraine and Corsica. Louis XVI had separated America from England and helped create there a great nation whose gratitude toward the French people was part of the heritage of the citizen. Even after the Revolution, it was in 1830 and in 1848, when kings were reigning, that there was a strong political, naval, and military organization. On the other hand, under the false monarchs, the Bonapartes, there was invasion or loss of territory. The two Empires had left France nothing but Sedan and Waterloo. Restoration of the monarchy was necessary, but only the right kind of monarchy. A true monarch would always be acting in the general interest of the country because the interest of the monarch was synonymous with that of the public good. He would make alliances that would be useful to the country, and keep his eyes always turned toward the Rhine. Since states needed leaders and guides as populations needed bread, it was the monarch who would provide the necessary leadership and be the example of his time as was Louis XIV, "type de sa race et figure de sa patrie."[6] The monarch could act quickly, could stand above party differences, and could make use of able advisers.

The fact that monarchy would strengthen the nation in this way did not mean that its powers would be extensive in all directions. Monarchy did not provide a fully made answer for good citizens or for national associations, or any ready-made solution, but simply the faculty of existing freely, of developing without constraint, of living in peace under just laws. The king re-established order and then reserved to himself the domain of pure politics which concerned him

[5] *Mes Idées politiques*, p. 281.
[6] Charles Maurras, *Louis XIV et la France*, Paris, 1936, p. 64.

alone: diplomacy and war, the important police and judicial posts.[7]

It was only under monarchy that decentralization could take place, for only the king could apply himself to the task of decentralization without risking anything for himself or for France.[8] Royalty would allow a thousand private groups to make their own law and rules. Only under Philip VIII, who would become the protector of *syndicats* as well as King of the United Provinces, could professional republics and local republics be organized. The king would be the head of the French Republics. Philip VIII could truly establish the French State because of his nationalism, his anti-Semitism, his military policy, his taste for authority, his views on decentralization. It is perhaps in this argument that the fundamental fallacy of Maurras' thesis lies, for it is difficult to see why a monarchy, absolute, hereditary, and not dependent on popularity, should create limitations to its own power and foster the growth of groups which might check it. Since power tends to be cumulative, Maurras' attempt to combine a self-limiting monarch with decentralization of administration is pure fantasy.

In October 1897, after his return from Greece and before the Dreyfus Affair had reached its climax, Maurras was already writing articles on the necessity for monarchy. But at first he anticipated the return of French monarchy only through a kind of Monk or Talleyrand,[9] and only later, after the Action Française movement was founded, did he begin to think that a movement of the kind could prepare the way for the successful conquest of power. But this self-styled realist was incredibly unrealistic about the power of the movement and its chances for success. The renaissance of the Royalist movement of which Maurras spoke was limited to a small group. His idea of the king as "father of all his subjects" was not one that was of especial appeal to the workers. His analysis and estimate of the historical activity of the monarchs was

[7] *La Démocratie religieuse*, pp. 73-74.
[8] *L'Etang de Berre*, p. 60.
[9] *Au Signe de Flore*, p. xvii.

inaccurate. He was unwilling to admit that the French kings had suppressed several ancient provinces—Maine, Anjou, Touraine, and Auvergne. Nor would he admit that, as M. Luethy has argued recently, it was not the 40 kings who made France, but 30 generations of administrative and judicial officials. Maurras set up a false equation of the 17th century as the great century of the French monarchy and as the great century of classical literature. But in the 19th and 20th centuries, he refused to draw any conclusions from the only powerful and securely based monarchy in Europe, the constitutional monarchy of Great Britain.

James Darmesteter once called Royalist writers "les chevaliers du gothique larmoyant." Certainly Maurras could be included in this category. The great gap in his ideas on monarchy was not simply the refusal to admit the unwillingness of the French people to accept the return of a monarch but the mysterious absence of any kind of discussion of the desirable qualities for the sovereign. It is true that Maurras never argued that good government was the outcome of the blood of the monarch, but solely that the hereditary sovereign would be in the position to govern well. Yet admitting that the king would not necessarily be outstanding in intelligence, culture, or virtue—a fair commentary on the available candidates for the throne—it is difficult to see how he would suddenly be directly interested in the public welfare. It is noticeable that apart from a few lines at one point Maurras never discusses the qualities the king should have. In those few lines his image of the king—young, an outdoor man rather than a scholar, a lover of the active life, a great hunter, shooter, aviator, an individual full of initiative and rapid in execution of his actions—was sufficient to stiffen any previously half-hearted opposition to the return of monarchy.

MAURRAS AND BARRÈS—NATIONALISM

If Maurras and Barrès disagreed on the need for monarchy, they agreed on the need for a strong nationalism, and were largely responsible for the development of a Nationalist movement in France. Maurras argued that it was necessary to create a theory of Frenchman as Fichte had created one for Germans. This theory was not simply one of patriotism, which was love of country, but one of nationalism, a readiness to defend it against the foreigner. To love one's country was not enough. It was necessary to defend eternal France against caprice or avidity.[10] Maurras always regarded his defense of Colonel Henry as "the best action, and in any case, the most useful of all those for which I had reason to rejoice."[11] After Colonel Henry's suicide, the first French blood to be spilled in the Dreyfus Affair, it was evident that national sentiment was divided and incapable of action. Since the Patrie Française was insufficient, it was necessary to create a new movement, the Action Française. Maurras admitted that his nationalism had begun as an aesthetic one with a love for the air and the sky of France. His cult of "la patrie" allied him with the great objects of the beautiful and the good. But his nationalism turned in a political direction.

Nationalism was not simply desirable subjectively, but an inescapable necessity, the great fact of the modern world. Since the disappearance of the Christian Republic of the Middle Ages, the nation was, from the secular point of view, the condition of the life of man and the setting for his highest and richest development. The nation rendered to citizens the same service that the *syndicat* rendered to producers: it was the organ of real rights. Nationalism was not a simple sentiment, but really the aspect, admission, and the exercise of a rational and mathematical obligation.[12]

True humanity began with what was near to us; not only was the nation natural, it was also rational and moral— the nation was the most complete and the most coherent manifestation of humanity. Humanity had never existed in itself; it had been realized in Roman unity, Christian unity, and in Maurras' day, in the framework of the nation. He objected to the fake cosmopolitanism of the stadium at the time of the Olympic Games in Athens. A race, a nation were

10 Charles Maurras and Lucien Moreau, "L'Action française," p. 969.
11 *Au Signe de Flore*, pp. 81-104.
12 *Pour un jeune français*, pp. 108-109.

obviously immortal substances. They disposed of an inexhaustible reserve of thoughts, hearts, and bodies. France was not a cloudy idea, but a dear reality, a reality coming from the soil and the blood of France, its traditions, interests, and sentiments.[13]

Nationality derived from human nature defined and qualified by society. It was attached to concrete phenomena. Its political expression, the nation state, was the vehicle of the good life. Belief in the state was not a mystical conception, but one of intelligence. The modern nation state was the heir to Greek and Roman civilization. In particular, France was the inheritor of this civilization. Man and Frenchman had become synonymous. Civilization was a particular genre of beauty and truth to which the French would be wise to attach themselves because it was more natural for them to conceive it, and they expresed it better than others. The French were well qualified to do this, and French history had nothing to envy in the most famous. It was probably the most brilliant in all modern Europe. If France was a goddess, she was a rational one, a nonabstract one. She had a body and a soul, a history, art, charming nature, and a magnanimous society of heroes.

The nation was the central point for the defense of the existence of France, its strengthening, its encouragement of traditions, and its resistance to the enemy, both foreign and internal. The most extensive point of view was, practically speaking, the nationalist point of view.[14] Nationalism attended to the defense of religion and society, but the reverse was not necessarily true. France was not a union of individuals who voted, but a body of families who lived together in a nation composed by history and based on geography.

Maurras spoke of the two precious traditions, one of blood and the other of the sayings and writings of Frenchmen.[15] At first he stressed the idea of race much more than he did at a later stage. In 1892, he had suggested that there was no

---

[13] *Enquête sur la monarchie*, pp. 463-474.

[14] *La Démocratie religieuse*, p. 384.

[15] Maurras, "Bourget en Amerique," *Gazette de France*, May 5, 1895.

idea more worthy of directing the lives of men or even of nations than race; it was the very foundation of the concept of the fatherland.[16] But as racists began to emphasize the supremacy of the Aryan race, Maurras began to stress the concept less and less. Later, he insisted that he opposed the Jews, not as a race but as a people, the source of individualism, idealism, cosmopolitanism. To Maurras, all Frenchmen, rich or poor, were patricians by virtue of participation in French traditions. Frenchmen, in fact, could be defined by the harmony of two dominant elements: the extreme vigor of a natural, ordered and enlightened *élan*, and the powers of the heart magnified by the thought which oriented them.

These traditions were strengthened by love of France. The good citizen ought to subordinate his interests to the good of the *patrie*. Patriotism meant allegiance to France without qualifications or conditions.[17] Those who said, "France before all" were patriots; those who said, "France, but" were humanitarians. For Maurras, France was the only political principle, and among Frenchmen all political questions had to be coordinated and resolved by relation to the nation. Attention must therefore be paid to external and internal safety.

Part of this attention to the needs of the nation would be the military reawakening of France, and the carrying out of *la revanche*. Maurras had experienced childhood fears of Germany, as had Barrès. He recalled that his parents' maid had threatened him with the Prussians when he misbehaved as a child, and that the children of his day all wanted to be soldiers. He always regretted that his deafness had forced him to give up the idea of the naval school on which his heart had been set and the dream of going to fire on some German port and destroying the entry to the Kiel Canal that was being built with the millions of the French indemnity. The task was to recover Alsace-Lorraine, and return these provinces to the natural society called France. At his trial near the end of his

16 Maurras, "Paul Bourget et Cosmopolis," *Gazette de France*, December 20, 1892, as cited in Roudiez, "Charles Maurras: The Formative Years," p. 212.

17 *L'Ordre et le désordre*, p. 11.

life, Maurras confessed, "All my political life, I have been in contact with the men of the east devoted to the idea of revenge."[18]

Another part of this reawakening would be the resistance to internal foreigners. Maurras had been struck on first arriving in Paris by the number of foreigners, many of whose names were Jewish, with the letters *K*, *W*, and *Z* in them. He was distressed at the interest in foreign culture and literature. He attacked any undue attention to a nonclassical culture, and attacked even Lemaître for his praise of Tolstoy's *Resurrection*.[19] He upheld the French language, internally and externally. Internally, he opposed the teaching of German in schools. Externally, he advocated the use of French, rather than Flemish, in Belgian schools. There was for him an inequality in languages, as in persons and nations, and French was at the apex.

Barrès agreed with Maurras in much of this analysis of nationalism, in the rejection of an emphasis on race, and in the plea for a stronger nation dedicated to *la revanche*, in which foreigners would be absent. Barrès was not a racist. He agreed that there were a French type, an English type, a German type, but not a race. Peoples were products of history. For Barrès there was no French race, but a French nation which continued to develop every day, a French people, a collectivity of political formation in which there was no one rallying point. The country was partly composed of Latins, partly of Gauls, partly of "soldiers of the Church"; at times it had been a great nation, the emancipator of peoples.[20]

More real than either earth or race as nationalist values was the spirit of each small *patrie*, and that spirit lay largely in language. The French *patrie* existed more assuredly through language than in territory, for it was the possession of the same language and common legends that constituted nationalities. Barrès came to realize that the true background of Frenchmen was a common nature, a social and historical

[18] *Le Procès Maurras*, p. 53.
[19] *Quand les français*, pp. 149-161.
[20] *Mes Cahiers*, iii:112; *Scènes*, pp. 81, 473.

product. It was linked to certain places and figures, certain places like Mount Sion and Domremy, where the spirit was more sensitive than elsewhere, and certain figures, who in themselves were models of heroism or action—figures such as Marchand, Gallieni, Morès, Napoleon, Pascal, and Joan of Arc. Joan of Arc was particularly important because she united both Lorraine and France, paganism (through the goddess Rosmertha who reigned on the hills of Sion) and Christianity.

Barrès advocated the creation of a *mystique* that would reunite all Frenchmen. What was the common definition and idea behind nationalism? Barrès' contribution to the solution was that it was the voice of the ancestors, the prolongation of the dead, the acceptance of a determinism. Making his views apparent in the letter written by Roemerspacher in *L'Appel au soldat*, Barrès regarded France as the result of a series of historic facts, accumulated resources, and a direction imposed on individual behavior in order to produce a favorable action by individuals and by the nation as a whole. Nationalism ruled the universe, and was an irresistible force emerging all over the world. Since nationalism was not simply a matter of sentiment but a rational, even a mathematical necessity, there was no liberty of thought in this matter. To be a Nationalist was the best service that a Frenchman could render to humanity.[21] In this way, a discipline would attach Frenchmen to what was truly eternal, and could be developed in a continuous way, so that nationalism and universalism would be harmonized.

The idea of country was beautiful, good, legitimate, and ought to make itself felt in social economy, politics, and public education.[22] But it was always necessary to remember the realities of life. The force of a country was proportional to the number of rifles that its citizens could command. It was vital for France to be strong and to assert itself against the foreigners. In 1884 Barrès was writing of the special task of

[21] *Scènes*, pp. 10, 104–112.
[22] *La Cocarde*, October 24, 1894, as cited in H. Clouard, "La 'Cocarde' de Barrès," *Revue Critique des idées et des livres*, February 10, 1910, p. 227.

France, which was to recapture the stolen territory, and in particular, Metz and Strasbourg. In this way, the spirit of militarism was linked with the idea of regionalism. French nationality was born of provincial "nationalities"—if one of these defaulted, the political construction that was France lost one of its basic elements. Moreover, individuals had to be attached to these provincial nationalities, for the feeling for country was always stronger in the soul of an *enraciné* than in that of a *déraciné*. But the Nationalist campaign was also designed to put France on guard against the cosmopolitan, or rather German, socialism which enervated the defense of the country. Barrès saw his role as that of the preserver of French culture.[23] The defense of French interests was effected through tradition, protection, and decentralization. The traditions adopted would be those proper to France, the protection must be given to French economic and political interests against the forces of international finance, foreign goods, and foreigners both internal and external, and decentralization would be a means to communal and provincial life. In this way, Lorraine would be protected from the Germans and the Midi from the Italians.

But nationalism was valuable not only for rational and religious reasons, but also as a means of exaltation, as a discipline of French thought, as a way of feeling and thinking. For Barrès the *Marseillaise* was important not so much for the words as for the mass of emotions it excited in his subconscious. It was necessary to recapture, to protect, to augment the energy inherited from ancestors. The nationalism of Barrès was a combination of material interests and the development of the soul, a prolongation of his egoism.

Barrès was the first to give the word *nationalism* its present political significance, in an article on July 4, 1892, and became identified with the idea during the Boulanger and Dreyfus Affairs. He regarded himself as the conscious spokesman for the discipline and direction that were necessary in the nationalist movement. It was disastrous that Boulangism, without that brain power that Bouteiller had provided for parliamentarianism, had remained nothing but a fever. But Barrès

[23] *Mes Cahiers*, II:250.

was obliged to admit that nationalism had not given him felicity, because he appreciated the impossibility of provincialism while French provinces were so arid, and the impossibility of imperialism along British lines when French nationality was so weak.[24] In a letter of October 18, 1901, he wrote that he was retiring from the sterile struggle and did not want to be either a candidate or deputy, for political nationalism was finished. What alone interested him was a certain national point of view to introduce into public affairs. He returned to his "true territory, which is to help maintain the standard of French thought."[25]

At the funeral of Barrès, Georges Valois whispered to Maurras that the national tribute "was the first official homage to nationalist thought." But Barrès' nationalism had been one of defense and retraction, not of expansion. It was the period when nationalism began turning inward, and became a means of internal strength rather than of external power. "The last Boulangist," Thibaudet called Barrès, but alas, he was one of the first, not the last.

It was in this period that French nationalism relinquished its always tentative associations with liberalism and became firmly attached to the Right. Maurras, with his concept of integral nationalism, Barrès with his deterministic acceptance of nationalism, both established the basis on which the movement would proceed, and introduced new elements that have not yet lost their dangerous powers. The spirit of militarism, the hostility to foreign nations, the economic and political protectionism, but above all, the denial of individual rights in the interests of the nation state, and the proscription of internal opposition and dissent, signified a radical departure from nationalism in its liberal period.

SOREL AND SYNDICALISM

For Sorel, the key to the emancipation of the individual and to a better society was syndicalism. At the end of his article, "L'Avenir socialiste des syndicats" in *Humanité nouvelle*, May,

---

[24] *Mes Cahiers*, iii:6, 107.

[25] Maurice Barrès, *Quelques Lettres politiques inédites*, ed. J. Caplain, Paris, 1924, p. 22.

1898, and reprinted in *Matériaux d'une théorie du prolétariat,* he had said, "The future of socialism lies in the autonomous development of working-class *syndicats.*"[26] But it would be some years before he became a revolutionary syndicalist. It was, he argued elsewhere in the same year,[27] the emancipation of the working class that would create, instruct, and organize new institutions. He regarded the labor unions as the most notable educative institutions the world had ever known, and thought that the essential thing was that the cooperatives develop new juridical ideas in the working class, ideas of mutual help and solidarity instead of rivalry and corruption. But in 1903, ceasing to believe in the value or possibility of proletarian political organizations, he dismissed the consumers' cooperatives as bodies in which all the vices of democracy were present, while the producers' cooperatives were oligarchic and functioned well only if they were directed in patronal fashion. Cooperatives lacked the spirit of revolt, and this spirit was essential to socialism.[28]

Syndicalism, Bertrand Russell has argued, is more concerned with procuring freedom in work than increasing material well-being. Sorel's argument for a new civilization was in fact an amplification of this thesis. Comparing contemporary France with the past, Sorel found it unfortunate that the traditional technique of artisans had been lost. It was regrettable that this was not an epoch like the 13th century, when art emanated so directly from the practice of technicians.[29] For Sorel, it was essential that young people be taught to love their work, to find intelligible everything taking place in the workshop, to consider what they made as works of art of which they could not be too careful. They would gain in responsibility, in ability to take initiative, in personal dignity. The sublime could exist only in perfected industry.

The new civilization would emerge through the process of production. The source of future law was in the beneficial

[26] *Matériaux,* p. 133.
[27] Georges Sorel, "La Crise du socialisme," *op.cit.,* p. 612.
[28] *Matériaux,* p. 114; *Introduction à l'économie moderne,* p. 179.
[29] Sorel, "Superstition socialiste," *op.cit.,* p. 762.

MONARCHY, NATIONALISM, SYNDICALISM

practices of the workshop; socialism would inherit not only the tools created by capitalism and science resulting from technical development, but also the procedures of cooperation present in factories.[30] If there was something of social excellence in human activity, it was the machine; it was more social than language itself. Capitalist workshops engendered not only the material conditions, but also the moral conditions of socialism. Capitalism created the heritage which socialism would receive: the men who would overturn the present regime, and the means of bringing about this destruction. At the same time, it would preserve the results obtained in capitalist production. A better productive method would be founded on the active collaboration of the worker, considered as a producer interested in the perfect success of his work.

Not only was the productive process desirable materially and the cooperation it engendered desirable socially, but production was important philosophically. The machine created an artificial milieu. This was desirable because individuals were free insofar as they could construct a mechanism of their own, and so create sequences having an order of their own. Since men knew only those things belonging to the artificial milieu, by extending the activity of men and inventing new machines, individuals could discover more of the unknown by enlarging the field of human cooperation with the energies of nature in the artificial milieu. Men knew only by creating, and the creation of more machines led to industrial development.[31] In this way, workers as inventors and creators of their work developed aesthetic sensibility, a love of work, and a revelation of the splendor of man's destiny.[32] To know man it was always necessary to consider him entirely as worker, and not to separate him from the apparatus from which he gained his livelihood.

The concern for production was therefore uppermost in the mind of Sorel. He thought it the honor of Marxism to

[30] Sorel, "Le Syndicalisme révolutionnaire," *op.cit.*, p. 277.
[31] Sorel, "L'Evolution créatrice," *Le Mouvement socialiste* (April 1908), 23:276.
[32] Sorel, "La Valeur sociale de l'art," *Revue de métaphysique et de morale* (1901), 9:278.

have founded all its sociological investigations on the consideration of production and not, as bourgeois caricatures of capitalism did, on the division of riches and consumption. Marx, in contrast to Blanqui, thought of a revolution made by a proletariat of producers who had acquired the economic capacity and the intelligence of work, under the very influences of the conditions of production.[33] For Sorel, there could never be too many productive forces in a country marching to socialism; even cartels furnished the means of creating a better base for the creation of socialism. Sorel, as well as all syndicalists, was not an anticapitalist as were the anarchists, because he considered the syndicalist movement as the direct heir of capitalism. He repeated the tribute that Marx had paid to the productive triumphs of capitalism. He opposed and regretted sabotage, a procedure of the *ancien régime*, which could never orient workers towards emancipation.

The process of production was morally as well as materially beneficial, and the development of the syndicalist movement would increase this element of morality. For Sorel as for Proudhon, work became the noblest privilege of man. He saw demoralization in store for those who did not work. His belief that the ambition of all democrats was to avoid work only increased his distaste for them. The revolutionary syndicalists desired to exalt the individuality of the life of the producer. It was very important to inspire in the worker the sentiment that he was an artist, controlling a machine the construction of which clearly showed that it itself was a work of art.[34] The analogy between the worker and the artist was that they were both creators, capable of bringing their visions to realization. But this was morally as well as aesthetically important. Sorel therefore for the first time linked the ideas of the worker who loves his work, the artist, and the freedom that was necessary for the producer.

Morality must not be imperiled. If the workers triumphed without having accomplished the moral evolutions that were indispensable, their regime would be abominable and the

33 *La Décomposition du Marxisme,* p. 45.
34 *Introduction,* p. 421.

world would be plunged again into suffering, brutality, and injustices as great as those of the present. But fortunately the *syndicats* were a powerful mechanism of moralization, united by a will of solidarity. Whereas political parties communicated enthusiasm to the working class for only a limited time, the *syndicats* created powerful and durable ties in the working class. The overturning of political institutions required a high degree of morality among the workers, and the necessary moral training could be obtained only in production and through the *syndicats*. The *syndicats*, rather than the democratic political bodies, were better fitted to play the role of the former social authorities.

The two methods that were vital for the syndicalist movement in this moral development were self-emancipation and struggle. The task of emancipation, Sorel argued in 1899, must be the task of the workers themselves.[35] A great change would be produced in the world when the proletariat had acquired, as the bourgeoisie had after the Revolution, the feeling that it was capable of thinking according to its own conditions of life. But the first rule of conduct for the proletariat was to remain exclusively working class, which meant the exclusion of intellectuals whose direction would have the effect of restoring hierarchies and dividing the body of workers. It also meant that the emancipation of the proletariat would be the work of those who took a serious part in the process of production, the workers, and not the politicians. The fault of social democracy was that it had submitted the workers to the politicians. It was the syndicalist movement which would intellectually free the working class from all respect for bourgeois nonsense.

The method of self-emancipation was struggle and violence. The originality of revolutionary syndicalism was that it founded the superiority it attributed to the working class on the qualities this class was to acquire in the social struggle. The proletariat could regenerate humanity because it was the only class which was, at that time, animated by a spirit of war, and consequently, the only one that was virile and

[35] Sorel, "L'Ethique du socialisme," *op.cit.*, p. 159.

capable of progress.[36] Sorel argued that what was really true and
original in Marxism was the idea that class struggle was the
essence of socialism. This was not a sociological conception
for the use of the learned. It was the ideological aspect of
a social war by the proletariat against the owners of industry; the *syndicat* was the instrument of social war. Sorel
always drew a distinction between the revolt of the poor,
a bourgeois conception, and class war, a proletarian one, in
the same way as he distinguished the "proletariat" from the
"oppressed."

The means of this struggle and violence was the strike.
Sorel admitted that at first he had suppressed a chapter he
had written on the desirability of the General Strike, and
had allowed it to be published only when the General Strike
was no longer considered as an anarchist insanity. He believed the General Strike to be the essential method for the
regeneration of society. It was not born out of intellectual
reflection, but out of practice, an episode in the social struggle. As distinct from political parties which generally defined
the reforms they wished to bring about, the General Strike
had the character of infinity, because it put to one side all
discussion of definite reforms and confronted men with a
catastrophe.[37] Sorel attempted to demonstrate the moral regeneration produced by such a catastrophe through his analogy between the syndicalist men of action, and the Christian
martyrs who had died for their faith and the monks who
had kept the faith alive. The revolutionary syndicalists, like
those monks and martyrs who had saved the Church, could
save socialism. The General Strike, constantly rejuvenated
by the feelings aroused by proletarian violence, produced an
epic state of mind.

In an essay of 1896,[38] Sorel had denied that the proletarian
revolution had to take the character of a war of extermina-
tion, and in *Le Procès de Socrate*, he had said that in general,

[36] Sorel, "Le Caractère religieux de socialisme," *Le Mouvement socialiste* (November 1906), 20:287.
[37] *Reflections on Violence*, pp. 27, 294.
[38] Sorel, "Etude sur Vico," *op.cit.*, p. 934.

men who appealed to violence were very feeble theoreticians. But, influenced by Proudhon, who "had hoped for a Napoleonic battle finally destroying the opponent,"[39] Sorel came to urge the necessity of violence. This violence, similar to the task of an army in which there was no brutality, massacre or hate against the bourgeoisie, and in which it was not necessary for blood to flow, was the only way in which European nations stupefied by humanitarianism, could recover their former energy.

In all this, Sorel idealized the proletariat and found in it all the desirable moral and creative qualities he thought necessary to end the decadence of society. He advocated the superior morality of the proletariat, and argued that syndicalism could not accept the idea that the historical mission of the proletariat was to imitate the middle class. Part of this rejection of bourgeois ideology was the result of Sorel's attitude toward freedom. There is a remarkable resemblance between this attitude of Sorel and the Hegelian-Marxian idea of alienation. Under capitalism, work was external to the worker, and was not part of his nature. Therefore, since the worker did not fulfill himself in his work, he had a feeling of misery and his physical and mental energy was undeveloped. For Sorel, freedom meant spontaneous activity, which was denied under capitalism. Therefore, just as for Marx, communism was the definitive resolution of the antagonism between man and nature and between man and man, the true solution of the conflict between existence and essence, between freedom and necessity, so for Sorel syndicalism was the solution.

Since Lewis Lorwin's discerning book, *Syndicalism in France*, many have argued that the idea of Sorel as a leader of revolutionary syndicalism is a myth, for the movement was essentially the outcome of French experience, the state of the unions, and the behavior of the worker. Certainly Sorel himself was always modest about his influence, and never claimed more than a thousand readers, even in the years 1905-1908, when he was closest to the movement.

[39] *Reflections on Violence*, p. 245.

260

But if the revolutionary enthusiasm of a minority of syndicalists had produced their theorist, their lack of success also quickly led to disillusionment. In 1906 the Sarrien ministry had forbidden the creation of any new *syndicats* of officials. In the same year Clemenceau crushed the coal strike, using 20,000 troops against the 40,000 miners. With a force of 45,000 troops behind him, he prevented the syndicalists from taking to the barricades on May Day. When in 1908 the attempted general strike call failed, and four killed and 50 wounded were casualties of the cavalry at Villeneuve-Saint-Georges, it was clear that a strong minister could control the syndicalist threat. Yet it was in these moments of struggle and anxiety that the core of Sorel's ideas lay.

For this "Tertullien of socialism," as Berth called him, the new evaluation of all moral values by the militant proletariat resulted in the notion of catastrophe.[40] His was the Jansenist spirit, martial and loath to compromise. For him, as Ascoli has suggested, the unique value of life rested in the moments of fervor, revolt, and faith.[41] It is interesting and perhaps revealing that a behaviorist like Elton Mayo reached the same conclusion as did Sorel on the need to integrate the worker with his work, by exactly opposite logic: the necessity of cooperation, not conflict, and by means of the manager rather than the worker. Sorel refused to concern himself with the aims of the syndicalist movement, or with the practical details of their implementation. In an age of the welfare state, in which the theory of syndicalism is absent, but in which the problem of workers' control and participation in the government of industry is a very real one, this lack of concern by Sorel is highly unfortunate. To argue, as did Sorel, that one could have only indeterminate views about the future,[42] expressed in the language of artistic imagination, meant granting to those who were prepared to be more articulate the right to initiate change. Moreover, his

---

[40] Sorel, "La Crise du socialisme," *op.cit.*, p. 611.

[41] Max Ascoli, *Georges Sorel*, p. 31.

[42] Sorel, "Les Théories de M. Durkheim," *Le Devenir social* (May 1895), 1:163.

disillusion with the syndicalist movement in 1911, when he wrote that syndicalism, which could have had a powerful ideology, had fallen into the hands of hyperdemagogues who did not understand ideas,[43] stripped the syndicalist idea of its most powerful intellectual advocate.

[43] Letter to Croce, January 25, 1911, *La Critica* (1928), 26:345.

CHAPTER XIII

CONCLUSION

IT HAS BEEN THE AIM of this work to examine the similarities in criticism that the extreme Left and Right made of liberal democracy in general and of the ideology and institutions of the Third Republic in particular. There was, among Sorel, Barrès, and Maurras, a natural if not inevitable link through Proudhon, with his views on democracy, the value of tradition and the family, and through Le Play, with his views on decentralization and on social authorities. When the close collaborator of Maurras, Jacques Bainville dedicated his *Bismarck and France* to Proudhon, it caused no surprise. Among them, the three writers were representative of the contemporary opposition to the Third Republic, and also were significant forerunners of an opposition that would prove more fatal in the future not only to France, but to other European nations. They aptly illustrated the dictum of Julien Benda that the modern age was typified by the intellectual organization of political hatreds.

Sorel, Maurras, and Barrès were writing in a country with a proud cultural heritage but one which was facing new, complex, and difficult internal and external problems that seemed insoluble. Born into a nation that had experienced a humiliating defeat either during their youth or early manhood, they were intensely concerned with the strength of their country. For Maurras, this strength could be renewed by a complete counter-revolution and a return to past rulers. For Barrès it would be through the energetic hero or the leader acting in and through the noblest traditions of the country. For Sorel, it was to be by a renewal of moral spirit. The work of these writers illustrates the modern French dilemma. In an epoch when strong executive leadership became indispensable, the country was compelled through the impetus of its own revolutionary traditions to frown on such leadership. At the same time, strong executive leaders had always been, if popular, undemocratic, in the sense of lacking in responsibility and accountability.

In the context of a humiliated country, the rise of mass movements and the beginning of extensive education, the emotional, intellectual, and institutional divisions in France gave rise to views dangerous for the future. The attack on the intellectuals began to mount, and with it the idea that political problems could be solved in ways other than by conscious application of reason. The true treason of the intellectuals was to attack the process of intellectualization. When to this was added the feeling of heightened nationalism, with its strong stress on militarism and defense against foreigners, the setting was laid not simply for antidemocratic but also for totalitarian movements. It was perhaps in this sense that Louis Aragon suggested that Barrès' books were the first examples in French of the modern political novel.[1]

It is interesting that the three writers were forerunners in the use of political terminology which becomes as confusing as helpful. We have agreed that a division between Left and Right can be drawn, but it is by no means easy to do so, especially in the discussion of extremists, since the attack on the moderate democratic position, though made for opposing reasons, is likely to embrace similar theses. The three writers illustrated the difficulty of such a division: the neo-Marxist attacked rationalism and liberal humanism, the disciple of Comte challenged the economic implications of the master's thought, the supporter of exuberant individualism upheld tradition. It is by their very complexity that these writers are interesting, not only for the understanding of French political life and thought, but for that of the western world as a whole.

The three writers all protested against the conception of the isolated man that they regarded as an integral part of democratic theory, either because to posit such an isolation was a mere intellectual exercise, the product of a cold, unrealistic, rationalistic process, or because it meant controverting the fact that societies were superior to and more important than the individual. The writers protested against the abstract nature of the underlying premises of a democratic

[1] Louis Aragon, *La Lumière de Stendhal*, Paris, 1954, p. 266.

system—its conceptions of natural rights, its assumption that government through a process of discussion can reach desirable solutions—and against the educational system that would be fostered.

The three writers were all opposed to the existing political institutions, used myths, consciously or otherwise, to justify this opposition, and were prepared to use violence to overthrow these institutions; the violence would come from a small group, an elite, either by direct action or by a coup. It was poetic justice that Clemenceau, Prime Minister in 1906, on the outbreak of a number of strikes in Paris, should arrest the leaders of the syndicalist, Nationalist, and monarchist groups for which Sorel, Barrès, and Maurras were the intellectual spokesmen, as responsible for a plot against the Republic. In fact, for a number of years in the first decade of the century, the Action Française flirted with the C.G.T. in the hope of overthrowing the Republic. Yet up to 1914 the political effect of the three writers was limited: Maurras' group at the Action Française was essentially one of literary figures; Barrès, after his Boulangist experience, isolated himself politically and in the Chamber; Sorel was unwilling or incapable of working with any organized political or social movement for long.

The differences among the writers were also significant. The essential and underlying difference between Maurras and Barrès on one side and Sorel on the other was their respective attitudes to politics and to the state, typical of the Right and the Left. The Right always stresses the importance of politics, and in fact for Maurras and Barrès it was important to change the political institutions and replace them by others, to decentralize in order to make the state as a whole stronger, more efficient, and freer. Sorel was hardly interested in the mechanics of politics, and indeed only a small part of his total output of articles and books was concerned with political problems as such. For Sorel, the state was an oppressive institution. Whereas force for Maurras and Barrès meant the capture of the state, violence for Sorel meant its destruction and the breaking up of authority.

This differing emphasis on the power of the state gave rise to another important difference of opinion, a conflicting point of view on the value of unity or scission. All three advocated the need for heroic action, but for Maurras and Barrès this would serve the interest of the nation while for Sorel it was desirable for moral regeneration. If the Nationalists concentrated on politics, Sorel concentrated on morals and economics. The Nationalists in fact had no economic doctrine as such, nor were they much concerned about it. Their suggestion for the need of corporations as opposed to *syndicats* was vague, but in the Rightist-Catholic tradition. Their world was closed, ordered, finite. That of Sorel had no real end, but was one of continuing development.

Maurras and Barrès would disagree on a number of important issues, including fundamental approach to problems. For Maurras, investigation was based on empiricism, rationalism, and classicism. Barrès thought that too large a place had been given to man, and in man to reason, to analysis.

Of the three writers it is Maurras who fits most easily into a recognizable pattern. Maurras was the classic 19th century, as distinct from the modern, counter-revolutionary. His desire was to return to what he thought was the peak of French civilization, the 17th century, and his view was that life ought not to have moved on from that period. Maurras, the would-be classicist, the seemingly dogmatic realist, was in fact the most romantic and the most unrealistic of the three writers. Maurras was provincial in the narrowest sense, concerned with the greatness of one civilization at one time and place.

Like Hobbes, Maurras was authoritarian but not totalitarian. He was authoritarian in his demand for an absolute political power and in his belief that there should be no opposition to this power, but at the same time he insisted that this power should not be exercised over all the affairs of the community and that the political power was not itself a religious phenomenon. Yet Catholic thinkers were right to fear the threat that Maurras represented to the Church both because the state would make use of religion for its own political advantage, and because the Church could be only a prop of the state, not an independent check to it. With Maurras everything had become political, everything was subject to political control, and the control was by a small particular group. The ultimate paradox in Maurras' argument is that political activity must of necessity be limited because of his refusal to allow dissent, and because order was to be imposed from above and was not the result of consent. For him the best guarantees of the rights of the humble were bound up with the health and good of the powerful.

Barrès and Sorel are not so easy to classify as is Maurras. Barrès, like Maurras, favored a revolution from the Right, but he differed from the latter in appealing to eternity rather than to yesterday, and in advocating return to the soul of the people. Of the three writers, Barrès anticipated most closely later antidemocratic ideas and movements, partly through his traditional nationalism on which the state was to be based, and partly through his advocacy of a leader supported by a mass counter-revolution.

Barrès, essentially bourgeois in his emphasis on clean, regular, ordered habits, in his recommendation of material independence in order both to escape dissipation and to ensure the existence of a solid class, was representative of those who felt the Revolution had been made against the nobility as well as against the monarchy. For him the nobility was a dead thing, not capable of rendering any particular service. But Barrès was equally opposed to the working-class movements that were developing and becoming a threat to established material and cultural possessions. As Jacques Madaule has argued, Barrès was too bourgeois to be a man of the Left.[2]

It is significant that Barrès had no economic or social policy as such, but only related economic and social problems to nationalism. By giving the worker a share in industry, he would be induced to be more willing to defend his country. Barrès' combinations of attitudes—bourgeois behavior and morals, antiplutocratic, antiaristocratic, and antiproletarian

[2] Jacques Madaule, *Le Nationalisme de Maurice Barrès,* Marseilles, 1943, passim.

leanings—together with his exaggerated nationalism was new in the 19th century, but common in the 20th.

Barrès' psychological determinism provided the underlying philosophy for his outlook. His emphasis on the individual's lack of freedom of thought or action, man's dependence on his dead ancestors and his native soil, his cult of French heroes, his attempt to revive historic regional organizations, his endeavor to use the Church as a social bulwark and as a means of exaltation—all had their allotted place in the strengthening of the nation.

In Barrès one finds all the themes of the modern counter-revolutionary: the stress on leadership, on action, on the call to arms, on the maintenance of a militarist spirit, the appeal to the soul of the people rather than to reason, the prescription of protection and national economic security, the attack on parties, the intolerance of dissent, and the subordination of the individual to the safety of the whole. Differing from Maurras in his reliance on mass support for political authority, Barrès would support any political movement that could restore stability and renovate French glory.

Like Barrès, Sorel defies easy classification. From Rousseau on, the man of the Left has supported the growth of democratic institutions and society, the trend towards equality, the emancipation of the working class. Sorel certainly advocated the last of these, but philosophically he was opposed to optimism, economically to plutocracy and to commerce, politically to the electoral system and to state enterprise, educationally to a system of integral education. For the Left, the motive of the social movement is the pursuit of equality or justice or the conviction of historical inevitability. For Sorel it was the renewal of moral energy or the struggle to produce the autonomous man who would become free by participating in what he loved, by construction of his own world, and by action upheld by the myth. Whereas the socialist movement is an urban manifestation, Sorel was a hater of cities. Whereas the Marxist believes that revolution takes place in a period of increasing poverty, Sorel believed it would take place through strikes in a period of prosperity. Whereas

Socialist movements are oriented politically toward the capture of the state power—if also implicitly to its destruction when captured—Sorel attacks all political movements and the economic solutions they proposed as founded on the omnipotence of the state. Sorel's advocacy of syndicalism and his consistent detestation of political preoccupation was a break in the historic link between socialism and democracy. Sorel cannot be classified wholly either as Left or Right, just as Proudhon to some extent is in this ambiguous position. Eclectic in his intellectual borrowings, attracted by different movements, owing political allegiance to none of them for more than a short time, with his unsystematic erudition, Sorel, part technocrat, part revolutionary, part conservative, is an outstanding example of the difficulty of drawing a distinction between Left and Right.

The criticism of the regime by the three writers was valid in many ways, especially in relation to the operation of political institutions and the educational system. But, even ignoring their neglect of economic problems, it is curious to see an attack launched on the culture and educational system of France when invention, scientific genius, and literature were at such an extraordinarily high level. Moreover, their attacks were often unfair. Maurras, for instance, urged that the Republic was incapable of centralizing power efficiently and also of decentralizing. It was incapable of making war and also incapable of avoiding it. He attacked the operation of the power of the state, but he also attacked the state whenever it refused to take action.

The irony of the case of the Nationalists is that they refused to agree that 19th century ideas on tradition sprang largely from German romanticism. Their nationalism became, not a symbol of freedom, but the doctrine of internal politics. Nationalism was not simply patriotism, but meant aggression against other countries and opposition to internal dissent. Narrowness replaced universalism. Sorel's criticism in 1894 of the Nationalist position was aptly made. At the beginning of the 19th century, he said, one called patriots those who fought for liberty and who defended collective interests against the rapacity of the privileged. Later, one meant the servile admirers of established governments. Under the fallacious pretext of patriotism, reactionaries of all kinds aspired to involve revolutionary France in a war, the clear result of which would be the triumph of capitalism.[3]

The Nationalists attempted and largely succeeded in gaining a monopoly on patriotism and militarism, and the moderate parties of the Republic, except in time of war, did not attempt to dispute this hold. It was forgotten that Déroulède had originally been a man of the Left. The Nationalist movement had some success in organizing an annual pilgrimage to the statue of Strasbourg, getting the anniversary of Joan of Arc accepted as a national festival. Lyautey had been virtually unchallenged in his attempt to get admittance to the Academy, and the three-year service law had been passed in 1910, against the bitter opposition of Jaurès. Yet the paradox remained, for Maurras at any rate, that while the Right appealed to patriotism, the monarchists had emigrated.

The proposed solutions of the writers were not so much inadequate as irrelevant. For instance, the interest of Barrès in social problems was largely to prevent division and class conflict and to obtain national unity, but it would be difficult to guess from his work that factories existed. The suggestions of the three writers were naïve when they were directed towards complex political and social problems. The essential defect in their argument was that in an age of increasing education, they were all concerned essentially with an elite, a ruling group that was limited, and which was not even, in Pareto's phrase, a circulating elite. Incapable of entering the real game of politics because their extremism made the formation of alliances with other groups or factions impossible, they remained politically isolated. But they also gave warning of future danger to political systems, and it is the tragedy of our times that the insights they had on the nature of political action and the lack of enthusiasm in and for the regime were not heeded.

[3] Georges Sorel, Book review of Leo Tolstoy, *L'Esprit Chrétien et le patriotisme*, *L'Ere Nouvelle* (October 1894), 2:212.

CONCLUSION

France ignored the lesson to be learned from this period, that for democratic societies to survive happily, they need both economic prosperity and ideological enthusiasm. Culturally superior though France was and brilliant as was its administrative organization, especially the Conseil d'Etat, the country's economic strength was not sufficient to support the growing claims of the French worker. Temporarily united with the regime at the time of its greatest peril, during the two Affairs, the workers could owe no deep allegiance to a regime which refused to grant them a greater share of its wealth. Above all the ideological appeal of democracy was limited to but a small part of the country, and if the masses have gone a-whoring after strange gods, this is a measure of the deficiency of liberal democracy. France has not yet ceased to pay the price for this deficiency, and liberal democracy has not yet found the answer to its problems.

BIBLIOGRAPHY

BIBLIOGRAPHY

The bibliography used for this book is divided in the following way:

1a) Books by Maurice Barrès.
1b) Articles by Maurice Barrès.
1c) Books concerning Barrès.
1d) Articles concerning Barrès.

2a) Books by Charles Maurras.
2b) Articles by Charles Maurras.
2c) Books concerning Maurras.
2d) Articles concerning Maurras.

3a) Books by Georges Sorel.
3b) Articles by Georges Sorel.
3c) Books concerning Sorel.
3d) Articles concerning Sorel.

4a) Books concerning more than one of the three writers.
4b) Articles concerning more than one of the three writers.

5) General works on French history.
6) General works on French literature.
7) General works on French working-class movements.
8) General works on Political Theory.

BIBLIOGRAPHY

1a) *BOOKS BY MAURICE BARRÈS*

Adieu à Moréas. Emile-Paul, Paris, 1910.

Alsace-Lorraine. Sansot, Paris, 1906.

Les Amitiés françaises. Juven, Paris, 1911.

Amori et dolori sacrum. Juven, Paris, 1903.

L'Appel au Soldat. Fasquelle, Paris, 1900.

Assainissement et fédéralisme. Librairie de la Revue Socialiste, Paris, 1895.

Le Bi-centenaire de J-J. Rousseau. Editions de l'Indépendance, Paris, 1912.

Mes Cahiers. 14 vols. Plon, Paris, 1929-1957.

Colette Baudoche (Augmented Edition). Plon, Paris, 1923.

La Colline Inspirée (Definitive Edition). Plon, Paris, 1922.

Dans le Cloaque. Emile-Paul, Paris, 1914.

Les Déracinés. 2 vols. Juven, Paris, 1897.

Du Sang, de la volupté et de la mort (New Edition). Emile-Paul, Paris, 1910.

En Provence. Editons du Cadran, Paris, 1930.

L'Ennemi des lois. Perrin, Paris, 1893.

Anatole France. Charavay, Paris, 1883.

Un Homme libre (New Edition). Fontemoing, Paris, 1905.

Huits Jours chez M. Renan (Second Edition). Perrin, Paris, 1890.

Le Jardin de Bérénice (Second Edition). Didier, Paris, 1891.

Le Jardin de Bérénice (Definitive Edition). Plon, Paris, 1921.

Une Journée parlementaire. Charpentier & Fasquelle, Paris, 1894.

Leurs Figures. Juven, Paris, 1902.

Pour la haute intelligence française (Thirteenth Edition). Plon, Paris, 1925.

Quelques lettres politiques inédites. J. Caplain, Editor. Goulet, Paris, 1924.

Sous l'oeil des barbares (New Edition). Didier, Paris, 1892.

Scènes et doctrines du nationalisme. Juven, Paris, 1902; Plon, Paris, 1925.

Taine et Renan. V. Giraud (ed.). Bossard, Paris, 1922.

Toute licence sauf contre l'amour. Perrin, Paris, 1892.

Les Traits éternels de la France. Oxford University Press, New Haven, 1918.

Trois stations de psychothérapie. Perrin, Paris, 1891.

Violons de Lorraine. Basserre, Bayonne, 1912.

Les Voyage de Sparte. Juven, Paris, 1906.

BIBLIOGRAPHY

PREFACES by Maurice Barrès to the following books:

Barrès, J-B. A., *Souvenirs d'un officier de la Grande Armée,*
Plon, Paris, 1923.
Ducray, Camille, *Paul Déroulède,* Ambert, Paris, 1914.
Pilant, Paul, *Le Patriotisme en France et à l'étranger,* Per-
rin, Paris, 1912.

1b) *ARTICLES BY MAURICE BARRÈS*

"A Propos de la réimpression de 'l'Homme Libre,'" *Revue
politique et littéraire* (September 10, 1904), 41:321-24.
"Paul Bourget," *Living Age* (February 9, 1924), 320:272-74.
"L'Elite intellectuelle et la démocratie," *Revue politique et
littéraire* (November 19, 1904), 41:645-46.
"Lettres de Maurice Barrès à Camille Jullian," *Revue philo-
mathique de Bordeaux et du sud-oeust* (January 1935),
38:1-9.
"Lettres de Maurice Barrès à Charles le Goffic," *Annales
de Bretagne* (1951), 58:19-88.
"M. le général Boulanger et la nouvelle génération," *La
Revue indépendante* (April 1888), 7:55-63.
"Notes d'un lettré mécontent," *Le Figaro—Supplément lit-
téraire* (May 26, 1888), p. 1.
"The Panama Scandal," *The Cosmopolitan* (June 1894),
17:203-10.

1c) *BOOKS CONCERNING BARRÈS*

Aragon, Louis, *La Lumière de Stendhal.* Denöel, Paris,
1954.
Beauclair, Henri, *Une Heure chez M. Barrès.* Tresse &
Stock, Paris, 1890.
Berlet, Charles, *Un Ami de Barrès—Stanislas de Guaita.*
Grasset, Paris, 1936.
Blanc-Péridier, A., *Maurice Barrès.* Spes, Paris, 1929.
Boisdeffre, Pierre de, *Métamorphose de la littérature.* Al-
satia, Paris, 1950.
Boisdeffre, Pierre de, *Barrès parmi nous.* Dumont, Paris,
1952.
Boisdeffre, Pierre de, *Des Vivants et des morts.* Editions
Universitaires, Paris, 1954.
Bonnefon, Jean de, *M. Auguste Maurice Barrès.* Société
d'Editions, Paris, 1908.
Bordeaux, Henry, *Le Retour de Barrès à sa terre et à ses
morts.* Plon, Paris, 1924.

BIBLIOGRAPHY

Bremond, Henri, *Maurice Barrès*. Bloud & Gay, Paris, 1924.

Clouard, Henri, *Bilan de Barrès*. Sequanna, Paris, 1943.

Cocteau, Jean, *La Noce massacrée*. A la Sirène, Paris, 1921.

Dietz, Jean, *Maurice Barrès*. La Renaissance du Livre, Paris, 1927.

Domenach, Jean-Marie, *Barrès par lui-même*. Editions du Seuil, Paris, 1954.

Empaytaz, Frédéric, *Reconnaissance à Barrès*. Les Presses Françaises, Paris, 1925.

Empaytaz, Frédéric (ed.), *Chroniques Barrésiennes*. 2 vols. Le Rouge et le Noir, Paris, 1928-29.

Faure-Biguet, J-N., *Maurice Barrès, son oeuvre*. La Nouvelle Revue Critique, Paris, 1924.

Fernandez, Ramon, *Barrès*. Editions du Livre Moderne, Paris, 1943.

Garreau, Albert, *Barrès, défenseur de la civilisation*. Editions des Loisirs, Paris, 1945.

Gillouin, René, *Maurice Barrès*. Sansot, Paris, 1907.

Gillouin, René, *Essais de critique littéraire et philosophique*. Grasset, Paris, 1913.

Gouhier, Urbain, *Notre Ami Barrès*. Montaigne, Paris, 1928.

Herluison, Jean, *Maurice Barrès et le problème de l'ordre*. Nouvelle Librairie Nationale, Paris, 1911.

Huneker, James, *Egoists*. Scribners, New York, 1910.

Jacquet, René, *Notre Maître Maurice Barrès*. Nilsson, Paris, 1900.

King, Sylvia M., *Maurice Barrès: la pensée Allemande et le problème du Rhin*. Champion, Paris, 1933.

Lalou, René, *Maurice Barrès*. Hatchette, Paris, 1950.

Madaule, Jacques, *Le Nationalisme de Maurice Barrès*. Editions du Sagittaire, Marseilles, 1943.

Massis, Henri, *La Pensée de Maurice Barrès*. Mercure de France, Paris, 1909.

Miéville, Henri, *La Pensée de Maurice Barrès*. Editions de la Nouvelle Revue Critique, Paris, 1934.

Mondor, Henri, *Maurice Barrès avant le quartier latin*. Ventadour, Paris, 1956.

Montherlant, Henry de, *Le Solstice de Juin*. Grasset, Paris, 1941.

Montherlant, Henry de, *Aux Fontaines du désir*. Grasset, Paris, 1927.

Moreau, Pierre, *Maurice Barrès*. Editions du Sagittaire, Paris, 1946.

Petitbon, Pierre-Henri, *Taine, Renan, Barrès*. Société d'Edition, "Les Belles Lettres," Paris, 1934.

Ross, Flora E., *Goethe in Modern France*. Illinois Studies in Language and Literature, Vol. 21. University of Illinois, Urbana, 1937.

Tharaud, Jérôme et Jean, *Mes Années chez Barrès*. Plon, Paris, 1928.

Thibaudet, Albert, *La Vie de Maurice Barrès*. Editions de la Nouvelle Revue Française, Paris, 1921.

1d) *ARTICLES CONCERNING MAURICE BARRÈS*

Baldensperger, Fernand, "L'Appel Goethéen chez Maurice Barrès," *Revue de littérature comparée* (January 1925), 5:103-38.

Bidou, Henry, "Parmi les Livres," *La Revue de Paris* (June 15, 1921), 28:867-83.

Blanche, J-E., "Maurice Barrès et le général Boulanger," *Les Nouvelles littéraires* (May 26, 1928).

Boisdeffre, Pierre de, "Justice pour Barrès," *Etudes* (January 1949), 260:331-50.

Bourget, Paul, "Maurice Barrès," *Revue des deux mondes* (December 15, 1923), vii.18:946-48.

Bourne, Randolph S., "Maurice Barrès and the Youth of France," *Atlantic Monthly* (1914), 114:394-99.

Braspart, Michel, "L'Amitié de Barrès," *La Nef* (August 1947), 4:59-63.

Brée, Germaine, "Marcel Proust et Maurice Barrès," *Romanic Review* (April 1949), 40:93-105.

Bremond, Henri, "L'Evolution littéraire de M. Maurice Barrès," *Revue des deux mondes* (February 15, 1908), 43:791-824.

Brogan, D. W., "Maurice Barrès: Formation et progrès d'un nationaliste," *La France libre* (January 15, 1942), 3:187-97.

Cheydleur, F. D., "Maurice Barrès: Author and Patriot," *North American Review* (March 1926), 223:150-56.

Cheydleur, F. D., "Maurice Barrès as a Romanticist," *Publications of the Modern Language Association of America* (1926), 41:462-87.

Clouard, Henri, "La 'Cocarde' de Barrès," *Revue Critique des idées et des livres* (February 10, 25; March 10, 1910), 8:205-30, 332-58, 397-419.

Clyne, Anthony, "Maurice Barrès," *Contemporary Review* (May 1920), 117:682-88.

Dietz, Jean, "Les Débuts de Maurice Barrès dans la vie politique (1888-91)," *La Revue hebdomadaire* (August 15, 1931), 40.33:267-84.

BIBLIOGRAPHY

Dietz, Jean, "Les Débuts de Maurice Barrès," *La Revue de Paris* (October 1, 1928), 35:616-26.

Dimnet, Ernest, "The Evolution of Maurice Barrès," *The Nineteenth Century* (October 1909), 66:634-44.

Domenach, Jean-Marie, "Barrès et les contradictions du nationalisme," *Esprit* (April 1954), 22:481-94.

Duclaux, Mary, "Maurice Barrès," *Quarterly Review* (July 1912), 217:110-35.

Duhourcau, François, "La Voix intérieure de Barrès d'après ses cahiers," *Revue des deux mondes* (September 15; October 1, 1928), vii.47:241-74, 585-621.

Eccles, F. Y., "Maurice Barrès," *Dublin Review* (October 1908), 143:244-63.

Falls, Cyril, "Maurice Barrès," *London Mercury* (November 1922), 7:64-75.

Frohock, W. H., "Maurice Barrès' Collaboration with the Action Française," *The Romanic Review* (April 1938), 29:167-69.

Giraud, Victor, "M. Maurice Barrès," *Revue des deux mondes* (January 1, 15; February 15, 1922), vii.7:47-78, 315-48, 881-907.

Guerard, Albert L., "Maurice Barrès and the Doctrine of Nationalism," *The Texas Review* (April 1916), 1:275-90.

Kanters, Robert, "Barrès invisible et présent," *La Nef* (August 1947), 4:64-72.

Launay, Robert, "Maurice Barrès à l'Action française," *Mercure de France* (February 1, 1924), 169:668-78.

Lynch, Hannah, "A Political Writer of France," *Contemporary Review* (September 1900), 78:381-88.

Mauriac, François, "En marge des cahiers de Barrès," *La Table ronde* (January 1950), 25:20-25.

Mondor, Henri, "La Jeunesse de Barrès," *La Revue de Paris* (January 1956), 63:5-23.

Montherlant, Henry de, "Barrès et notre Temps," *Hommes et mondes* (July 1950), 12:354-64.

Moreau, Pierre, "La Jeunesse de Maurice Barrès," *Revue des cours et conférences* (January 15, 1936), 37:199-210.

Parodi, D., "La Doctrine politique et sociale de M. Maurice Barrès," *La Revue du mois* (January 1907), 3:18-36.

Putnam, George F., "The Meaning of Barrésisme," *Western Political Quarterly* (June 1954), 7:161-82.

Rey, Jean, "Une Campaigne electorale en 1889: revisionniste candidat," *Candide* (April 30, 1936), p. 5.

Thibaudet, Albert, "La Mort de Maurice Barrès," *La Nouvelle revue française* (January 1, 1924), 22:5-24.

281

Thibaudet, Albert, "Barrès à Sion-Vaudémont," *La Nouvelle revue française* (October 1, 1928), 26:568-76.

Thorold, Algar, "The Ideas of Maurice Barrès," *Edinburgh Review* (January 1916), 223:83-99.

Vettard, Camille, "Maurice Barrès et Jules Soury," *Mercure de France* (March 15, 1924), 170:685-95.

Vielé-Griffin, Francis, "La Délimitation du 'Barrésisme,'" *Mercure de France* (March 16, 1912), 96:225-29.

Virtanen, Reino, "Barrès and Pascal," *Publications of the Modern Language Association of America* (1947), 62:802-23.

Three journals devoted an entire issue to Barrès:

La Plume (April 1, 1891).

Revue Critique des idées et des livres (December 25, 1923).

La Table ronde (March 1957).

2a) BOOKS BY CHARLES MAURRAS

L'Allée des philosophes. Crès, Paris, 1924.

Les Amants de Venise (New Edition). Boccard, Paris, 1917.

L'Anglais qui a connu la France. Les Cahiers de Paris, Paris, 1928.

Anatole France, politique et poète. Plon, Paris, 1924.

Anthinéa (New Edition). Champion, Paris, 1919.

Antigone, Vierge-Mère de l'ordre. Aeschlimann, Geneva, 1948.

Au Signe de Flore. Les Oeuvres Répresentatives, Paris, 1931.

L'Avenir de l'intelligence. Nouvelle Librairie Nationale, Paris, 1918.

Maurice Barrès. A la Girouette, Paris, 1948.

Le Bibliophile Barthou. Editions du Capitole, Paris, 1929.

La Critique des lettres. Nouvelle Librairie Nationale, Paris, n.d.

Le Chemin de paradis (Third Edition). Boccard, Paris, 1921.

De la Colère à la justice. Editions du Milieu du Monde, Geneva, 1942.

La Contre-révolution spontanée. Lardanchet, Paris, 1943.

Un Debat sur le romantisme (Written with Raymond de La Tailhède), Flammarion, Paris, 1928.

La Démocratie religieuse. Nouvelle Librairie Nationale, Paris, 1921.

BIBLIOGRAPHY

De Démos à César. 2 vols. Editions du Capitole, Paris, 1930.

La Dentelle du rempart. Grasset, Paris, 1937.

Dictionnaire politique et critique. 5 vols. Cité des Livres, Paris, 1932-34.

Enquête sur la monarchie (Definitive Edition). Nouvelle Librairie Nationale, Paris, 1924.

L'Etang de Berre. Champion, Paris, 1915.

L'Idée de la décentralisation. L'Action Française, Paris, 1919.

Kiel et Tanger. Nouvelle Librairie Nationale, Paris, 1921.

Louis XIV et la France. Les Editions du Cadran, Paris, 1936.

Mademoiselle Monk. Stock, Paris, 1923.

Maîtres et témoins de ma vie d'esprit. Flammarion, Paris, 1954.

Mes Idées politiques. Fayard, Paris, 1937.

Oeuvres capitales. 4 vols. Flammarion, Paris, 1954.

L'Ordre et le désordre. Self, Paris, 1948.

Pages littéraires choisies. Champion, Paris, 1922.

Poèmes, portraits, jugements et opinions. Nouvelle Librairie Nationale, Paris, 1919.

Pour un jeune français. Amiot-Dumont, Paris, 1949.

Pour un réveil français. A l'Ombre des Cyprès, n.p., 1943.

Les Princes des nuées. Plon, Paris, 1933.

Principes. A la cité des livres, Paris, 1931.

Le Procès Maurras. Michel, Paris, 1946.

Prologue d'un essai sur la critique. La Porte Etroite, Paris, 1932.

Quand les français ne s'aimaient pas. Nouvelle Librairie Nationale, Paris, 1916.

Réflexions sur l'ordre en France. Au Pigeonnier, Paris, 1927.

Réflexions sur la révolution de 1789. Editions Self, Paris, 1948.

Réponse à André Gide. Editions de "La Seule France," Paris, 1948.

La République de Martigues. Les Editions du Cadran, Paris, 1929.

La République ne peut pas décentraliser. Nouvelle Librairie Nationale, Paris, 1923.

Tombeaux. Nouvelle Librairie Nationale, Paris, 1921.

Tragi-comédie de ma surdité. Messonet, Aix-en-Provence, 1951.

Trois Idées politiques. Crès, Paris, 1923.

Le Voyage d'Athènes. Flammarion, Paris, 1929.

2b) *ARTICLES BY CHARLES MAURRAS*

In the *Action française* there is an article almost every day by Maurras either under his own name or as "Criton."

"L'Action française" (written with Lucien Moreau), *Le Correspondant* (June 10, 1908), 231:959-81.

"L'Avenir de l'ordre," *La Revue universelle* (April 1920), 1:11-25.

"Maurice Barrès," *La Contemporaine* (October 1901), 1:73-89.

"De l'Autorité legitime: le Droit national et le droit démocratique," *La Revue universelle* (June 1924), 6:657-71.

"Les Droits de l'homme et la philosophie naturelle au XIX^{ieme} siècle," *La Revue hebdomadaire* (November 1899), 12:506-30.

"L'Evolution des idées sociales," *La Réforme sociale* (January 16, February 1, 16, 1891), 21:125-31, 200-208, 277-94.

"Les Idées royalistes," *La Revue hebdomadaire* (March 1910), 3:34-58.

"La Personne du Roi," *Revue critique des idées et des livres* (August 25, 1911), 14:385-411.

"Souvenirs Politiques: L'Affaire Dreyfus et la ligue de la patrie française," *La Revue universelle* (May 15, June 1, 1930), 41:385-401, 559-89.

"Sur les idées de Rousseau," *Revue critique des idées et des livres* (June 25, 1912), 17:648-52.

2c) *BOOKS CONCERNING MAURRAS*

Arbellot, Simon, *Maurras, homme d'action.* Denoel and Steele, Paris, 1937.

Beau de Loménie, Emmanuel, *Maurras et son Système.* E. T. L., Bourg, 1953.

Benjamin, René, *Charles Maurras, ce fils de la mer.* Plon, Paris, 1932.

Bordeaux, Henry, *Charles Maurras et l'académie française.* Editions du Conquistador, Paris, 1955.

Bordeaux, Henry, et al., *Charles Maurras 1868-1952.* Plon, Paris, 1953.

Buthman, William Curt, *The Rise of Integral Nationalism in France.* Columbia University Press, New York, 1939.

Chabaneix, Paul, *Charles Maurras: l'homme, le penseur, le chef.* Millon, La Rochelle, 1937.

Clavière, Maurice, *Charles Maurras ou la restauration des valeurs humaines.* Lesfauries, Paris, 1939.

Cormier, Aristide, *Mes Entretiens de prêtre avec Charles Maurras*. Plon, Paris, 1953.

Cormier, Aristide, *La Vie intérieure de Charles Maurras*. Plon, Paris, 1955.

Daudet, Léon, *Vers le Roi*. Nouvelle Librairie Nationale, Paris, 1921.

Daudet, Léon, *Charles Maurras et son temps*. Flammarion, Paris, 1930.

Dimier, Louis, *Vingt ans d'action française*. Nouvelle Librairie Nationale, Paris, 1926.

Gérin-Ricard, Lazare de, *Les Idées politiques de Joseph de Maistre et la doctrine de Maurras*. Millon, La Rochelle, 1929.

Hupin, Gérard, *Un Grand défenseur de la civilisation, Charles Maurras*. Editions Universitaires, Paris, 1956.

Larpent, Georges, *Pour Connaître Charles Maurras*. Librairie de l'Action Française, Paris, 1926.

Lièvre, Pierre, Maurras. Le Divan, Paris, 1925.

Maritain, Jacques, *Une Opinion sur Charles Maurras et le devoir des Catholiques*. Plon, Paris, 1926.

Massis, Henri, *Maurras et notre temps*. 2 vols. La Palatine, Paris-Geneva, 1951.

Mourre, Michel, *Charles Maurras*. Editions Universitaires, Paris, 1953.

Muret, C. T., *French Royalist Doctrines since the Revolution*. Columbia University Dissertations, Vol. 307. Columbia University Press, New York, 1933.

Pado, Dominique, *Maurras, Béraud, Brasillach*. Pathé, Monaco, 1945.

Raynaud, Ernest, *Souvenirs de police*. Payot, Paris, 1923.

Roche, Alphonse V., *Les Idées traditionalistes en France de Rivarol à Charles Maurras*. Illinois Studies in Languages and Literature, Vol. 21. University of Illinois, Urbana, 1937.

Roudiez, Leon S., "Charles Maurras: the Formative Years," Unpublished doctoral dissertation. Columbia University, New York, 1950.

Roudiez, Leon S., *Maurras jusqu'à l'action française*. Bonne, Paris, 1957.

Roux, Marie de, *Charles Maurras et le nationalisme de l'action française*. Grasset, Paris, 1928.

Segard, Achille, *Charles Maurras et les idées royalistes*. Fayard, Paris, 1919.

Selincourt, Basil de, *The English Secret and other Essays*. Oxford University Press, London, 1923.

BIBLIOGRAPHY

Thibaudet, Albert, *Les Idées de Charles Maurras*. Gallimard, Paris, 1919.

Truc, Gonzague, *Charles Maurras et son temps*. Bossard, Paris, 1918.

Truc, Gonzague, *Apologie pour l'Action française*. Bossard, Paris, 1927.

Vallat, Xavier, *Charles Maurras: numéro d'ecrou 8321*. Plon, Paris, 1953.

2d) *ARTICLES CONCERNING MAURRAS*

Balfour, R. E., "The Action Française Movement," *Cambridge Historical Journal* (1930), 3:182-205.

Bordeaux, Henry, et al., "Hommage à Charles Maurras," *La Revue universelle* (January 1937), 68.

Brogan, D. W., "The Nationalist Doctrine of M. Charles Maurras," *Politica* (February 1935), 1:286-311.

Charpentier, John, "Charles Maurras," *Mercure de France* (September 1, 1930), 222:331-34.

Chatterton-Hill, Georges, "The Royalist Revival in France," *The Nineteenth Century* (July 1914), 76:29-50.

Corrigan, Beatrice, "Charles Maurras: Philosopher of Nationalism," *Queens Quarterly* (Autumn 1945), 52:288-98.

Crito, "Charles Maurras and the English," *The Nineteenth Century* (March 1943), 133:115-22.

Dimnet, Ernest, "Neo-royalist Movement in France," *The Nineteenth Century* (August 1908), 64:287-93.

D'Oléon, R., "L'Idée de nation dans l'oeuvre de Charles Maurras," *La Revue universelle* (January 1, 1939), 76.19:12-25.

Fidao, M. J-E., "Les Postulats de 'l'Action française,' " *Le Correspondant* (December 10, 1905), 221:927-58.

Flat, Paul, "Quelques Idées de M. Charles Maurras," *Revue politique et littéraire* (December 14, 1912), 50:750-52.

Gwynn, Denis, "A Prophet of Reaction: Charles Maurras," *Studies* (December 1922), 11:523-40 (March 1923), 12:45-60.

Kemp, Robert, "Charles Maurras, prince des nuées," *Les Nouvelles littéraires* (November 20, 1952), No. 1316, p. 5.

Lamy, Etienne, " 'L'Action française' et 'Le Correspondant,' " *Le Correspondant* (December 10, 1907), 229:984-1005.

Lamy, Etienne, "Quelques Précisions," *Le Correspondant* (June 10, 1908), 231:982-88.

Lasserre, Pierre, "Charles Maurras et la Renaissance Classique," *Mercure de France* (June 1902), 42.150:589-612.

286

Maulnier, Thierry, "Charles Maurras est Mort," *La Table ronde* (January 1953), No. 61:163-72.
Nickerson, Hoffman, "Maurras," *The American Review* (December 1934), 4:155-72.
Parodi, D., "L'Action française," *"Pages libres"* (May 30, June 6, 1908), 15:585-96, 617-32.
Petrie, Charles, "Action française," *The English Review* (August 1927), No. 225:184-90.
Planhol, René de, "Points de Vue divers sur Charles Maurras," *La Revue critique des idées et des livres* (June 10, 1920), 28:522-34.
Roudiez, Leon S., "The Early Poetic Activities of Charles Maurras," *The French Review* (January 1951), 24:197-208.
Rouquette, Robert, "Charles Maurras et la Papauté," *Etudes* (June 1953), 277:392-405.
Rousseaux, André, "Charles Maurras ou l'exilé de l'éternel," *Revue de Paris* (March 1, 1939), 46.2:103-13.
Tucker, W. R., "The Legacy of Charles Maurras," *Journal of Politics* (November 1955), 17:570-89.
Virtanen, Reino, "Nietzsche and the Action Française," *Journal of the History of Ideas* (April 1950), 11:191-214.
Voguë, Marquis de, "L'Action Française et le Correspondant," *Le Correspondant* (June 10, 1908), 231:989-92.
Whitridge, Arnold, "Charles Maurras," *North American Review* (June 1926), 223:333-44.

3a) BOOKS BY GEORGES SOREL

D'Aristote à Marx (L'Ancienne et la nouvelle métaphysique). Rivière, Paris, 1935.
L'Avenir socialiste des syndicats. Jacques, Paris, 1898.
La Décomposition du Marxisme (Third Edition). Rivière, Paris, 1925.
Les Illusions du progrès (Fourth Edition). Rivière, Paris, 1927.
Introduction à l'Economie moderne (Second Edition). Rivière, Paris, 1922.
Lettres à Paul Delesalle:1914-24. Grasset, Paris, 1947.
Matériaux d'un théorie du prolétariat (Third Edition). Rivière, Paris, 1929.
Le Procès de Socrate. Alcan, Paris, 1889.
Reflections on Violence. Allen & Unwin, London, 1916. (Translation and preface by T. E. Hulme.)

Reflections on Violence. Smith, New York, 1941. (Trans. T. E. Hulme.)

Reflections on Violence. Free Press, Glencoe, 1950. (Preface by E. A. Shils.)

La Révolution Dreyfusienne (Second Edition). Rivière, Paris, 1911.

La Ruine du monde antique (Third Edition). Rivière, Paris, 1933.

Le Système historique de Renan. Jacques, Paris, 1906.

PREFACES by Georges Sorel to the following books:

Berth, Edouard, *Les Méfaits des intellectuels.* Rivière, Paris, 1914.

Labriola, Antonio, *Essais sur la conception matérialiste de l'histoire.* Giard & Brière, Paris, 1897.

Labriola, Arturo, *Karl Marx, l'économiste, le socialiste.* Rivière, Paris, 1910. (Translated into French by Edouard Berth.)

Pelloutier, Ferdinand, *Histoire des bourses du travail.* Schleicher, Paris, 1902.

Seligman, E. R. A., *L'Interprétation économique de l'histoire.* Rivière, Paris, 1911.

A speech "L'Ethique du Socialisme" delivered in February 1899 is printed in Georges Sorel et al., *Morale sociale,* Alcan, Paris, 1909.

3b) *ARTICLES BY GEORGES SOREL*

L'Action Française:
"Le Réveil de l'âme Française," April 14, 1910, pp. 1-2.
Cahiers de la quinzaine:
"Quelque mots sur Proudhon," 2nd series, No. 13, June 22, 1901.
"Socialismes nationaux," 3rd series, No. 14, April 22, 1902.
Le Devenir social:
"Les Théories de M. Durkheim," April 1895, 1:1-26.
                              May 1895, 1:148-80.
"Review of Dr. Legrain," *Dégénérescence sociale et alcoolisme,* October 1895, 1:673-77.
"Superstition socialiste," November 1895, 1:729-64.
"Etudes d'économie rurale après M. Zolla" (pseudonym "F"), January 1896, 2:15-33.

"Progrès et développement" (pseudonym "B"), February 1896, 2:153-74.

March 1896, 2:193-207.

"La Science dans l'éducation," February 1896, 2:110-41.

March 1896, 2:208-39.

April 1896, 2:339-65.

May 1896, 2:425-61.

"L'Idéalisme de M. Brunetière" (pseudonym "J. David"), June 1896, 2:500-16.

"Les Sentiments sociaux" (pseudonym 'X"), August-September 1896, 2:673-95.

"Etude sur Vico," October 1896, 2:785-817.

November 1896, 2:906-41.

December 1896, 2:1013-46.

"La Dépression économique" (pseudonym "F"), November 1896, 2:942-70.

"Contre une critique anarchiste" (pseudonym "H"), May 1897, 3:440-58.

"Sociologie de la suggestion" (pseudonym "X"), August-September 1897, 3:673-89.

"Pro e contro il socialismo," October 1897, 3:854-88.

L'Ere nouvelle:

"La Fin du paganisme," October 1894.

Journal des économistes:

"Sur la théorie marxiste de la valeur," May 1897, 30:22-31.

Le Mouvement socialiste:

"Morale et socialisme," March 1, 1899, 1:207-13.

"Conseils du travail et paix sociale," January 1, 1901, 5:36-41.

"Notes additionnelles à 'l'Avenir socialiste des syndicats,' " September 1, 1905, 17:5-16.

"Le Syndicalisme révolutionnaire," November 1, 1905, 17:265-80.

"Les 'Droits acquis' de Lassalle," April 15, 1906, 18:476-85.

"Grandeur et décadence de Rome," July 1906, 19:244-68.

"Le Caractère religieux de socialisme," November 1906, 20:282-90.

"Le Prétendu socialisme juridique," April 1907, 21:321-48.

"Le Socialisme en 1907," May 1907, 21.

"J-J. Rousseau," June 1907, 21:507-32.

"La Crise morale et religieuse," July 15, 1907, 22:13-37.

"L'Evolution créatrice," October 1907, 22:257-83; Decem-

ber 1907, 22:478-95; January 1908, 23:34-53; March 1908, 23:184-95; April 1908, 23:276-95.
"La Politique Américaine," June 15, 1908, 23:49-56.
"Les Intellectuels à Athènes," September 15, 1908, 24:214-35.
"Pages Libres":
    "Les Grèves de Montceau-les-Mines et leur signification," March 2, 1901, 9:169-73.
    "Proudhon," May 4, 1901, 18:399-402.
    "Pour Proudhon," June 8, 1901, 23:503-05.
Revue critique des idées et des livres:
    Two letters to Georges Valois, May 1908, 1:145-56.
    "Modernisme dans la religion et dans le socialisme," August 10, 1908, 2:177-204.
Revue de métaphysique et de morale:
    "Y-a-t-il de l'utopie dans le Marxisme," March 1899, 7:152-75.
    "La Valeur sociale de l'art," May 1901, 9:251-78.
    "La Crise de la pensée Catholique," 1902, 10:523-51.
    "Sur Divers aspects de la mécanique," 1903, 11:716-48.
    "Les Préoccupations des physiciens modernes," 1905, 13:859-89.
    "La Religion d'aujourd'hui," 1909, 17:240-73, 413-47.
    "Vues sur les problèmes de la philosophie," 1910, 18:581-613; 1911, 19:64-99.
Revue internationale de sociologie:
    "Les Polémiques pour l'interprétation du Marxisme," April 1900, 8:262-84.
    May 1900, 8:348-69.
Revue philosophique:
    "Essai sur la philosophie de Proudhon," June 1892, 33:622-38; July 1892, 34:41-68.
    "Science et socialisme," May 1893, 35:509-11.
Revue politique et parlementaire:
    "La Crise du socialisme," December 1898, 18:598-612.
    "Les Dissensions de la socialdémocratie en Allemagne," July 1900, 25:33-66.
La Revue socialiste:
    "Les Aspects juridiques du socialisme," October 1900, 32:385-415; November 1900, 32:558-85.
    "Economie et agriculture," March 1901, 33:289-301.
    April 1901, 33:421-41.
"Essai sur l'état et l'eglise," August, September, October 1901, 34:129-55, 325-43, 402-21. (Issued later as a separate brochure, *De l'Eglise et de l'état.*)

"Idées socialistes et faits economiques au xix⁰ siècle,"
March, April, May 1902, 35:295-318, 385-410, 519-44.
"Les Syndicats industriels et leur signification," July,
August 1902, 36:41-65, 156-80.
La Science sociale:
"Les Divers types de sociétés coopératives," September
1899, 28:172-201.

3c) *BOOKS CONCERNING SOREL*

Andreu, Pierre, *Notre Maître M. Sorel.* Grasset, Paris, 1953.

Angel, Pierre, *Essais sur Georges Sorel.* Rivière, Paris, 1936.

Ascoli, Max, *Georges Sorel.* Delesalle, Paris, 1921.

Cheydleur, Frédéric, *Essai sur l'evolution des doctrines de Georges Sorel.* Saint-Bruno, Grenoble, 1914.

Deroo, Jean, *Une Expérience sociologique, Georges Sorel.* Rivière, Paris, 1939.

Elliott, W. Y., *The Pragmatic Revolt in Politics.* Macmillan, New York, 1928.

Humphrey, Richard Dale, *The Thought of Georges Sorel as an Anti-intellectual Conception of History.* Harvard University Press, Cambridge, 1951.

Lytle, Scott H., *Historical Materialism and the Social Myth.* Unpublished doctoral dissertation. Cornell University, Ithaca, 1948.

Marcu, Valeriu, *Men and Forces in Our Time.* Harrap, London, 1931.

Meisel, James H., *The Genesis of Georges Sorel.* Wahr, Ann Arbor, 1951.

Péguy, Marcel, *La Rupture de Charles Péguy et de Georges Sorel.* Cahiers de la Quinzaine, 1930.

Perrin, P-L-M. J., *Les Idées sociales de Georges Sorel.* Angélis, Algiers, 1925.

Pirou, Gaetan, *Georges Sorel.* Rivière, Paris, 1927.

Pomerance, Irwin, *The Moral Utopianism of Georges Sorel.* Unpublished doctoral dissertation. Columbia University, New York, 1950.

Rennes, Jacques, *Georges Sorel et le syndicalisme révolutionnaire.* Editions Liberté, Paris, 1936.

Sartre, Victor, *Georges Sorel.* Spes, Paris, 1937.

Variot, Jean, *Propos de Georges Sorel.* Editions de la Nouvelle Française, Paris, 1935.

Wanner, Jean, *L'Idée de décadence dans le pensée de Georges Sorel.* Roth, Lausanne, 1943.

3d) *ARTICLES CONCERNING SOREL*

Andreu, Pierre, "Un Inédit de Georges Sorel," *La Table ronde* (December 1948), 12:2128-36.

Andreu, Pierre, "Bergson et Sorel," *Les Etudes Bergsoniennes* (1952), 3:41-78.

Berth, Edouard, "G. Sorel," *Clarté* (September 15, 1922), 21:495-96.

Berth, Edouard, "Le Tertullien du socialisme," *La Rivoluzione liberale* (December 14, 1922).

Borkenau, Franz, "Sorel, Pareto, Spengler," *Horizon* (June 1942), 5:420-31.

Croce, Benedetto (ed.), "Lettere di Georges Sorel a Benedetto Croce," *La Critica* (1927), 25:38-52, 101-08, 168-76, 300-12, 360-72. (1928), 26:31-39, 92-108, 187-97, 334-48, 432-42. (1929), 27:47-52, 114-25, 289-97, 353-61, 438-46. (1930), 28:42-51, 118-21, 189-95.

Croce, Benedetto, "Cristianesimo, socialismo, e metodo storico," *La Critica* (July 1907), 5:317-30.

Dimnet, Ernest, "A French Defence of Violence," *The Forum* (November 1909), 42:413-22.

Molléans, Edouard, "Le Visage de Georges Sorel," *Revue d'histoire économique et sociale* (1940-47), 26:97-112.

Guy-Grand, Georges, "Georges Sorel et les problèmes contemporains," *La Grande revue* (December 1922), 110:293-324.

Lasserre, Pierre, "Georges Sorel, théoricien de l'impérialisme," *Revue des deux mondes* (September 1, 1927), 41:144-66.

Lee, Vernon, "M. Sorel and the 'Syndicalist Myth,'" *The Fortnightly Review* (October 1911), 96:664-80.

Massis, Henri, "Les Idées sociales de M. Georges Sorel," *Mercure de France* (February 16, 1910), 83:610-21.

Meisel, James H., "Georges Sorel's Last Myth," *Journal of Politics* (February 1950), 12:52-65.

Meisel, James H., "Disciples and Dissenters," *South Atlantic Quarterly* (April 1950), 49:159-74.

Michelet, Victor-Emile, "Deux Médaillons," *Mercure de France* (June 15, 1938), 284:590-93.

Munson, Gorham B., "Georges Sorel: Mythmaker for the Social Revolution," *The Modern Quarterly* (Winter 1931), 6:93-96.

Parmée, Douglas, "Georges Sorel: a Reconsideration," *The Cambridge Journal* (March 1952), 5:355-73.

Reclus, Maurice, "Doctrine et influence de Georges Sorel,"

Les Nouvelles Littéraires (November 10, 1928).

Saint Chamant, Jean de, "L'Actualité de Georges Sorel," *La Grande Revue* (January 1938), 153:308-22.

Salome, René, "Le Lyrisme de M. Georges Sorel," *Revue des jeunes* (January 25, 1923), 13:150-70.

Valois, Georges, "Monarchie et classe ouvrière," *Revue critique des idées et des livres* (May 1908), 1:145-56.

4a) *BOOKS CONCERNING MORE THAN ONE OF THE WRITERS*

Bernanos, Georges, *Nous Autres Français*. Gallimard, Paris, 1939.

Berth, Edouard, *Les Méfaits des intellectuels*. Rivière, Paris, 1914.

Blum, Léon, *Oeuvre, 1891-1905*. Michel, Paris, 1954.

Bordeaux, Henry, *Portraits d'hommes, Volume 1*. Plon, Paris, 1924.

Bordeaux, Henry, *Reconstructeurs et Mainteneurs*. Plon, Paris, 1954.

Brasillach, Robert, *Portraits*. Plon, Paris, 1935.

Brodin, Pierre, *Présences Contemporaines*. Debresse, Paris, 1955.

Brogan, D. W., *French Personalities and Problems*. Knopf, New York, 1947.

Burke, Kenneth, "The Allies of Humanism Abroad," in *The Critique of Humanism*, C. Hartley Grattan (ed.). Brewer & Warren, New York, 1930.

Burnham, James, *The Machiavellians*. Day, New York, 1943.

Chamson, André, *L'Homme contre l'histoire*. Grasset, Paris, 1927.

Dumont-Wilden, L., *Le Crépuscule des maîtres*. La Renaissance du livre, Brussels, 1947.

Faÿ, Bernard, *Panorama de la littérature Française*. Kra, Paris, 1925.

Frescobaldi, Dino, *La Controrivoluzione*. L'Arco, Florence, 1949.

Gérin Ricard, Lazare de, and Louis Truc, *Histoire de l'Action Française*. Valdes, Paris, 1949.

Gide, André, *Prétextes*. Mercure de France, Paris, 1913.

Gide, André, *Incidences*. Editions de la Nouvelle Revue Française, Paris, 1924.

Gillouin, René, *Idées et figures d'aujourd'hui*. Grasset, Paris, 1919.

Gillouin, René, *Trois crises*. Grasset, Paris, 1929.

Guy-Grand, Georges, *La Philosophie nationaliste*. Grasset, Paris, 1911.

Guy-Grand, Georges, *Le Procès de la démocratie*. Colin, Paris, 1911.

Guy-Grand, Georges, *Le Conflit des idées dans la France d'aujourd'hui*. Rivière, Paris, 1921.

Havard de la Montagne, Robert, *Histoire de "l'Action Française."* Amiot-Dumont, Paris, 1950.

Hayes, C. J. H., *France, a Nation of Patriots*. Columbia University Press, New York, 1930.

Hayes, C. J. H., *The Historical Evolution of Modern Nationalism*. Smith, New York, 1931.

Henriot, Emile, *Maîtres d'hier et contemporains*. Michel, Paris, 1956.

Johannet, René, *Itinéraires d'intellectuels*. Nouvelle Librairie Nationale, Paris, 1921.

Labasse, Jean, *Hommes de droit, hommes de gauche*. Economie et Humanisme, Paris, 1947.

Latzarus, Louis, *La France veut-elle un roi?* Editions du Siècle, Paris, 1926.

Massis, Henri, *Jugements, Volume 1*. Plon, Paris, 1923.

Massis, Henri, *Evocations*. Plon, Paris, 1931.

Massis, Henri, *Débats, Volume 1*. Plon, Paris, 1934.

Maurel, André, *Souvenirs d'un écrivain, 1883-1914*. Hachette, Paris, 1925.

Mauriac, Claude, *Hommes et idées d'aujourd'hui*. Michel, Paris, 1953.

Mauriac, François, *Mes Grands hommes*. Editions du Rocher, Monaco, 1949.

Mauriac, François, *Ecrits intimes*. La Palatine, Geneva, 1953.

Mirambel, André, *La Comédie du nationalisme intégral*. Grasset, Paris, 1947.

Moreau, Pierre, *Le Victorieux vingtième siècle*. Plon, Paris, 1925.

Parodi, D., *La Philosophie contemporaine en France*. Alcan, Paris, 1919.

Parodi, D., *Traditionalisme et démocratie* (Second Edition). Colin, Paris, 1924.

Péguy, Charles, *Oeuvres Completes, 1873-1914*. Editions de la Nouvelle Revue Français, Paris, 1916-55.

Rémond, René, *La Droite en France de 1815 à nos jours*. Aubier, Paris, 1954.

Rivière, Jacques, and Alain-Fournier, *Correspondance 1905-1914*. 4 vols. Gallimard, Paris, 1926.

Saurat, Denis, *Tendances*. Editions du Monde Moderne, Paris, 1928.

Segard, Achille, *Les Voluptueux et les hommes d'action*. Société d'Editions Littéraires et Artistiques, Paris, 1900.

Soury, Jules, *Une Campaigne nationaliste*. Plon, Paris, 1902.

Tharaud, Jérome and Jean, *La Vie et la mort de Déroulède*. Emile-Paul, Paris, 1914.

Thibaudet, Albert, *Les Princes Lorrains*. Grasset, Paris, 1924.

Thibaudet, Albert, *Les Idées politiques de la France*. Stock, Paris, 1932.

Valois, Georges, *D'un Siècle à un autre*. Nouvelle Librairie Nationale, Paris, 1922.

Valois, Georges, *L'Homme qui vient* (Definitive Edition). Nouvelle Librairie Nationale, Paris, 1923.

Valois, Georges, *Contre le mensonge et la calomnie*. Nouvelle Librairie Nationale, Paris, 1926.

Vaugeois, Henri, *Notre Pays*. Nouvelle Librairie Nationale, Paris, 1916.

Vignaux, Paul, *Traditionalisme et syndicalisme*. Editions de la Maison Française, New York, 1943.

4b) *ARTICLES CONCERNING MORE THAN ONE OF THE THREE WRITERS*

Gillouin, René, "Maurras, Lemaître, Barrès-Apologètes," *Mercure de France* (November 1, 1916), 118:47-60.

Gregh, Fernand, "Trois Figures," *Revue de Paris* (November 1951), 58:63-64.

Jaques, Robert S., "The Significance of Bergson for Recent Political Thought and Movements in France," *Transactions of the Royal Society of Canada* (May 1932), 26:5-12.

Kammerer, Gladys, "The Political Theory of Vichy," *Journal of Politics* (November 5, 1943), 5:407-34.

Lagardelle, H., "Monarchistes et syndicalistes," *Le Mouvement socialiste* (January 1911), 29:52-55.

Longford, W. W., "The Vatican, France, and l'Action Française," *The Nineteenth Century* (November 1927), 102:611-23.

Lovejoy, Arthur O., "The Practical Tendencies of Bergsonism," *International Journal of Ethics* (April 1913), 23:253-74. (July 1913), 23:419-42.

Maulnier, Thierry, "Towards a New Classicism?", *Horizon* (November 1945), 12:301-09.

Metraux, Eva, "Trends in French Thought during the Third Republic," *Science and Society* (Summer 1941), 5:207-21.

Raynaud, Ernest, "L'Ecole romane française," *Mercure de France* (May 1895), 14:131-45.

Roux, Marie de, "Un Critique du nationalisme, M. Georges Guy-Grand," *Revue critique des idées et des livres* (February 10, 1912), 16:257-66.

Sanborn, Alvan F., "The New Nationalism in France," *The Forum* (January 1914), 47:9-26.

Schnurer, Herman, "The Intellectual Sources of French Fascism," *Antioch Review* (March 1941), 1:35-49.

Spronck, Maurice, " 'L'Esprit Nouveau' des révolutionnaires," *Le Correspondant* (January 10, 1909), 198:35-64.

Tixier, Gilbert, "Les Notions de droite et de gauche en France," *Revue politique et parlementaire* (May 1954), Number 638:119-30.

5) *GENERAL WORKS ON FRENCH HISTORY*

Arendt, Hannah, "From the Dreyfus Affair to France Today," in *Essays on Anti-Semitism,* pp. 173-217, ed. K. S. Pinson (Second Edition). Conference on Jewish Relations, New York, 1942.

Aron, Raymond, *L'Homme contre les tyrans.* Gallimard, Paris, 1946.

Aron, Raymond, *Espoir et peur du siècle.* Calmann-Lévy, Paris, 1957.

Aron, Raymond, *The Opium of the Intellectuals.* Secker & Warburg, London, 1957.

Aron, Robert, *Précis de l'unité française.* Charlot, Paris, 1945.

Bainville, Jacques, *La Troisième République.* Fayard, Paris, 1935.

Barlatier, Pierre, *L'Aventure tragi-comique du grand général Boulanger.* La Bibliothèque Française, Paris, 1949.

Beau de Loménie, E., *Les Responsabilités des dynasties bourgeoises, Volume 2.* Denoël, Paris, 1947.

Bérenger, Henri, *L'Aristocratie intellectuelle.* Colin, Paris, 1895.

Bérenger, Henri, *La France intellectuelle.* Colin, Paris, 1899.

Berl, Emmanuel, *Mort de la pensée bourgeoise.* Grasset, Paris, 1929.

Bernanos, Georges, *A Diary of my Times.* Macmillan, New York, 1938.

Bernanos, Georges, *La Grande peur des bien-pensants.* Grasset, Paris, 1931.

Bloch, Marc, *Strange Defeat.* Trans. Gerard Hopkins. Oxford University Press, London, 1949.

Blum, Léon, *Souvenirs sur l'affaire.* Gallimard, Paris, 1935.

Bouju, Paul M., and Henri Dubois, *La Troisième République 1870-1940.* Presses Universitaires de France, Paris, 1952.

Bourgin, Hubert, *De Jaurès à Léon Blum: L'école normale et la politique.* Fayard, Paris, 1938.

Brogan, D. W., *France under the Republic.* Harper, New York, 1940.

Byrnes, Robert F., *Anti-Semitism in Modern France, Volume 1.* Rutgers University Press, New Brunswick, 1950.

Chapman, Guy, *The Dreyfus Case.* Hart-Davis, London, 1955.

Charensol, G., *L'Affaire Dreyfus et la Troisième République.* Kra, Paris, 1930.

Chastenet, Jacques, *Histoire de la Troisième République.* 3 vols. Hatchette, Paris, 1952-55.

Clough, S. B., *France: a History of National Economics 1789-1939.* Scribners, New York, 1939.

Dansette, Adrien, *Le Boulangisme 1886-1890.* Perrin, Paris, 1938.

Daudet, Léon, *l'Entre-deux-guerres.* Nouvelle Librairie Nationale, Paris, 1915.

Daudet, Léon, *Le Stupide XIX siècle.* Nouvelle Librairie Nationale, Paris, 1922.

Daudet, Léon, *Panorama de la III république* (Second Edition). Gallimard, Paris, 1936.

Earle, E. M. (ed.), *Modern France: Problems of the Third and Fourth Republics.* Princeton University Press, Princeton, 1951.

Fisher, Herbert, *Studies in History and Politics.* Clarendon Press, Oxford, 1920.

Girardet, Raoul, *La Société militaire dans la France contemporaine 1815-1939.* Plon, Paris, 1953.

Goguel, François, *La Politique des partis sous la Troisième République.* Editions du Seuil, Paris, 1946.

Goguel, François, *Géographie des elections françaises de 1870 à 1951* Colin, Paris, 1951.

Goguel, François, *Le Régime politique français.* Editions du Seuil, Paris, 1955.

Gooch, G. P., *Studies in Modern History.* Longmans, Green, London, 1931.

Gooch, R. K., *Regionalism in France*. The Century Company, New York, 1931.

Guedalla, Philip, *The Two Marshals: Bazaine, Pétain*. Reynal and Hitchcock, New York, 1943.

Guérard, Albert Léon, *French Civilisation in the Nineteenth Century*. Fisher Unwin, London, 1914.

Halasz, Nicholas, *Captain Dreyfus*. Simon & Schuster, New York, 1955.

Halévy, Daniel, *Apologie pour notre passé*. Cahiers de la Quinzaine, Paris, 1910.

Halévy, Daniel, *La République des comités*. Grasset, Paris, 1934.

Halévy, Daniel, *Pour l'Etude de la Troisième République*. Grasset, Paris, 1937.

Halévy, Daniel, *Péguy et "les Cahiers de la quinzaine."* Longmans, Green, New York, 1947.

Halévy, Elie, *L'Ere des tyrannies*. Gallimard, Paris, 1938.

Headings, Mildred J., *French Freemasonry under the Third Republic*. Johns Hopkins University Historical Studies, No. 66, 1948-49. Johns Hopkins Press, Baltimore, 1949.

Jaurès, Jean, *Les Preuves*. La Petite République, Paris, 1898.

Jouvenel, Robert de, *La République des camarades*. Grasset, Paris, 1914.

Kohn, Hans, *The Making of the Modern French Mind*. Van Nostrand, New York, 1955.

Leyret, Henry, *La Tyrannie des politiciens*. Cornely, Paris, 1910.

Leyret, Henry, *La République et les politiciens*. Charpentier, Paris, 1909.

"Lysis" (Eugene Le Tailleur), *Les Capitalistes français contre la France*. Michel, Paris, 1916.

Manevy, Raymond, *La Presse de la III république*. Foret, Paris, 1955.

Marcellin, L., *Politique et politiciens d'avant guerre*. La Renaissance du Livre, Paris, 1924.

Ogburn, W. F. and W. Jaffé, *The Economic Development of Post-war France*. Columbia University Press, New York, 1929.

Paléologue, Maurice, *An Intimate Journal of the Dreyfus Case*. Criterion Books, New York, 1957.

Proust, Marcel, *Jean Santeuil*. Weidenfeld and Nicolson, London, 1955.

Reclus, Maurice, *La Troisième République de 1870 à 1918*. Fayard, Paris, 1945.

Schram, Stuart, *Protestantism and Politics in France.* Cor-
bière, Alençon, 1954.
Scott, John A., *Republican Ideas and the Liberal Tradition
in France 1870-1914.* Columbia University Press, New
York, 1951.
Seippel, Paul, *Les Deux Frances et leurs origines his-
toriques.* Alcan, Paris, 1905.
Sembat, Marcel, *Faites un roi; sinon faites la paix.* Figuière,
Paris, 1913.
Siegfried, André, *Tableau politique de la France de l'ouest
sous la Troisième République.* Colin, Paris, 1913.
Siegfried, André, *France: a Study in Nationality.* Yale Uni-
versity Press, New Haven, 1930.
Siegfried, André, *Mes Souvenirs de la Troisième République.*
Editions du Grand Siècle, Paris, 1946.
Soltau, Roger, *French Parties and Politics 1871-1921.* Ox-
ford University Press, London, 1930.
Thibaudet, Albert, *La République des professeurs.* Grasset,
Paris, 1927.
Zévaès, Alexandre, *Au Temps du Boulangisme.* Gallimard,
Paris, 1930.
Zévaès, Alexandre, *L'Affaire Dreyfus.* Editions de la Nou-
velle Revue Critique, Paris, 1931.

ARTICLES ON FRENCH HISTORY OR POLITICS

Andreani, Pierre, "La Formation du parti radical-socialiste,"
Revue politique et parlementaire (January 1952), 614:33-
41.
Anon, "General Boulanger: an Object-Lesson in French
Politics," *Blackwood's Magazine* (February 1895), 952:
297-305.
Anon, "Anti-clericalism in France," *Dublin Review* (April
1907), 140:351-70.
Bastid, P., "Quelques traits du régime parlementaire en
France sous la III république," *Revue internationale
d'histoire politique et constitutionelle* (April 1954), New
Series No. 14:145-52.
Belfort, Roland, "General Boulanger's Love Tragedy," *The
Nineteenth Century* (March 1929), 105:413-27.
Benda, Julien, "Note sur la réaction," *N. R. F.* (August 1,
1929), 191:149-82.
Benda, Julien, "The Enemies of Democracy in France,"
Foreign Affairs (January 1935), 13:284-94.
Bertier de Sauvigny, G. de, "Population Movements and

Population Changes in 19th Century France," *Review of Politics* (January 1957), 19:37-47.

Bruchard, Henry de, "Le Marquis de Morès: un héros de l'antisémitisme," *Revue critique des idées et des livres* (May 10, 1911), 13:273-85.

Byrnes, Robert F., "Morès, 'The First National Socialist,' " *The Review of Politics* (July 1950), 12:341-62.

Byrnes, Robert F., "The French Christian Democrats in the 1890's: their Appearance and their Failure," *Catholic Historical Review* (October 1950), 36:286-306.

Byrnes, Robert F., "The French Publishing Industry and its Crisis in the 1890's," *Journal of Modern History* (September 1951), 23:232-42.

Cairns, John C., "Politics and Foreign Policy: the French Parliament 1911-14," *Canadian Historical Review* (September 1953), 34:245-76.

Cairns, John C., "International Politics and the Military Mind," *Journal of Modern History* (September 1953), 25:273-85.

Clough, S. B., "Retardative Factors in French Economic Development," *Journal of Economic History* (1946), supplement 6:91-102.

Dansette, Adrien, "The Regimentation of French Catholicism," *Review of Politics* (January 1953), 15:34-52.

Dorphlen, Andreas, "Tsar Alexander III and the Boulanger Crisis in France," *Journal of Modern History* (June 1951), 23:122-36.

Ducattillon, J. V., "The Church in the Third Republic," *Review of Politics* (1944), 6:74-85.

Dumas, Jacques, "The Present State of the Land System in France," *Economic Journal* (March 1909), 19:32-50.

Fisher, H. A. L., "French Nationalism," *Hibbert Journal* (January 1917), 15:217-29.

Goguel, François, "Political Instability in France," *Foreign Affairs* (October 1954), 33:111-22.

Goguel, François, "The Historical Background of Contemporary French Politics," *Yale French Studies* (1955), 15:30-37.

Gooch, Robert K., "The Antiparliamentary Movement in France," *American Political Science Review* (August 1927), 21:552-72.

Guyot, Yves, "The Dreyfus Drama and its Significance," *The Nineteenth Century* (January 1899), 45:149-72.

Halévy, Daniel, "Un Entretien sur la démocratie," *"Pages libres"* (January 25, 1908), 15:91-100.

BIBLIOGRAPHY

Hargreaves, J. D., "Entente Manquée: Anglo-French Relations 1895-96," *Cambridge Historical Journal* (1953), 11:65-92.

Heinberg, John G., "Personnel of French Cabinets 1871-1930," *American Political Science Review* (May 1931), 25:389-96.

Landes, David S., "French Entrepreneurship and Industrial Growth in the 19th Century," *Journal of Economic History* (May 1949), 9:45-61.

Leaman, Bertha, "The Influence of Domestic Policy on Foreign Affairs in France 1898-1905," *Journal of Modern History* (December 1942), 14:449-79.

Monod, G., "Contemporary Life and Thought in France," *Contemporary Review* (June 1888), 53:902-20.

Mortimer, Raymond, "Books in General," *New Statesman and Nation* (August 1, 1942), 24:78.

Piou, Jacques, "Le Boulangisme," *La Revue de Paris* (March 15, 1932), 39.2:301-20.

Reclus, Maurice, "Jules Ferry et la doctrine coloniale," *Revue politique et parlementaire* (November 1946), 561:148-62.

Reclus, Maurice, "Quelques aspects de la Troisième République 1879-1918," *Revue politique et parlementaire* (January 1948), 574:33-49.

Rist, Charles, "Nos Ressources financières," *La Revue de Paris* (December 1, 1915), 22.23:657-72.

Rochefort, Henri, "The Boulangist Movement," *The Fortnightly Review* (July 1888), 44:10-23.

Rouquette, Robert, "The Evolution of the French Church," *Thought* (Spring 1953), 28:5-18.

Siegfried, André, "The French Democratic Tradition," *Foreign Affairs* (July 1939), 17:649-62.

Siegfried, Andre, "Une Crise ministerielle en 1887," *Hommes et mondes* (April 1950), 11:477-500.

Stead, W. T., "France and her 'Brav Général,'" *Contemporary Review* (June 1889), 55:910-28.

Stead, W. T., "Character Sketch: Boulanger," *Review of Reviews* (October 1890), 2:323-31.

Steevens, G. W., "France as affected by the Dreyfus Case," *Harpers Monthly* (October 1899), 99:792-98.

Tricor, "The Coming Social Revolution in France," *Contemporary Review* (January 1899), 75:106-22.

Varenne, Francis, "La Défaite de Georges Clemenceau à Draguignan en 1893," *Revue politique et parlementaire* (March 1955), 215:255-59.

Willoughby, W. F., "Labour Legislation in France under the Third Republic," *Quarterly Journal of Economics* (May 1901), 15:390-415; (August 1901), 15:551-77.

Winnacker, R. A., "The Influence of the Dreyfus Affair on the Political Development of France," *Papers of the Michigan Academy of Science, Arts and Letters* (1935), 21:465-78.

Winnacker, R. A., "The Délégation des gauches: A Successful Attempt at Managing a Parliamentary Coalition," *Journal of Modern History* (December 1937), 9:449-70.

Winnacker, R. A., "The Third French Republic 1870-1914," *Journal of Modern History* (September 1938), 10:372-409.

Wolf, Lucien, "Antisemitism and the Dreyfus Case," *The Fortnightly Review* (January 1898), 69:135-46.

Zévaès, Alexandre, "Clemenceau et Jaurès," *Revue politique et parlementaire* (June 1951), 609:230-41.

6) *GENERAL WORKS ON FRENCH LITERATURE*

Agathon (Henri Massis and Alfred de Tarde), *Les Jeunes gens d'aujourd'hui*. Plon, Paris, 1919.

Aldington, Richard, *Introduction to Mistral*. Heineman, London, 1956.

Benda, Julien, *Belphégor*. Emile-Paul Frères, Paris, 1918.

Benda, Julien, *The Treason of the Intellectuals*. Trans. Richard Aldington, Morrow, New York, 1928.

Bloch, Jean-Richard, *Carnaval est Mort* (Fourth Edition). Editions de la Nouvelle Revue Française, Paris, 1920.

Curtius, Ernst Robert, *The Civilisation of France*. Trans. Olive Wyon. Allen & Unwin, London, 1932.

Delhorbe, Cécile, *L'Affaire Dreyfus et les écrivains français*. Editions Victor Attinger, Paris, 1932.

Franck, Henri, *La Danse devant l'arche*. Editions de la Nouvelle Revue Française, Paris, 1912.

Hubert, Renée Riese, *The Dreyfus Affair and the French Novel*. Eagle Enterprises, Cambridge, 1951.

Lasserre, Pierre, *Le Romantisme Français*. Société du Mercure de France, Paris, 1907.

Lazare, Bernard, *Figures contemporaines*. Perrin, Paris, 1895.

Lucas, F. L., *The Decline and Fall of the Romantic Ideal*. Cambridge University Press, Cambridge, 1936.

Martin du Gard, Roger, *Summer 1914*. Trans. Stuart Gilbert. Viking Press, New York, 1941.

Martin du Gard, Roger, *Jean Barois*. Trans. Stuart Gilbert. Viking Press, New York, 1949.

Michaud, Régis, *Modern Thought and Literature in France*. Funk & Wagnalls, New York, 1934.

Peyre, Henri, *Le Classicisme français*. Editions de la Maison Française, New York, 1942.

Peyre, Henri, "Literature and Philosophy in Contemporary France," in *Ideological Differences and World Order*, pp. 269-96, F. S. C. Northrop (ed.). Yale University Press, New Haven, 1949.

Praz, Mario, *The Romantic Agony*. Meridian Books, New York, 1956.

Randall, Earle Stanley, *The Jewish Character in the French Novel 1870-1914*. Banta, Menasha, 1941.

Sartre, Jean-Paul, *What is Literature?* Trans. Bernard Frechtman. Philosophical Library, New York, 1949.

Tharaud, Jérôme and Jean, *Notre Cher Péguy*. Plon, Paris, 1926.

Wright, C. H. C., *The Background of Modern French Literature*. Ginn, Boston, 1926.

ARTICLES ON FRENCH LITERATURE

Cobban, Alfred, "The Historical Significance of Marcel Proust," *Cambridge Journal* (July 1948), 1:613-22.

Darmesteter, Mary Jane, "The Social Novel in France," *Contemporary Review* (June 1899), 75:800-813.

Douglas, Wallace W., "The Meaning of 'Myth' in Modern Criticism," *Modern Philology* (May 1953), 50:232-42.

Gallie, W. B., "Péguy the Moralist," *French Studies* (January 1948), 2:68-82.

Guy-Grand, Georges, "Le Conflit des croyances et les moeurs littéraires dans la France d'avant-guerre," *Mercure de France* (July 16, 1919), 134:193-222.

Jones, P. Mansell, "Intellectual Reaction in France," *Hibbert Journal* (October 1926), 25:159-71.

MacMahon, A., "Catholic Ideals in Modern French Fiction," *American Catholic Quarterly Review* (October 1912), 37:671-717.

Nugent, Robert, "Baudelaire and the Criticism of Decadence," *Philological Quarterly* (April 1957), 36:234-43.

Rohden, P. R., "Die Rolle des Hommes de Lettres in der Französischen Politik," *Historische Zeitschrift* (1932), 147:63-69.

7) GENERAL WORKS ON FRENCH WORKING CLASS MOVEMENTS

Beracha, S., *Le Marxisme après Marx.* Rivière, Paris, 1937.
Berth, Edouard, *Les Derniers aspects du socialisme.* Rivière, Paris, 1923.
Berth, Edouard, *La Fin d'une culture.* Rivière, Paris, 1927.
Berth, Edouard, *Du "Capital" aux "Réflexions sur la violence."* Rivière, Paris, 1932.
Bouglé, C., *Syndicalisme et démocratie.* Cornély, Paris, 1908.
Challaye, Félicien, *Syndicalisme révolutionnaire et syndicalisme réformiste.* Alcan, Paris, 1909.
Cole, G. D. H., *Socialist Thought, Volume 3: The Second International 1889-1914.* 2 vols. Macmillan, London, 1956.
Collinet, Michel, *Esprit du syndicalisme.* Les Editions Ouvrières, Paris, 1951.
Dolléans, Edouard, *Histoire du mouvement ouvrier.* 2 vols. Colin, Paris, 1939.
Eastman, Max, *Marxism, is it Science?* Norton, New York, 1940.
Elbow, Matthew H., *French Corporative Theory 1789-1948.* Columbia University Press, New York, 1953.
Estey, James A., *Revolutionary Syndicalism.* King, London, 1913.
Ferré, Max, *Histoire du mouvement syndicaliste révolutionnaire chez les instituteurs.* Société Universitaire d'Editions et de Librairie, Paris, 1955.
Guy-Grand, Georges, *La Philosophie syndicaliste.* Grasset, Paris, 1911.
Joll, James, *The Second International 1889-1914.* Weidenfeld & Nicolson, London, 1955.
Labriola, A., et al., *Syndicalisme et socialisme.* Rivière, Paris, 1908.
Lorwin, Lewis L., *Syndicalism in France* (Second Edition). Columbia University Press, New York, 1914.
Lorwin, Val R., *The French Labor Movement.* Harvard University Press, Cambridge, 1954.
Louis, Paul, *Histoire du socialisme en France 1789-1945.* Rivière, Paris, 1946.
Maitron, J., *Le Syndicalisme révolutionnaire: Paul Delesalle.* Les Editions Ouvrières, Paris, 1952.
May, André, *Les Origines du syndicalisme révolutionnaire.* Jouve, Paris, 1913.
Moreau, Georges, *Essai sur les théories et l'histoire du syndicalisme ouvrier en France.* Rivière, Paris, 1925.

Pareto, Vilfredo, *Les Systèmes socialistes*. Giard, Paris, 1926.

Pirou, G., *Proudhonisme et syndicalisme révolutionnaire*. Rousseau, Paris, 1910.

Ralea, Michel, *L'Idée de révolution dans les doctrines socialistes*. Rivière, Paris, 1923.

Russell, Bertrand, *Proposed Roads to Freedom*. Holt, New York, 1919.

Saposs, David J., *The Labor Movement in Post-War France*. Columbia University Press, New York, 1931.

Scott, J. W., *Syndicalism and Philosophical Realism*. Black, London, 1919.

Todorovitch, Dragoslav B., *Le Droit syndical et les doctrines syndicalistes*. Bière, Bordeaux, 1934.

Wu-Wu, Sheng, *Le Conflit des tendances dans le syndicalisme français contemporain*. Librairie Russe et Française, Paris, 1932.

Zévaès, Alexandre, *Histoire du socialisme et du communisme en France*. Editions France-Empire, Paris, 1947.

Zévaès, Alexandre, *Notes et souvenirs d'un militant*. Rivière, Paris, 1913.

Zévaès, Alexandre, *Une Génération*. Rivière, Paris, 1922.

ARTICLES ON FRENCH WORKING CLASS MOVEMENTS

Bernstein, Samuel, "Jules Guesde, Pioneer of Marxism in France," *Science and Society* (Winter 1940), 4:29-56.

Bernstein, Samuel, "Jean Jaurès and the Problem of War," *Science and Society* (Summer 1940), 4:127-64.

Bouglé, C., "Syndicalistes et Bergsoniens," *La Revue du mois* (April 1909), 7:403-16.

Collinet, Michel, "Masses et Militants," *Revue d'histoire économique et sociale* (1951), 29:65-73.

Dimnet, Ernest, "Syndicalism and its Philosophy," *Atlantic Monthly* (January 1913), 3:17-30.

Ehrmann, Henry W., "Jean Jaurès—Last of the Great Tribunes," *Social Research* (September 1949), 16:332-43.

Elliott, W. Y., "The Political Application of Romanticism," *Political Science Quarterly* (1924), 39:234-64.

Kelso, Maxwell R., "The Inception of the Modern French Labor Movement 1871-79: a Reappraisal," *Journal of Modern History* (June 1936), 8:173-93.

Lafargue, Paul, "Socialism in France from 1876 to 1896," *Fortnightly Review* (September 1897), 68:445-58.

Lagardelle, Hubert, "Le Socialisme et l'affaire Dreyfus,"

Le Mouvement Socialiste (February 15, 1899), 1:155-68; (March 15, 1899), 1:285-99.

Mott, R. L., "The Political Theory of Syndicalism," *Political Science Quarterly* (1922), 37:25-40.

Passage, Henri du, "Le Syndicalisme révolutionnaire," *Etudes* (January 1913), 134:433-50, 627-45.

Pirou, Gaetan, "A Propos du syndicalisme révolutionnaire: théoriciens et militants," *Revue politique et parlementaire* (October 10, 1911), 70:130-42.

Scaife, Walter B., "Organized Labor in France," *Forum* (June 1900), 29:455-64.

Seilhac, Leon de, "Le Syndicalisme révolutionnaire et la C. G. T.," *Le Correspondant* (June 25, 1908), 231:1258-81.

Williams, T. Rhondda, "Syndicalism in France and its Relation to the Philosophy of Bergson," *Hibbert Journal* (January 1914), 12:389-403.

8) *GENERAL WORKS ON POLITICAL THEORY*

Barker, Ernest, *Reflections on Government*. Oxford University Press, London, 1942.

Cassirer, Ernst, *The Myth of the State*. Doubleday, New York, 1955.

Faguet, Emile, *The Dread of Responsibility*. Trans. E. J. Putnam. Putnam, New York, 1914.

Faguet, Emile, *The Cult of Incompetence*. Trans. Beatrice Barstow. Dutton, New York, 1914.

Friedrich, Carl J., *The New Belief in the Common Man*. Little, Brown, Boston, 1942.

Friedrich, Carl J. (ed.) *Totalitarianism*. Harvard University Press, Cambridge, 1954.

Jouvenel, Bertrand de, *Sovereignty*. University of Chicago Press, Chicago, 1957.

Kolnai, Aurel, *The War Against the West*. Viking Press, New York, 1938.

Laski, H. J., *Authority in the Modern State*. Yale University Press, New Haven, 1919.

MacIver, Robert M., *The Web of Government*. Macmillan, New York, 1947.

Mayer, J. P., *Political Thought in France from Sièyes to Sorel*. Faber & Faber, London, 1943.

Merriam, Charles E., *The New Democracy and the New Despotism*. McGraw-Hill, New York, 1939.

Mannheim, Karl, *Essays on Sociology and Social Psychology*. Oxford University Press, London, 1953.

BIBLIOGRAPHY

Neumann, Sigmund, *Permanent Revolution*. Harper, New York, 1942.

Rader, Melvin, *No Compromise*. Macmillan, New York, 1939.

Soltau, Roger, *French Political Thought in the 19th Century*. Yale University Press, New Haven, 1931.

Watkins, Frederick M., *The Political Tradition of the West*. Harvard University Press, Cambridge, 1957.

INDEX

Action Française, 10, 37, 42, 45, 53, 60, 61, 63, 71, 94, 95, 96, 124, 144, 206, 225, 246, 248, 265
Albert, Marcellin, 18
alcoholism, 17-18
Amouretti, F., 162
anarchism, 20
anticlericalism, 20
antidemocratic thought, Chapter IV, 148
antimilitarism, 40, 42
antiparliamentarianism, 25, 78-79
antirepublicanism, 3, 25, 28, 38-39, 45, 46, 59, 62, Chapter IX
anti-Semitism, 10, 28, 36, 37, 55, 89, 97, 208, 210-20
Aragon, Louis, 264
aristocracy, 74-75
Aristotle, 68, 90, 130, 238
army, 38-40, 227-29
Aron, Raymond, 102
Ascoli, Max, 176, 261
Auriol, Vincent, 61

Bagehot, Walter, 22
Bainville, Jacques, 63, 199, 207, 225, 263
Barker, Ernest, 172
Barrès, Maurice, acceptance, 109; action, 138; ambition, 56; antidemocratic, 64-65; antirepublican, 78-79, 174; anti-Semitic, 55, 97, 203, 213-14; aristocracy, 74; Boulanger, 23, 26, 137, 138, 150, 172, 193, 253; bourgeois, 267; Catholicism, 222-24; character, 54; coldness, 55; conformity, 149; conservative, 7, 111; corruption, 185-86; culte-du-moi, 57, 71, 104; death, 112-13; decadence, 99; decentralization, 158-60; deracine, 109-10; dilettante, 58; discipline, 108-09, 113; Dreyfus Affair, 23, 33-34, 44, 56, 91, 110, 149, 204, 205, 253; early success, 54; earth and the dead, 113; education, 78, 166-69; elan, 115, 137-38; elite, 71; energy,

136; exaltation, 105; fraternity, 90; French Revolution, 82-83; friendships, 34, 56; Germany, 111, 253; game of politics, 54, 56, 58, 177, 180-81; hatred, 138; immigration, 213; individualism, 64, 105-06, 264; influences, 11; intelligence, 135-36; interest in science, 59; justice, 90-91; lack of policy, 147; limitation, 109; Lorraine, 54, 105-06, 108, 110-12, 229; monarchy, 74; nationalism, 7, 10, 48, 58, 59, 95, 105-06, 111, 252-54; need for certainty, 100; plutocracy, 187; politicians, 158, 180; race, 213; reason, 105, 107; relations with Maurras, 45-46; romanticism, 58, 124; romanticist, 59; Rousseau, 83, 109; rural virtues, 229; Socialism, 137-38, 267; tradition, 100, 106-07, 110; travel, 110; unity, 150
Baudelaire, 49, 62, 104, 204
Benda, Julien, 97, 216, 263
Bergson, Henri, 51, 52, 61, 75, 127, 129, 130, 142, 216
Berlin, Isaiah, 136
Bernanos, Georges, 35, 60, 225
Berth, Edouard, 48, 53, 142, 261
Bismarck, 24, 194, 201
Blanquists, 33
Blum, Léon, 33, 36, 44, 54, 55, 238
Boisdeffre, General de, 34, 37, 43
Bonald, de, 62, 68, 85, 94, 184, 199
Bonnemain, Marguerite de, 28
Boulanger, General, 25-26, 39, 239
Boulangism, 4, 6, 22, 49, 82, 97, 122; antiparliamentary, 33; anti-Semitism, 24, 28; character, 25-26; failure, 30-31; mass appeal, 25; popularity, 30; press, 30; program, 27; relations with Church, 27; relations with monarchists, 26; supported by Barrès, 26; support from anarchists, 26; urban nature, 26
Bourgeois, Léon, 6, 41, 82, 190, 197, 207

309

INDEX

Goguel, François, 14, 31
Goncourts, 40
Greece, 62, 102, 112, 116, 124, 199
Guérin, 36, 95
Guesde, Jules, 19, 20, 33, 41
Guy-Grand, Georges, 145, 238

Halévy, Daniel, 35, 44, 97, 198
Hanotaux, Gabriel, 10, 40, 201
Hegel, 12, 152
heroism, 75
Herr, Lucien, 10, 41, 229
Herriot, Edouard, 54
Herzl, T., 37
Hobbes, 88, 123, 266
Hulme, T. E., 52, 124

immigration, 16
intellectuals, Chapter VII

James, William, 42, 52, 56, 143
Jaurès, Jean, 10, 22, 34, 41, 61,
  177, 189, 191, 200, 241, 269, 270
Jews, see anti-Semitism
Jouvenel, Bertrand de, 176
Jouvenel, Robert de, 17

Kant, 12, 70, 166, 169, 200

Lagardelle, Hubert, 141
Lamennais, 92
la revanche, 24, 251
Lasserre, Pierre, 60, 63, 74, 106,
  124, 199
La Tour du Pin, 120, 152, 162, 218,
  238
League of Patriots, 32, 95
Left, 5, 31, 43-44, 82, 99, 145, 263-
  64
Le Bon, 52
Leo XIII, 38, 61
Lemaître, Jules, 34, 95, 110, 251
Le Play, 94, 123, 152, 184, 263
Littré, 36
Lorwin, Lewis, 260
Loynes, Madame de, 95
Loyola, 105
Luethy, Herbert, 247
Lyautey, Marshal, 39, 270

MacIver, R., 95

Maistre, Joseph de, 11, 62, 68, 184,
  227
Mannheim, Karl, 146, 149
Marx, Karl, 30, 47, 52, 68, 102, 120,
  130, 152, 232
Masons, 207-08
Mauriac, François, 11
Maurras, Charles, 6, 59-63; ancien
  régime, 161; antidemocratic, 64,
  68-71, 86, 148, 181; antiparliamentary, 79; antirepublican,
  160-61, 173-74, 194-97; anti-
  Semitic, 62, 89, 93, 123, 214-18,
  250; aristocracy, 74; army, 227-
  28; attack on Bergson, 61; authority, 238; Catholicism, 61,
  224-26, 266; classicism, 62, 100,
  120-24, 198; colonies, 196; continuity, 244; counter-revolution,
  7, 83-86, 93-95, 99-100, 266;
  Dreyfus Affair, 23, 83, 93, 121,
  181, 194, 195, 215-16, 227, 235,
  246, 248; deafness, 60; decentralization, 160-63; dictatorship, 239;
  disowned by Pretender, 61; education, 60, 169; elan, 145, 250;
  elite, 73-75; empiricism, 234;
  England, 71, 195; equality, 69,
  89-90; Etats Confédérés, 78, 89,
  206, 207, 240; Felibrige, 62, 162;
  force, 144; foreigners, 67-68;
  fraternity, 69, 91; Germany, 71,
  200, 250; Greece, 62, 112, 124,
  199; heredity, 240; hierarchy, 69,
  88; individualism, 69, 77, 88,
  264; influence, 63, 96; influences
  on, 6, 7, 11; intransigence, 60;
  justice, 91; liberty, 69, 87-89;
  masons, 207-08; Métèques, 206-
  07; monarchy, 74, 163, 242-47;
  nationalism, 112, 200-01; need
  for certainty, 100; order, 121,
  145, 236, 245; parties, 184; plutocracy, 187; political science,
  233-41; Protestantism, 83-84, 86,
  90, 93, 123, 209-10; provinces,
  162; put on Index, 61; race, 214,
  249; realism, 236; reason, 94-95;
  relations with Barrès, 45-46; relations with Sorel, 48; romanti-

311

INDEX

ground, 51; bourgeoisie, 117, 139, 140, 141, 153; changeable views, 51; Christianity, 139, 143, 222; classicism, 56, 167; corruption, 186; criticism of Barrès and Maurras, 48; culture, 102; decentralization, 156; demagoguery, 182; Dreyfus Affair, 23, 141, 153, 156, 179, 186, 211; education, 170; elan, 99, 142; elite, 72-73, 144; equality, 66; erudition, 52; family, 102, 119; fraternity, 66; freedom, 260; French Revolution, 86; General Strike, 131, 154, 258-59; Greeks, 102, 116; heroism, 141-42, 154; individualism, 264; intellectualism, 127-29, 131; intellectuals, 131-35, 183-84; Jews, 210-11; law, 115-20; liberty, 66; machine, 256; Marxism, 118, 141, 256; monarchy, 47; morals, 68, 98-99, 104, 115-20; mystery, 129; myth, 129-31, 143; nationalism, 7, 46; need for certainty, 100; optimism, 67, 128; pacifism, 140; parties, 183-84; pessimism, 128, 132; plutocracy, 187; politicians, 177-78; production, 256-57; progress, 67; proletariat, 118, 135, 143, 170, 176, 258, 260; rationalism, 66, 131; reformism, 141; relations with Maurras and Barrès, 47-48; relations with monarchists, 47; rural virtues, 230-32; scission, 153; self-emancipation, 258; sex, 119; socialism, 102, 178-80, 183; sovereignty of the people, 91-92; state, 156-57, 167, 175; syndicalism, 7, 47, 53, 74, 141, 157, 254-62, 269; towns, 141; trade unions, 141; traditions, 72, 100, 102-03; unsystematic, 51; worker, 257-58

Soury, Jules, 204
Spencer, Herbert, 123
Spinoza, 238
Stendhal, 11, 48, 106
strikes, 19-20
syndicalism, 21, *see* Sorel

Taine, 10, 46, 52, 63, 82, 84, 86, 106, 109, 161, 166, 184
Tawney, R. H., 228
Thibaubet, Albert, 41, 55, 159, 229, 254
Thierry Maulnier, 63
Thiers, 4, 19
Tocqueville, de, 39, 52, 124, 161
tradition, 12, 100, 102-04, 106-07, 110

unity, 150, 151, 243

Valois, Georges, 46, 47, 60, 254
Variot, Jean, 47, 49, 53
Vaugeois, 68, 76, 96, 199, 225
Veuillot, 227
Vico, 130

Wagner, 207
Waldeck-Rousseau, 6, 156, 191
Wallas, Graham, 80, 131
Weil, Simone, 99
Weygand, General, 37
working conditions, 18-19

Zola, Emile, 15, 34, 35, 41, 177, 202

313

DATE DUE

APR 20 '67			
MAR 19 '69			